LYRA MYSTICA

AN ANTHOLOGY
OF MYSTICAL VERSE

Edited by
CHARLES CARROLL ALBERTSON

Introduction by
WILLIAM RALPH INGE
Dean of St. Paul's

NEW YORK
THE MACMILLAN COMPANY
1932

Copyright, 1932,
BY THE MACMILLAN COMPANY

All rights reserved—no part of this book may be reproduced in any form without permission in writing from the publisher, except by a reviewer who wishes to quote brief passages in connection with a review written for inclusion in magazine or newspaper.

Set up and printed. Published March, 1932.

PRINTED IN THE UNITED STATES OF AMERICA
BY THE STRATFORD PRESS, INC., NEW YORK

To Permelia

"I have seen the Eternal in thy face."

ACKNOWLEDGMENTS

The editor of *Lyra Mystica* wishes to tender his sincere thanks to the following persons, magazines, newspapers, and publishers, American and foreign, for their courtesy in granting permission to reprint copyrighted poems:

Mrs. A. St. John Adcock; Augusta Albertson; Karle Wilson Baker; Dr. Clara Barrus for "Waiting" by John Burroughs; Mrs. Theodore Beck; Aubrey F. G. Bell; William Rose Benét; Laurence Binyon; Gamaliel Bradford; Robert Bridges; executors of the estate for three poems by Thomas Edward Brown; Maxwell Struthers Burt; Richard Burton; Witter Bynner; Mrs. Katherine M. Carruth for "Each in His Own Tongue" by William H. Carruth; Paul Claudel; Myles E. Conolly; Grace Coolidge; Richard Lew Dawson; Anna de Bary; Margaret Deland; Lorna de Lucchi; Babette Deutsch; John Drinkwater; William Dudley Foulke; Neil Fraser-Tytler; Rose Fyleman; Zona Gale; Kahlil Gibran; Charlotte Perkins Gilman; Harold E. Goad; Grace Duffield Goodwin; Eva Gore-Booth; Arthur Guiterman; Kenneth Guthrie; Molly Anderson Haley; executors of the estate of W. E. Henley; executors of the estate for three poems by Gerard Manley Hopkins; Edith M. Howe; J. S. Hoyland; Harriet Jay for two extracts from "The City of Dream" by Robert Buchanan, Thomas S. Jones, Jr.; David Starr

Acknowledgments

Jordan; Helen Keller; Harry Kemp; Aline Kilmer; Henry Herbert Knibbs; Richard Le Gallienne; H. Elvet Lewis; Ludwig Lewisohn; Vachel Lindsay; Francis A. Litz, Executor, for three poems by John Bannister Tabb; Edwin Markham; John Masefield; Madeline Mason-Manheim; Wilfrid Meynell for seven poems by Alice Meynell and three poems by Francis Thompson; Edna St. Vincent Millay; Angela Morgan; Kenneth Morris; John G. Neihardt; Joseph Fort Newton; D. H. S. Nicholson; Reynold Alleyne Nicholson; Alfred Noyes; James Oppenheim; Herbert E. Palmer; E. S. Parker; Derek Patmore for "Sponsa Dei" by Coventry Kersey Dighton Patmore; E. Allison Peers; Pennsylvania Company, Executor, for two poems from *Poems* by Florence Earle Coates; Cale Young Rice; Mrs. J. M. Robb; Edwin A. Robinson; Henry Morton Robinson; Madeleine Caron Rock; Sir James Rennell Rodd; Sir Ronald Ross; George William Russell (A. E.); Arthur L. Salmon; Siegfried Sassoon; Clinton Scollard; Mrs. William Sharp for six poems from *The Hills of Dream: Threnodies, Songs, and Later Poems* by Fiona Macleod (William Sharp); Solomon Solis-Cohen; W. Force Stead; James Stephens; Jane T. Stoddart; Charles W. Stork; Rabindranath Tagore; Sara Teasdale; Charles H. Towne; Katharine Tynan; Evelyn Underhill; Henry van Dyke; Robert Stephen Vere de Vere for "Implicit Faith" by Aubrey Thomas Vere de Vere; Sir William Watson; Willard Wattles; Edith Wharton; Margaret Widdemer; Avrahm Yarmolinsky; William Butler Yeats; Marya Zaturenska

Acknowledgments

America for "Quo Vadis" by Myles E. Conolly; Asia for "Autumn" by Rabindranath Tagore; The Atlantic Monthly for "Life" by Edith Wharton and "On a Subway Express" by Chester Firkins; The Bookman for "A Star Map" by Sara Teasdale; The Churchman for "Miracles" by Molly Anderson Haley; The Commonweal for "The Final Faith" by George Sterling; Harper's Magazine for "Deaf" by Margaret Deland; Lippincott's Magazine for "De Mortuis Nil nisi Bonum" by Richard Realf; The New Adelphi for "The Pilgrim" by Herbert E. Palmer; The New York Times for "The Frozen Grail" by Elsa Barker; The Outlook for "The Guest" by Joseph Fort Newton and "The White Comrade" by Robert Haven Schauffler; Poetry of Today for "The Fringe of Heaven" from *The Dawn Patrol* by Paul R. Bewsher; The Saturday Review (London) for "On Christmas Eve" by W. Force Stead; The Spectator for "Christ in Flanders" by L. W.; The Theosophical Path for "Dusk" by Kenneth Morris

George Allen & Unwin, Ltd. for "Over the City" and "So Thin a Veil" from *Towards Democracy* by Edward Carpenter

The America-Scandinavia Foundation for "Evening Song" from *A Book of Danish Verse* by B. S. Ingeman

D. Appleton & Company for "Life" from *Artemis to Actæon* by Edith Wharton; "Silence" from *Selected Poems* by Charles Hanson Towne; "To a Waterfowl" by William Cullen Bryant

Basil Blackwell for "Turris Eburnea" from *The*

Acknowledgments

Little City by Wilfred Rowland Childe; "Quiet" from *The Quiet Spirit* by J. S. Muirhead

William Blackwood & Sons for "The Origin of Life" and "Paradox" from *Collected Poems*, Vol. I, by Alfred Noyes

Albert and Charles Boni, Inc. for "A Pagan Reinvokes the Twenty-third Psalm" from *After Disillusion* by Robert Wolfe (copyright 1923 by Thomas Seltzer, Inc.)

Brentano's for "Prayer" from *Hill Fragments* by Madeline Mason-Manheim; "The Voice of Christmas" by Harry Kemp

Cambridge University Press for "Passionate, with Longing in My Eyes" by Lâlla from Sir Richard Carnac Temple's work, *The Word of Lâlla the Prophetess*

The Century Co. for "A Litany for Latter Day Mystics" and "A Rhapsodist's Song" from *Selected Plays and Poems* by Cale Young Rice; "The Servants" and "The Pilgrims" from *Ashes and Sparks* by Richard Wightman

The Challenge, Limited for "O Thou, in Whom We Live and Breathe," "Father, We Thank Thee," "O Thou Who Lovest with Divine Passion" from *Prayers Written for Use in an Indian College* by J. S. Hoyland

The Clarendon Press for "Johannes Milton Senex" from *The Spirit of Man* by Robert Bridges

Constable & Co. for "Sonnet" by George Santayana

J. M. Dent & Sons Ltd. for "Seeking God" and "A New Hymn for Solitude" by Edward Dowden; "Adrift" by Mrs. Edward Dowden; "Uxbridge

Acknowledgments

Road," "Immanence," and "Supersensual" from *Immanence* by Evelyn Underhill; Mrs. Theodore Beck's translations from Jacopone da Todi

Dodd, Mead & Company, Inc. for "Veni Creator" and "Vestigia" by Bliss Carman; "The Messenger" by Richard Hovey; "Kinship" and "A Song of Thanksgiving" by Angela Morgan; Arthur Symons' translations from St. Teresa and St. John of the Cross; "The Poet's Prayer" from *New Poems* by Stephen Phillips

Doubleday, Doran and Company for "In Praise of Common Things," "Growth" and "Trust" from *Selected Poems of Lizette Woodworth Reese;* from "Passage to India" and from "Prayer of Columbus" from *Leaves of Grass* by Walt Whitman; "The Gift" from *Selected Poems* by Aline Kilmer; "The Soldier in France" from *Poems, Essays and Letters of Joyce Kilmer*

E. P. Dutton & Co., Inc. for four Quatrains from *A Persian Anthology* translated by Edward Granville Browne; from "Thoughts of God" by Francis Ridley Havergal; "Lost and Found," "Obedience" and "A Prayer for the Past" by George MacDonald; "By Every Ebb" and "Acceptance" from *Lanterns in Gethsemane* by Willard Wattles; "Crying, Abba Father" from *The Invisible Playmate* by William Canton; "Immanence," "Supersensual" and "Uxbridge Road" from *Immanence* by Evelyn Underhill; "Ploughman at the Plough" by Louis Golding; "The Pavilions of Peace" and "Introit" from *The Book of Grace* by Grace Rhys

Acknowledgments

Paul Elder & Co. for "Sonnet" from *Sonnets of Spinsterhood* by Snow Longley

Funk & Wagnalls Company for "The Word" from *Poems by Richard Realf*

Haldeman-Julius Publications for Ludwig Lewisohn's translation of "Rapture" by Stefan George

Harcourt, Brace and Company, Inc. for "Barter" from *Cross Currents* and "The Other Place" from *Collected Poems* by Margaret Widdemer

Harper & Brothers for "In the Hospital" from *The Light Guitar* by Arthur Guiterman; "God's World" from *Renascence and Other Poems* by Edna St. Vincent Millay

William Heinemann, Ltd. for three translations by Arthur Symons from St. Teresa and St. John of the Cross; "Of Children" and "Of Reason and Passion" from *The Prophet* by Kahlil Gibran; "Sonnets" and from "The Everlasting Mercy" by John Masefield; "In Salutation to the Eternal Peace" and "The Soul's Prayer" by Sarojini Naidu; Lorna de Lucchi's translation of "L'Infinito" by Giacomo Leopardi; "Off Shore" from *Swinburne's Collected Poetical Works*

Hodder & Stoughton Ltd. for "God of the Open Air" by Henry van Dyke; "Immortality" from *Collected Poems* by A. St. John Adcock

Henry Holt and Company for "The Anodyne" and "An Air of Coolness Plays upon His Face" by Sarah N. Cleghorn from *Fellow Captains* by Cleghorn and Fisher

Houghton Mifflin Company for "Borderlands" and "Summum Bonum" from *Happy Ending* by Louise

Acknowledgments

Imogen Guiney; "God Is Not Dumb" and "Longing" from "Bibliolatres" in *Lowell's Poetical Works*; "In the Silence" and "The Source" by Josephine Preston Peabody; "Crossing the Bar," "The Higher Pantheism," "In Memoriam" and "The Human Cry" by Alfred, Lord Tennyson; "A Prayer" by John Drinkwater; "The World We Live In," "Immortal" and "Our Christ" by Lucy Larcom; "The Problem" from *Threnody* by Ralph Waldo Emerson; from "A Century of Indian Epigrams" by Paul Elmer More; "The Hill Born" from *In the High Hills* by Maxwell Struthers Burt; "I Vex Me Not" by Thomas Bailey Aldrich; "Starlight" by Edward Rowland Sill; "Prospice" from "Abt Vogler" by Robert Browning; "Holy Land," "The Invisible" and "Undying Light" by Richard Watson Gilder; "I Stood within the Heart of God" by William Vaughn Moody; "The Eternal Goodness" by John Greenleaf Whittier

The Incorporated Society of Authors, Composers, and Playwrights for "The Flying Wheel," "The Image," "Sanctuaries," "Of an Orchard" and "Sheep and Lambs" by Katharine Tynan

International Publishers Co. for "The Prophet" by Alexander Sergeyevich Pushkin from *Russian Poetry*

Jewish Publication Society for translations by Nina Salaman and Israel Zangwill

Alfred A. Knopf, Inc. for "A Little Hill among New Hampshire Hills" from *The New World* by Witter Bynner; "The Cry of Man" by James Oppenheim; "Of Children" and "Of Reason and Passion"

Acknowledgments

from *The Prophet* by Kahlil Gibran; "This Corruptible" by Elinor Wylie

John Lane, The Bodley Head, Limited for "The Poet's Prayer" from *New Poems* by Stephen Phillips; from "Out of the Silence" by James Rhoades; "The Immortal Hour" from *Poems* by Rachel Annand Taylor

Little, Brown & Company for "Chartless" from *Poems* and "My Faith Is Larger than the Hills," "Dost Thou Remember Me?" and "Eternity, I'm Coming" from *Further Poems* by Emily Dickinson; "Yea, Every Day He Comes" by Susan Coolidge

Horace Liveright for extracts from "The Confessions of St. Augustine" translated and annotated by J. G. Pilkington

Longmans, Green & Co. Limited and/or Longmans, Green & Co. for "The Quest" by Eva Gore-Booth; "Shadows" by Vladimir Solovev from *The Spirit of Man* by Robert Bridges; "Lo, as Some Bard" from *St. Paul* and "A Cosmic Outlook" and "A Last Appeal" from *Collected Poems* by Frederick William Henry Myers; "I Went to Sleep; and Now I am Refreshed" by John Henry Newman

Lothrop, Lee and Shepard Co. for "God's Garden" from *Dumb in June* by Richard Burton

A. C. McClurg & Co. for "At Beach St. Mary" by Frank W. Gunsaulus

Erskine Macdonald, Ltd. for "The Fringe of Heaven" from *The Dawn Patrol and Other Poems of an Aviator* by Paul R. Bewsher

Macmillan & Co., Ltd. and/or The Macmillan Company for "A Vision of Beauty," "The City," "The Twilight of Earth," "The Divine Vision" and "By

Acknowledgments

the Margin of the Great Deep" by George William Russell (A. E.); "My Garden," "Land, Ho!" and "Specula" by Thomas Edward Brown; "The Voice of God" from *Collected Poems* by James Stephens; "The Oarsmen" and another extract from *Fruit-Gathering* by Rabindranath Tagore; "He Who Is Meek and Contented," "My Lord Hides Himself" and "O Servant, Where Dost Thou Seek Me?" from Kabir's *Poems* translated by Rabindranath Tagore; "Thick Is the Darkness" from *Poems* by W. E. Henley; "Flower in the Crannied Wall" and extract from "The Ancient Sage" from *Collected Poems* by Alfred, Lord Tennyson; "East London" and "Lines Written in Kensington Gardens" by Matthew Arnold; "Heart of God" from *Collected Poems* by Vachel Lindsay; from "The Everlasting Mercy" by John Masefield; "Envoy" and "Prayer for Pain" by John G. Neihardt; "I Had a Dream Last Night" from "Captain Craig" in *Collected Poems* by Edwin Arlington Robinson; "Sheep and Lambs," "Of an Orchard," "The Image" and "Sanctuaries" by Katherine Tynan; "A Chant out of Doors," "Out of the Dark" and "Sonnets of the New Birth" (3) by Marguerite Wilkinson; "Contours" and "The Secret Way" from *The Secret Way* by Zona Gale; "The Voice" by Sara Teasdale

The Manual Arts Press for "The Craftsman's Creed" by James P. Haney

Elkin Mathews & Marrot for "After St. Augustine" by Mary E. Coleridge

Mercure de France for "The Holy Face" from *La Ville* in *Théâtre* by Paul Claudel

Methuen & Co. Ltd. for "Enough" from *A Small*

Acknowledgments

Cruse by Rose Fyleman; Quatrains from *A Persian Anthology* translated by Edward Granville Browne; translations of Luis de León by Aubrey F. G. Bell, adapted by E. Allison Peers, from *Spanish Mysticism*

The Mosher Press for "Deo Adventante," "An Invocation" and "The Prism of Life" by John Addington Symonds; "Sonnets" (6) by Thomas S. Jones, Jr.

The Oxford University Press for "God's Grandeur," "Pied Beauty" and "The Wreck of the Deutschland" by Gerard Manley Hopkins; "A Ballad of the Center" from *The Oxford Book of Mystical Verse*; "Johannes Milton Senex" from *The Spirit of Man* by Robert Bridges; "Quatrains" from *Studies in Islamic Mysticism* by Reynold Alleyne Nicholson

The Poetry Bookshop, London, for "Where the Blessed Feet Have Trod" by Michael Field

G. P. Putnam's Sons for "Symbol" and "Who Walks With Beauty" from *Ships in Harbor* by David Morton

The Rosenbach Company for "I Know That My Redeemer Liveth" and "Oh, Lord, Where Shall I Find Thee?" from *When Love Passed By and Other Verses* by Solomon Solis-Cohen

Charles Scribner's Sons for "No Distant Lord" by Maltbie D. Babcock; "God of the Open Road" by Henry van Dyke; from "Florida Sunday," from "The Marshes of Glynn" and "A Song of the Future" from *The Poems of Sidney Lanier*; "Christmas Night," "To a Daisy," "A General Communion," "I Am the Way," "To the Mother of Christ the Son of Man," "The Treasure" and "The Unknown God" from *Collected Poems* by Alice Meynell; "Sonnet" by George San-

Acknowledgments

tayana; "Life" from *Artemis to Actæon* by Edith Wharton; "I Do Not Fear" by John Hall Wheelock; "Desiderium Indesideratum," "The Hound of Heaven" and "The Kingdom of God" by Francis Thompson; "Thick Is the Darkness" from *Collected Poems* by William Ernest Henley

Martin Secker for "God's World" from *Renascence and Other Poems* by Edna St. Vincent Millay

Sidgwick & Jackson, Ltd. for "A Prayer" from *Collected Poems* by John Drinkwater

Society for Promoting Christian Knowledge for "The Goal in Sight" by Christina Rossetti

Frederick A. Stokes Company for "The Paradox" and "The Origin of Life" from *Collected Poems*, Vol. I, by Alfred Noyes; "The Secret Garden" by Robert Nichols

The Talbot Press Ltd. for "The Quest" by James H. Cousins; "I See His Blood upon the Rose" from *Complete Poems of Joseph Mary Plunkett*

The Viking Press Inc. for "To the Victor" from *The Vaunt of Man* by William Ellery Leonard, copyright 1912 by B. W. Huebsch

World Book Company for "Men Told Me, Lord" from *The Days of a Man* by David Starr Jordan

Yale University Press for "Pronouns" from *The Burning Bush* by Karle Wilson Baker; "The Falconer of God" from *The Falconer of God and Other Poems* by William Rose Benét

Man is a stream whose source is hidden. Always our being is descending into us from we know not whence.

RALPH WALDO EMERSON

Mysticism is the ferment of the faiths, the forerunner of spiritual liberty, the inaccessible refuge of the nobler heretics, the inspirer, through poetry, of countless youth who know no metaphysics, the teacher, through the devotional books, of the despairing, the comforter of those who are weary of finitude. It has determined, directly or indirectly, more than half of the technical theology of the church.

JOSIAH ROYCE

Mystical experience does not supply concrete information. It does not bring new finite facts, new items that can be used in a description of "the scenery and circumstance" of the realm beyond our sense horizons. It is the awareness of a Presence, the consciousness of a Beyond, the discovery, as James puts it, that "we are continuous with a More of the same quality, which is operative in us and in touch with us."

RUFUS M. JONES

EDITOR'S NOTE

In addition to the more formal but grateful acknowledgments which appear on another page, the editor here records his deep appreciation of the assistance of many friends, American and foreign. He is especially indebted to Mr. Henry Morton Robinson, of Stockbridge, New York, for his constructive criticism and discriminating counsel; to Miss Jane T. Stoddart, of London, a member of the staff of the *British Weekly*, whose acquaintance with the literature of Spanish and German mysticism is unequaled; to Mr. Thomas S. Jones, Jr., of New York, who is both a poet and a specialist in the knowledge of mystical verse; and to Miss Anna M. Colcord, of Brooklyn, and Miss Rosalie de Veaux, of New York, secretaries, for their painstaking and accurate work of research in public libraries and private collections, and their expert skill in the preparation of the several drafts of the manuscript, and the various indices.

The compilation of such an anthology involves an enormous amount of labor. Correspondence with authors and publishers, and inquiries as to the sources of unidentified material cover years of time.

The editor is under obligation to the makers of other anthologies, such as Messrs. Nicholson and Lee's *Ox-*

Editor's Note

ford Book of English Mystical Verse, easily first in the list of anthologies of this order; Irene Hunter's *American Mystical Verse*; Mark Van Doren's *Anthology of World Poetry*; *Twentieth-Century Poetry*, edited by John Drinkwater, Henry Seidel Canby, and William Rose Benét; *The Oxford Book of English Verse*, edited by Sir Arthur Quiller-Couch; A. Methuen's *Anthology of Modern Verse*; *The World's Great Religious Poetry*, edited by Caroline Miles Hill; *Lyra Germanica*, translated by Catherine Drinkwater; Walter De La Mare's *Come Hither*; *The Bronze Treasury*, edited by Harry Kemp; *Redemption, An Anthology of the Cross*, edited by George H. Stuart; Louis Untermeyer's *Modern British Poetry, American Poetry Since 1900*; *A Celtic Anthology*, edited by Grace Rhys; *New Voices*, edited by Marguerite Wilkinson; Robert Bridges' *The Spirit of Man*; R. H. Strachan's *The Soul of Modern Poetry*; James Hope Moulton's *Early Religious Poetry of the Hebrews*; E. G. King's *Early Religious Poetry of Persia*; Edward Granville Browne's *A Persian Anthology*; W. Robertson Nicoll's *Songs of Rest*; Robert Haven Schauffler's *The Poetry Cure*; *The Humbler Poets*, edited by Wallace and Frances Rice; *A Book of Danish Verse*, selected and annotated by Oluf Friis; Jessie B. Rittenhouse's *The Little Book of Modern Verse, The Second Book of Modern Verse, The Third Book of Modern Verse*, and *The Little Book of Modern British Verse*; William Kingsland's *An Anthology of Mysticism* (mainly prose); Reynold Alleyne Nicholson's *Studies in Islamic Mysticism*; Herbert J. C. Grierson's *Metaphysical Lyrics and Poems of the*

Editor's Note

Seventeenth Century; Volney Streamer's *Voices of Doubt and Trust.*

Due credit is given to authors, translators, and publishers in the list of formal acknowledgements and, to many of them, additionally in an appendix of notes. The editor has met with uniform and immeasurable kindness on the part of writers and publishers. Even with the utmost diligence, in the effort to ascertain the names of publishers of certain poems and data concerning their authors, there remain titles concerning which no definite information was available. If any author's or publisher's rights have been invaded, the editor offers apology.

C. C. A.

INTRODUCTION

What is Mysticism? There have been many definitions, some good, some bad. The following may help to dispel some erroneous impressions, still too prevalent, about the meaning of a word which is often very loosely used.

The scholastic mystic, Bonaventura, says: "Mysticism is the extension of the mind to God by way of love's longing." Pfleiderer says: "Mysticism is the immediate feeling of the unity of the self with God; it is nothing, therefore, but the fundamental feeling of religion, the religious life at its very heart and centre. But what makes the mystical a special tendency inside religion is the endeavor to fix the immediateness of the life in God as such, and to find a permanent abode in the abstract inwardness of the life of pious feeling." (Here, however, there are, in my opinion, two errors. We should read "communion" for "unity"; Mysticism does not destroy the distinction between the human and the divine, though its ultimate end is to leave behind whatever separates us from God. And the poet-mystics, with whom we are dealing in this book, are not content with "abstract inwardness"; they find symbols and footprints of the divine in all that is good, true, and beautiful on earth.) Professor Pringle-Patterson says more fairly: "Mysticism appears in connexion with the en-

Introduction

deavor of the human mind to grasp the divine essence or the ultimate reality of things, and to enjoy the blessedness of actual communion with the highest. The first is the philosophic side of Mysticism; the second its religious side. The thought that is most intensely present with the mystic is that of a supreme all-pervading and indwelling Power, in whom all things are one. On the practical side, Mysticism maintains the possibility of direct intercourse with this Being of beings. God ceases to be an object and becomes an experience." Charles Kingsley says that "the great Mysticism is the belief which is becoming every day stronger with me, that all symmetrical natural objects are types of some spiritual truth or existence. This feeling of being surrounded by truths which I cannot grasp amounts to indescribable awe sometimes. Oh, to see, if but for a moment, the whole harmony of the great system! To hear once the music which the whole universe makes as it performs His bidding." (A good profession of Mysticism of the objective type.) R. L. Nettleship, of Oxford, writes: "True Mysticism is the consciousness that everything we experience is an element, and only an element, in fact, i.e., that in being what it is it is symbolic of something more." Still more searching is the splendid saying of Isaac Penington, one of the early Quakers: "Every truth is a shadow, except the last. But every truth is substance in its own place, though it be but a shadow in another place. And the shadow is a true shadow, as the substance is a true substance." (This emphasizes that Mysticism is a *quest*, a progressive initiation into the divine mysteries. At

Introduction

each stage, we say, like the Indian sage, of what we are leaving behind us, "Neti, Neti"; "Not this—this is not good enough to be true." Yet what we are rejecting was not worthless; it was "substance in its own place.") Lastly, Frank Granger says: "Mysticism is that attitude of mind which divines and moves towards the spiritual in the common things of life, not a partial and occasional operation of the mind under the guidance of far-fetched analogies."

There are several paths up the hill of the Lord. They meet at the top, in the beatific vision, but the tracks start from different sides. Some mystics are philosophers, like Plotinus, Eckhart, and Boehme. It is of these that Goethe was thinking when he said that 'Mysticism is the scholastic of the heart, the dialectic of the feelings.' For mystical philosophy is based on religious experience, carefully prepared for by bodily, mental, and moral discipline. Others, the mystics of the cloister, detach themselves entirely from the world, and look to trances and ecstasies as the reward of intense concentration on acts of devotion and contemplation. Many regard this as the most typical form of Mysticism. But there are others who, as some of the definitions which I have quoted prove, honor earth as "the shadow of heaven," and nature as a book "which heavenly truth imparts." Among these are many of the poet-mystics from whom this Anthology is taken.

The parallel between the artistic and the religious representation of things is very significant. Both are essentially unselfish. The selfish man has eyes only for the things which serve or baffle him in his schemes.

Introduction

To all else, whether within him or without, he is blind. But art is the wide world's memory of things. In the same way religion views things under the form of eternity and not as they give us pleasure or pain. Both art and religion make free use of the imagination, creating concrete images which symbolise the invisible. Some sympathetic critics of Mysticism, like Josiah Royce, have found an inconsistency in this readiness to use symbols, since a craving for immediacy is above all else characteristic of the mystical quest. But there is no contradiction. The mystic, if he is in deadly earnest, has no taste for what Wordsworth calls "loose types of things through all degrees." Pretty or playful fancies do not attract him. Nature, he thinks, half reveals and half conceals its Maker; and the mystic longs to tear the heart out of all experience.

Some of the poems in this volume express the symbolism of the nature-mystics; others the raptures of contemplative devotion. The cloistered mystic has sometimes to resort to the language of the earthly loves which he has renounced for a more austere and spiritual devotion. In the poetry of the Sufis a kind of sublimated eroticism is apparent; but Christian Mysticism is on the whole very free from this perversion. It may be that the saints of the cloister have penetrated most deeply into the joys and agonies of the mystical state; but these rare experiences are strictly not transferable. Language was not made to describe them, and memory can reproduce them very imperfectly. Such visions and revelations are not only the reward of a very special and terribly severe discipline; they belong also to a

Introduction

special temperament. It is a mistake to confine our attention to these extreme cases, as if they only could teach us what Mysticism means. In very various degrees, all truly religious persons are mystics; for the typical mystical experience is not trance or ecstasy; it is the act of prayer, when we are really praying and feel that our prayers are being heard.

It is natural that in a selection made for English readers the large majority of the poems should be by English and American writers. Some may think, quite wrongly, that our literature is not likely to be rich in this kind of poetry. The Anglo-Saxon is often said to be essentially practical, and his philosophy, if he has one, to be empirical, or, as it is now called, pragmatist. This notion, which is commonly held on the Continent of Europe, is no doubt made plausible by the national prosperity of Great Britain in the nineteenth century, and of America in the twentieth. It has been pointed out by several writers that Calvinism, which is not a poetical creed, has adapted itself more easily than other forms of Christianity to modern industrialism, so that the societies in which it has flourished, such as Scotland and the United States, have exhibited a very prosperous but not very beautiful civilization. But this judgment is superficial, and if passed upon the genius of the Anglo-Saxons generally, it is false. The typical Briton or American is not a materialist. There is probably no other language which can boast so great a wealth of imaginative literature. The Anglo-Saxon mind has a rather special affinity with Platonism, a tendency which is shown in much of our best poetry as well as in the

Introduction

general trend of our philosophy, if Professor Dewey will pardon me for saying so. And the best part of our national wisdom, our clearest visions of the invisible, are enshrined in our poetry. Our poetry, more decidedly than that of other nations, tends to be serious, moral, and often religious in its aim. Some of our poets have aspired, with Milton, to justify the ways of God to man; others, like Wordsworth, have considered the object of poetry to be "general and operative truth." Not that poetry can usurp the place of theology or of philosophy; though Mr. Yeats has boldly said that "whatever of philosophy has been made poetry is alone permanent." This reminds us of Maeterlinck's dictum that Mysticism is the true antiseptic in literature; "a book grows old in consequence of its anti-mysticism." Plato is immortal certainly not as a systematic philosopher, but as an inspired prose poet or prophet. In religion too the profoundest intuitions of faith are expressed poetically in myths and symbols, which the heavy hand of the dogmatist turns into flat historical recitals.

"Some form of song or musical language," says that fine critic, Principal Shairp of St. Andrews, "is the best possible adumbration of spiritual verities."

In the early middle ages the Irishman, John Scotus Erigena, translated the mystical treatises of Dionysius the Areopagite (really a Christian Neoplatonist of the fifth century) and we are told that the book "ran across England like deer." John the Scot was an isolated figure; but in the fourteenth century we find a remarkable group of English mystics—the unknown

Introduction

author of "The Cloud of Unknowing," Richard Rolle of Hampole, who wrote poetry, unfortunately too archaic in diction for this volume, and the exquisite Julian of Norwich, whose "Revelations" are one of the most perfect gems of mediæval literature.

At the Renaissance, Greek, and Plato, came back into their own, and we have Sidney's sonnets, and Spenser's "Hymn of Heavenly Beauty." Robert Southwell, whose fine poem on the Sacrament of the Altar is included in this collection, was a contemporary of Shakespeare. The mystical tradition is continued by John Donne, Dean of St. Paul's (1573-1631) a somewhat enigmatical figure, but a true poet; by Francis Quarles (1592-1644), a quaint writer with considerable charm; and by the ever popular George Herbert (1593-1632), a genuine saint of the Anglican Church. By the side of Herbert we usually place two other names—Welshmen like himself, Henry Vaughan (1641-1695), and Thomas Traherne; the latter hardly known until a few years ago, but now a favorite with many readers. Richard Crashaw (1613-1649) is another short-lived mystical poet of the same century, an unequal writer, with flashes of genuine inspiration, as in his noble "Hymn to the Name and Honor of the Admirable Saint Teresa." Crashaw became a Roman Catholic; Herbert, Vaughan, and Traherne are deeply imbued with the mind of the English Church, which Palgrave describes as characterized by "broad scholarly learning, liberal acceptance of art and culture, a faith rational, deeply founded and fervent." Contemporary with these poets was the remarkable group of Cambridge Plato-

Introduction

nists, some of whom were genuine mystics. They are important in the chain of the Platonic tradition in England, but with the exception of Henry More, in whom, as Southey says, "uncouth as he is, there are passages of the highest feeling and exquisite beauty," they wrote hardly any poetry. It is only necessary to mention them here in order that we may realize how strong, in that period of civil and religious strife, was the appeal of philosophical Mysticism to the religious thought of the time. This was also the age when George Fox founded the Society of Friends, a purely mystical sect, which from that time to this has taken the lead in almost every movement to apply Christian principles to practical problems. But the Quakers have not contributed much to poetry.

The eighteenth century adds little to the literature of Mysticism, whether in prose or verse. It was an unmystical age; though William Law, one of the most masculine and eloquent of our divines, came under the spell of Jacob Boehme. The temper of that age, with its appeal to common sense and reason, and the dread of what it called enthusiasm, was unfavorable to fervent and imaginative poetry of every kind. The eighteenth century produced many fine hymns, in which pious emotion finds vent; but the most successful hymns do not as a rule rank very high as literature. Perhaps the best are those of Bishop Ken; but Watts, Charles Wesley, and others deserve honorable mention. Watts' "Cradle Song" has a tender grace which has seldom been surpassed, and Toplady's much-loved hymn, "Rock of Ages," glows with a sublime simplicity of self-sur-

Introduction

render. The Olney Hymns of Cowper are very unequal; but the poetry of Mysticism is enriched by "Hark, my soul; it is the Lord"; "Sometimes a light surprises," and "Far from the world, O Lord, I flee."

William Blake stands by himself in the eighteenth century, as he would have done in any other period. A lonely mystic, to whom the unseen alone was the real, but who used both pen and pencil to record his strange visions, his daring speculations, his natural tenderness and simplicity, he holds a unique position in the history of British literature and art. To some extent he seems to belong to the romantic period which followed the Age of Rationalism.

To this revival we now turn. Keble and Newman are its two chief sacred poets. In Keble the muse of Herbert and Vaughan seems to have returned to England; Newman's poetry is at times of a finer quality, but gentleness and liberality are not among his gifts. However, the poetry of Mysticism at the opening of the nineteenth century is represented by greater names than these, and of these the greatest is William Wordsworth, who was, and wished to be, a religious teacher. "I wish," he said, "to be considered as a teacher, or as nothing." He was a born Platonist, who believed that all true beauty is heavenly, immortal, and spiritual, though it sheds gleams of loveliness on this lower world. It is by communion with this spiritual beauty, revealing itself to pure and loving hearts, and the mind of man is cleansed and elevated. But in reality it is not the *beauty* of nature—such as ravished the mind of Keats—which appealed most to Wordsworth. It is

Introduction

the sense of eternal and all-pervading Life—of an universe animated throughout, and obeying one law. His religion is not quite pantheism but panentheism, or universal divine immanence. Shelley and Coleridge are more pantheistic than Wordsworth, who found in the contemplation of impersonal external nature a revelation of a personal God. By long discipline and meditation he had gained the power "to see into the life of things." He gives us no stock-taking of nature's picturesque effects: his stage is bare of scenery and contains only actors. His scheme of life resembles that of Novalis, who says: "Let him who would arrive at the knowledge of nature train his moral sense; let him act and conceive in accordance with the noble essence of his soul; and as of itself nature will become open to him." Wordsworth himself speaks of "a sinking inward into ourselves from thought to thought, a steady remonstrance and a high resolve. Let the youth go back, as occasion will permit, to nature and to solitude. A world of fresh sensations will gradually open upon him, as instead of being propelled restlessly toward others in admiration or too hasty love, he makes it his prime business to understand himself." He was an ascetic of an unfamiliar type, and his Mysticism, profound as it is, owes little to the human love in which Robert Browning found the opening of heaven's gates. The well-known lines in which he describes "the sense sublime of something far more deeply interfused—a motion and a spirit that impels all thinking things, all objects of all thought, and rolls through all things" express the innermost core of Wordsworth's Mysticism.

Introduction

Robert Browning, on the other hand, is the mystic of *personality*. "Do you care much for nature?" he was asked. "Yes, a great deal," he replied, "but for human beings a great deal more." The mystical element in his message is his belief in *love* as the constitutive principle of life—love, "the spark which God gave us from His fire of fires." He is the hierophant of love's mysteries, and love, for him, as for Plato, begins as Eros, not as the Christian *caritas* which has cast Eros behind it. "So let us say—not, since we know, we love, but rather, since we love, we know enough." It is a sentiment which the mediaeval mystics of the cloister would have approved; but their notion of love was very different from his.

Browning's great contemporary, Tennyson, is in reality the less mystical of the two. His biography shows that he was no stranger to the mystical trance, and his beautiful poem, "The Ancient Sage" shows an acute understanding and appreciation of Mysticism; but his ethics are definitely Victorian, prosaic, and anti-mystical. For him, the quest of the Holy Grail has as much to do with the wrecking of King Arthur's great scheme as the unfaithfulness of Guinevere. This is not said in disparagement of a very great poet, who has successfully survived the vulgar belittling of his genius in the generation after his death.

The Anthology to which this Introduction is a preface contains selections from a multitude of lesser names, chiefly in our own period. Some of them are far from negligible as poetry; and their inclusion has the advantage of showing how much that type of thought

Introduction

and feeling which has been called Mysticism means to our generation. In particular this book will reveal to many readers in Great Britain the beauty and value of American poetry.

Longfellow, and to a less extent Whittier, have long been favorites in England, where E. A. Poe and Walt Whitman also have many admirers. But I agree with that accomplished critic, Alfred Noyes, that neither in this country nor in America has adequate recognition been given to Emerson as a poet. Even if we grant, as I think we must, that a life so shielded from anxiety, sorrow and sickness, and surrounded by highly cultivated society of the type most congenial to him, was excluded by his great good fortune from a knowledge of the bitter problems of existence; even if it is much more true of him than of Wordsworth (of whom Matthew Arnold made the criticism) that he "averts his eyes from half of human fate," Emerson's best poems have a message of their own, and a lofty beauty of their own, which ought to have been more widely recognized. I feel the same about Lowell, who understood Mysticism, and whose idealism is made the more attractive by his brave and manly outlook upon life. Another mystical poet who should be better known on this side of the Atlantic is Sidney Lanier, whose Shakespearean sonnets combine fine and delicate feeling with a perfection of technique comparable with Shakespeare's own. There are other American names in this collection which will arouse interest and admiration.

One of the most remarkable things about mystical literature is its uniformity. Like the sublime subjects

Introduction

with which it deals, Mysticism seems to be independent of space and time. The mystics all speak the same language; their testimony agrees in the most surprising manner. This book contains specimens of Oriental Mysticism, from India and Persia. These were written long ago; they were written under circumstances very unlike our own; they are not even the work of Christians. And yet they are hardly distinguishable from some modern mystical poetry written in America or in the west of Europe. Rightly considered, this phenomenon should increase our respect for and confidence in the testimony of the mystics. They have followed the same path, seeking the same goal; and when they tell us what they have seen, we find that these explorers of the high places of the spiritual life do not differ greatly from one another. The philosopher Plotinus, baffled, as all visionaries are, by the impossibility of putting on paper those wonderful experiences which Saint Paul says "it is not lawful for man to utter," several times repeats, "The vision is for him who will seek it." Live as I have lived, and you will see what I have seen. Mystics not only admit, they insist on the inadequacy of their descriptions; and yet we can recognize the same chart of the land that is very far off, the same experience of purification, of enlightenment, of alternate rapture and dereliction, the same recurrent images of blinding light and murky darkness, of growing detachment from all earthly interests, of simplification leading up to the ineffable experience of losing the separate self and becoming united with God Himself. It is the fashion to explain

Introduction

all this psychologically—to write well-documented treatises, scientific in form, on the varieties of religious experience. Some of these books are as valuable as they are interesting, but let the reader bear one thing in mind. The psychologist's point of view is not that of the mystic himself. The psychologist investigates mystical phenomena merely as states of consciousness. He does not ask whether these states of consciousness point to any objective field of truth outside themselves. He abstains from asking this question, and in refusing to ask it he often seems to have decided for himself in the negative. He tries to account for visions and revelations without going beyond the subjective condition of the visionary's mind.

But this is not the attitude of the mystic himself. He cares nothing for states of consciousness. He stakes his all on the power of the human soul to see the invisible, to live and breathe in the eternal world, and at last to behold God face to face. If this hope is illusory—if Plato was wrong in his noble confidence that "the fully real can be fully known," the mystic would be the first to admit that his whole life is a mistake, that he has been hunting shadows and living in delusion. But he tells us that he knows, with ever-increasing certainty, that his quest has not been vain. Is there any reason why we should not believe him?

Is it necessary for us, after what has been said, to reply to Samuel Johnson's dictum that poetry is not the proper vehicle for spiritual truth? "Poetry," he says, "loses its lustre and its power, because it is applied to the decoration of something more excellent than itself. All that pious verse can do is to help the memory, and delight the ear, and for these purposes it may be very useful, but it supplies nothing to the mind. The ideas of Christian theology are too simple for eloquence, too sacred for fiction, and too majestic for ornament." The great lexicographer belonged to his own generation, and was not a good judge of some kinds of poetry. We shall rather agree with Palgrave that "nowhere is the power and magic of poetry as an art more naturally in place or better employed than when her inspiring muses are Faith, Hope, and Love—when her subjects are those incomparably highest and most vital interests to mankind, which may be briefly summed up as right conduct here, and its reward hereafter." To the mystic, however, the reward of right conduct is not deferred. His earth is that part of heaven in which his lot is cast; his God is not far away, but closer than breathing and nearer than hands and feet; to him the whole creation is a hymn of praise sung by the Divine Word to the glory of God the Father; and if he sings himself, it is in the spirit of Milton's prayer "At a Solemn Music":

O may we soon again renew that song,
And keep in tune with heaven, till God ere long
To His celestial concert us unite,
To live with Him, and sing in endless morn of light.

W. R. Inge.

Saint Paul's Deanery.
London.

CONTENTS

Acceptance. *Willard Wattles*	450
Adrift. *Mrs. Edward Dowden*	160
Adventante Deo. *John Addington Symonds*	134
After St. Augustine. *Mary Elizabeth Coleridge*	262
Air of coolness plays upon his face, An. *Sarah N. Cleghorn*	283
All are but parts. *Alexander Pope*	95
All in all. *John Bannister Tabb*	227
All these things live. From *The Wisdom of Ben-Sira*	9
All things are full of God. *John Stuart Blackie*	153
Amendment. *Thomas Traherne*	80
Ancient sage, The (from). *Alfred, Lord Tennyson*	128
And how shall I call upon my God? *St. Augustine*	17
Anodyne, The. *Sarah N. Cleghorn*	284
At Beach St. Mary. *Frank W. Gunsaulus*	252
Auguries of innocence. *William Blake*	99
Autumn. *Rabindranath Tagore*	300
Ballade of the centre, A. *Anonymous*	211
Barter. *Margaret Widdemer*	456
Beauty. *Plato*	7
Before action. *William Noel Hodgson*	398
Before the dawn. *Alice Mary Buckton*	375

Contents

Birth. *Charlotte Perkins Gilman*	393
Borderlands. *Louise Imogen Guiney*	262
Burning Babe, The. *Robert Southwell*	63
By every ebb. *Willard Wattles*	450
By Severn's banks. *Arthur L. Salmon*	340
By the margin of the great deep. *George William Russell (A. E.)*	353
By those heights we dare to dare. *Sir James Rennell Rodd*	339
Calm Soul of all things. *Matthew Arnold*	117
Canticle of the sun. *St. Francis of Assisi*	23
Century of Indian epigrams, A (from). *Paul Elmer More*	411
Chant out of doors, A. *Marguerite Wilkinson*	285
Chartless. *Emily Dickinson*	174
Christ and the pagan. *John Bannister Tabb*	228
Christ in Flanders. *L. W.*	309
Christmas night. *Alice Meynell*	234
Circuit of being, The. *Anonymous*	148
City, The. *George William Russell (A. E.)*	360
City of dream, The (two extracts). *Robert Buchanan*	150, 151
City of God, The. *Francis Turner Palgrave*	139
Cliff, The. *Eric Ericson*	203
Colloquy, A. *Laurence Binyon*	315
Confession. *Paul Verlaine*	112
Contours. *Zona Gale*	391
Cosmic outlook, A. *Frederick William Henry Myers*	218
Craftsman's creed, A. *James P. Haney*	398

Contents

Crossing the bar. *Alfred, Lord Tennyson*	132
Crying Abba, Father. *William Canton*	229
Cry of man, The. *James Oppenheim*	420
Dance chant, A. *Anonymous*	199
Deaf. *Margaret Deland*	383
Death. *Anonymous*	171
Death is before me today. *Anonymous*	1
Deep sea soundings. *Sarah Williams*	459
De mortuis nil nisi bonum. *Richard Realf*	164
Desiderium indesideratum. *Francis Thompson*	257
Desire. *William Sharp (Fiona Macleod)*	248
Divine image, The. *William Blake*	98
Divine Lover, The (from). *Phineas Fletcher*	67
Divine vision, The. *George William Russell (A. E.)*	354
Dominus illuminatio mea. *R. D. Blackmore*	117
Dost thou remember me? *Emily Dickinson*	173
Doubt. *Helen Hunt Jackson*	177
Dusk. *Kenneth Morris*	414
Dwelling-place, The. *Henry Vaughan*	88
Each in his own tongue. *William H. Carruth*	261
East London. *Matthew Arnold*	116
Elder sacrament, The. *Charles Wharton Stork*	438
Elixir, The. *George Herbert*	69
Enough. *Rose Fyleman*	323
Envoi, L'. *John G. Neihardt*	417
Eternal Goodness, The. *John Greenleaf Whittier*	197
Eternity, I'm coming. *Emily Dickinson*	172
Evening song. *B. S. Ingeman*	115
Eventide. *Caroline Atherton Mason*	187
Everlasting Mercy, The (from). *John Masefield*	328

xliii

Contents

Every day of life, The. *Annie Sophia Waples*	311
Ev'n like two little bank-dividing brooks. *Francis Quarles*	68
Excursion, The (from). *William Wordsworth*	145
Faith. *Richard Lew Dawson*	382
Falconer of God, The. *William Rose Benét*	373
Falterings toward the unknown God. *Charles Wharton Stork*	440
Father, we thank Thee. *J. S. Hoyland*	345
Final faith, The. *George Sterling*	280
Final thought, The (from). *Maurice Thompson*	194
First flight. *Clinton Scollard*	434
Florida Sunday (from). *Sidney Lanier*	179
Flower in the crannied wall. *Alfred, Lord Tennyson*	133
Flying wheel, The. *Katharine Tynan*	271
For I have learned to look on nature. *William Wordsworth*	146
For I know that my Redeemer liveth. *Solomon Solis-Cohen*	364
Fringe of heaven, The. *Paul R. Bewsher*	314
Frozen grail, The. *Elsa Barker*	372
Fruit-gathering (from). *Rabindranath Tagore*	299
General communion, A. *Alice Meynell*	235
Gift, The. *Aline Kilmer*	406
Gift of intelligence, The. *Jan van Ruysbroeck*	46
Give way! *Charlotte Perkins Gilman*	392
Glory of the grass, The. *Claire Wallace Flynn*	386
Goal in sight, The. *Christina Rossetti*	141
God. *Gamaliel Bradford*	375

Contents

Goddess's song from "Al Aaraaf," The. *Edgar Allan Poe*	188
God is not dumb. *James Russell Lowell*	186
God makes a path. *Roger Williams*	90
God of the open air. *Henry van Dyke*	449
God's garden. *Richard Eugene Burton*	378
God's grandeur. *Gerard Manley Hopkins*	154
God's world. *Edna St. Vincent Millay*	410
Go not away. *Mary Clemmer Ames*	167
Great art Thou, O Lord. *St. Augustine*	15
Great voice, The. *Clinton Scollard*	434
Growth. *Lizette Woodworth Reese*	427
Guest, The. *Augusta Albertson*	366
Guest, The. *Harriet M. Kimball*	178
Heart of God. *Vachel Lindsay*	284
Heathen hymn, A. *Sir Lewis Morris*	207
Heavenly life, The. *Luis de León*	57
He is made one with nature. *Percy Bysshe Shelley*	101
He is the light. *Henry Herbert Knibbs*	406
He is the Lonely Greatness of the world. *Madeleine Caron Rock*	338
He who is meek and contented. *Kabir*	53
Hidden life. *Charles G. Ames*	166
Higher pantheism, The. *Alfred, Lord Tennyson*	130
Hill-born, The. *Maxwell Struthers Burt*	377
Holy Face, The. *Paul Claudel*	302
Holy land. *Richard Watson Gilder*	223
Hound of heaven, The. *Francis Thompson*	253
Human cry, The. *Alfred, Lord Tennyson*	131
Hymn of Sivaite Puritans. *Anonymous*	18

Contents

Hymn to Aton. *Akhenaton (Amenhotep IV)*	1
Hymn to heavenly beauty (from). *Edmund Spenser*	65
Hymn to intellectual beauty. *Percy Bysshe Shelley*	104
Hymn to Zeus. *Æschylus*	5
I am the way. *Alice Meynell*	236
I cannot find Thee. *Eliza Scudder*	202
Icarus. *Anonymous*	66
I died. *Jalal ud-Din Rumi*	22
I do not fear. *John Hall Wheelock*	454
If, Lord, Thy love for me is strong. *St. Teresa*	56
If there had anywhere appeared. *Richard Chenevix Trench*	134
I gaze aloof. *Thomas Whytehead*	148
I had a dream last night. *Edwin Arlington Robinson*	431
I have a life with Christ to live. *John Campbell Shairp*	149
I have lifted my eyes. *Charles Poole Cleaves*	380
I know not. *Elizabeth Gibson*	323
I lived my days apart. *Siegfried Sassoon*	341
Image, The. *Katharine Tynan*	269
Immanence. *Evelyn Underhill*	308
Immortal. *Lucy Larcom*	184
Immortal hour, The. *Rachel Annand Taylor*	350
Immortality. *A. St. John Adcock*	313
Implicit faith. *Aubrey Thomas de Vere*	201
Ineffable Love Divine. *Jacopone da Todi*	24
Infinito, L'. *Giacomo Leopardi*	110
In God my soul reposes. *Theodore Fechner*	114

Contents

In praise of common things. *Lizette Woodworth Reese*	425
In salutation to the eternal peace. *Sarojini Naidu*	300
Inspiration. From *Ode VI of Solomon*	9
Inspirations. *William James Dawson*	242
In summer fields. *Christina Catherine Fraser-Tytler*	350
Interpreter, An. *John Bannister Tabb*	228
In the garden of the Lord. *Helen Keller*	403
In the hospital. *Arthur Guiterman*	396
In the silence. *Josephine Preston Peabody*	282
In thine own heart. *Johann Scheffler (Angelus Silesius)*	75
In this, O nature, yield. *Sir Ronald Ross*	348
Introit. *Grace Rhys*	274
Invention. *Sir William Watson*	313
Invisible, The. *Richard Watson Gilder*	225
Invocation. *Ibn Gabirol*	19
Invocation, An. *John Addington Symonds*	135
I see His blood upon the rose. *Joseph M. Plunkett*	292
I stood within the heart of God. *William Vaughn Moody*	279
It were not hard, we think, to serve Him. *Margaret Seebach*	342
I vex me not. *Thomas Bailey Aldrich*	209
I went to sleep; and now I am refreshed. *John Henry Newman*	127
I will hearken what the Lord God will speak. *Thomas à Kempis*	48
Johannes Milton Senex. *Robert Bridges*	226
Kingdom of God, The. *Francis Thompson*	257

xlvii

Contents

Kinship. *Angela Morgan*	411
Knight of Jesus, The. *Henry Suso*	47
Land, ho! *Thomas Edward Brown*	161
Last appeal, A. *Frederick William Henry Myers*	219
Last lines. *Emily Brontë*	119
Let us beside the river rest awhile. *William James Dawson*	243
Let us hasten, let us fly. *Aristophanes*	6
Life. *Edith Wharton*	451
Life and death. *Laura Spencer Porter*	189
Life's evening. *William Dudley Foulke*	388
Light. *M. Elizabeth Crouse*	190
Lines written in her breviary. *St. Teresa*	56
Litany for latter-day mystics, A. *Cale Young Rice*	430
Little bird I am, A. *Jeanne Marie Guyon*	73
Little hill among New Hampshire hills, A. *Witter Bynner*	378
Living flame of love. *St. John of the Cross*	55
Lo, as some bard. *Frederick William Henry Myers*	220
Longing. *James Russell Lowell*	185
Lord, I have shut my door. *Mary E. Atkinson*	168
Lord is my portion, The. *Jehudah Halevi*	22
Lord is my shepherd, The. *David, King of Judah and Israel*	2
Lost and found. *George MacDonald*	206
Love. *St. Paul*	11
Love bade me welcome. *George Herbert*	71
Love holds me. *Grace Duffield Goodwin*	395
Marshes of Glynn, The (from). *Sidney Lanier*	180

Contents

Men told me, Lord! *David Starr Jordan*	233
Messenger, The. *Richard Hovey*	176
Milton (from). *William Blake*	97
Miracles. *Molly Anderson Haley*	397
My faith is larger than the hills. *Emily Dickinson*	173
My garden. *Thomas Edward Brown*	163
My Lord hides Himself. *Kabir*	52
Mystic's prayer, The. *William Sharp (Fiona Macleod)*	248
New hymn for solitude, A. *Edward Dowden*	222
Night is come, The. *Sir Thomas Browne*	77
Night of stars, A. *Luis de León*	59
No distant Lord. *Maltbie D. Babcock*	168
Now that I have grown to manhood. *Heinrich Heine*	107
Oarsmen, The. *Rabindranath Tagore*	297
Obedience. *George MacDonald*	205
Obscure night of the soul, The. *St. John of the Cross*	53
Ode: intimations of immortality (from). *William Wordsworth*	142
Ode to God. *Gavrila Románovich Derzhávin*	90
Of an orchard. *Katharine Tynan*	270
Of children. *Kahlil Gibran*	289
Off shore. *Algernon Charles Swinburne*	212
Of reason and passion. *Kahlil Gibran*	290
Of the blessed sacrament of the aulter. *Robert Southwell*	62
O Lord Thou hast searched me. *David, King of Judah and Israel*	3

Contents

O Lord, where shall I find Thee? *Solomon Solis-Cohen*	362
O Love Divine and Great. *Jacopone da Todi*	41
On a subway express. *Chester Firkins*	385
On Christmas eve. *W. Force Stead*	343
On Saint Teresa. *Richard Crashaw*	78
Open door, The. *Grace Coolidge*	381
Ordeal, The. *Thomas S. Jones, Jr.*	403
Origin of life, The. *Alfred Noyes*	333
O servant, where dost thou seek Me? *Kabir*	52
O splendour of God! *Dante*	44
O soul of mine, how noble wert thou made! *Jacopone da Todi*	37
Other place, The. *Margaret Widdemer*	455
O Thou, in whom we live and breathe. *J. S. Hoyland*	344
O Thou who lovest with divine passion. *J. S. Hoyland*	347
Our Christ. *Lucy Larcom*	183
Out of the dark. *Marguerite Wilkinson*	286
Out of the silence (from). *James Rhoades*	216
Over all presides the Universal Soul. *Plotinus*	12
Over the city. *Edward Carpenter*	316
Overtones. *William Alexander Percy*	425
Pagan re-invokes the twenty-third psalm, A. *Robert Wolfe*	461
Pagan's prayer, A. *Alice Brown*	377
Paradox, The. *Alfred Noyes*	335
Parting, The. *Thomas S. Jones, Jr.*	402
Passage to India (from). *Walt Whitman*	195
Passer-by, The. *Mabel Earle*	384

Contents

Passionate, with longing in mine eyes. *Lâlla*	45
Patmos. *Edith M. Thomas*	241
Pavilions of peace, The. *Grace Rhys*	273
Peace. *Heinrich Heine*	108
Per aspera. *Florence Earle Coates*	233
Perfection. *Francis Carlin*	352
Pied beauty. *Gerard Manley Hopkins*	159
Pilgrim, The. *Herbert E. Palmer*	337
Pilgrim, The. *Richard Wightman*	457
Ploughman at the plough. *Louis Golding*	324
Poet's prayer, The. *Stephen Phillips*	276
Prayer, A. *John Drinkwater*	321
Prayer. *C. F.*	296
Prayer. *Thomas S. Jones, Jr.*	401
Prayer. *Madeline Mason-Manheim*	409
Prayer. *Alfred, Lord Tennyson*	133
Prayer for pain. *John G. Neihardt*	418
Prayer for the past, A. *George MacDonald*	203
Prayer of Columbus (from). *Walt Whitman*	195
Prism of life, The. *John Addington Symonds*	137
Problem, The. *Ralph Waldo Emerson*	176
Pronouns. *Karle Wilson Baker*	371
Prophet, The. *Alexander Sergeyevich Pushkin*	111
Prospice. *Robert Browning*	122
Psalm. *Jessie E. Sampter*	432
Pulley, The. *George Herbert*	71
Quatrains. *Abu Saʿid Ibn Abiʾl-Khayr*	20
Quest, The. *James H. Cousins*	160
Quest, The. *Eva Gore-Booth*	353
Quest, The. *Joseph Fort Newton*	419

Contents

Quiet. *John Spencer Muirhead*	416
Quo vadis? *Myles E. Conolly*	381
Rapture. *Stefan George*	304
Rapture, The. *Thomas Traherne*	82
Redemption. *Frederick William Orde Ward*	312
Refuge. *Thomas S. Jones, Jr.*	401
Renunciation. *Mark W. Call*	379
Reply. *Sir Ronald Ross*	348
Reply of Socrates, The. *Edith M. Thomas*	240
Retreate, The. *Henry Vaughan*	87
Revelation. *Edwin Markham*	408
Rhapsodist's song, A. *Cale Young Rice*	428
Rose and God, The. *Charles Wharton Stork*	444
Rose of the world, The. *William Butler Yeats*	352
Rune of age, The. *William Sharp (Fiona Macleod)*	248
Saint Francis. *Thomas S. Jones, Jr.*	400
Saint John of the Cross. *Thomas S. Jones, Jr.*	399
Sanctuaries. *Katharine Tynan*	267
Sanctuary. *Clinton Scollard*	435
Seasons, The (from). *James Thomson*	94
Second crucifixion, The. *Richard Le Gallienne*	325
Secret garden, The. *Robert Nichols*	331
Secret way, The. *Zona Gale*	388
Seeking God. *Edward Dowden*	222
Seek no more abroad, say I. *Joseph Beaumont*	77
Seen and the unseen, The. *Abram J. Ryan*	191
Servants, The. *Richard Wightman*	458
Shadows. *Vladimir Solovev*	116
Sheep and lambs. *Katharine Tynan*	270

Contents

Silence. *Charles Hanson Towne*	448
Soldier in France, The. *Joyce Kilmer*	292
Song, A. *Richard Crashaw*	78
Song of thanksgiving, A. *Angela Morgan*	413
Song of the future, A. *Sidney Lanier*	182
Sonnet. *Snow Longley*	408
Sonnet. *George Santayana*	366
Sonnets. *John Masefield*	329
Sonnets of the new birth, 2, 4, 12. *Marguerite Wilkinson*	287
Sonnet to Laura. *Petrarch*	45
So thin a veil. *Edward Carpenter*	317
Soul is in the body as the pilot in the ship, The. *Plotinus*	14
Soul's prayer, The. *Sarojini Naidu*	301
Soul's travelling, The (from). *Elizabeth Barrett Browning*	120
Source, The. *Josephine Preston Peabody*	281
Speak, Lord, for Thy servant heareth. *Thomas à Kempis*	50
Spectrum, The. *Cosmo Monkhouse*	215
Specula. *Thomas Edward Brown*	162
Sponsa Dei. *Coventry Kersey Dighton Patmore*	137
Spring's sacrament. *Harold E. Goad*	395
Starlight. *Edward Rowland Sill*	278
Star map, A. *Sara Teasdale*	447
Starry host, The. *John Lancaster Spalding*	193
Summum bonum. *Louise Imogen Guiney*	263
Supersensual. *Evelyn Underhill*	307
Symbol. *David Morton*	416

Contents

Tenebrae. *Lawrence Wilson*	460
Therefore to whom turn I but to Thee? *Robert Browning*	123
There is one mind. *Samuel Taylor Coleridge*	100
They are all gone into the world of light. *Henry Vaughan*	89
They list for me the things I may not know. *Anonymous*	210
Thick is the darkness. *William Ernest Henley*	126
This corruptible. *Elinor Wylie*	293
This I ask Thee. *Zoroaster*	5
Thou art of all created things. *Pedro Calderón de la Barca*	72
Thou canst choose the eastern circle. *Ruth Temple Lindsay*	327
Thoughts of God, The (from). *Frances Ridley Havergal*	125
Threnody (from). *Ralph Waldo Emerson*	174
Thy joy in sorrow. *Chauncey Hare Townshend*	448
'Tis not the skill of human art. *Jeanne Marie Guyon*	75
To a daisy. *Alice Meynell*	239
To a waterfowl. *William Cullen Bryant*	169
To be old. *Helen Eldred Storke*	446
To the mother of Christ the Son of Man. *Alice Meynell*	236
To the victor. *William Ellery Leonard*	407
Transfiguration. *Henry W. Warren*	206
Treasure, The. *Alice Meynell*	237
Trust. *Lizette Woodworth Reese*	427

Contents

Turris eburnea. *Wilfred Rowland Childe*	317
Twilight of earth, The. *George William Russell (A. E.)*	357
Two mysteries, The. *Mary Mapes Dodge*	214
Under a Wiltshire apple tree. *Anna de Bary*	319
Undying light. *Richard Watson Gilder*	224
Universal prayer, The. *Alexander Pope*	95
Unknown God, The. *Alice Meynell*	238
Up-hill. *Christina Rossetti*	141
Uxbridge road. *Evelyn Underhill*	305
Valley of silence, The. *William Sharp (Fiona Macleod)*	250
Veni Creator. *Bliss Carman*	265
Vestigia. *Bliss Carman*	264
Vision, The. *Thomas Traherne*	82
Visionary, The. *Emily Brontë*	118
Vision of beauty, A. *George William Russell (A. E.)*	355
Voice, The. *Sara Teasdale*	446
Voice of God, The. *James Stephens*	343
Voices of Christmas, The. *Harry Kemp*	404
Waiting. *John Burroughs*	213
We are not cast away. *Plotinus*	13
We may ascend to Him. *Plotinus*	15
Where is God? *Robert Collyer*	163
Where shall I find Thee? *Jehudah Halevi*	20
Where the blessed feet have trod. *Michael Field*	232
White Comrade, The. *Robert Haven Schauffler*	435
White peace, The. *William Sharp (Fiona Macleod)*	251

Contents

White star of time. *William Sharp (Fiona Macleod)*	251
Who walks with beauty. *David Morton*	415
With whom is no variableness, neither shadow of turning. *Arthur Hugh Clough*	125
Word, The. *Richard Realf*	164
World, The. *Henry Vaughan*	85
World we live in, The. *Lucy Larcom*	185
Wreck of the Deutschland, The. *Gerard Manley Hopkins*	155
Written in a volume of the Imitation of Christ. *Marya Zaturenska*	462
Yea every day He comes. *Susan Coolidge*	171
Yes, it was the mountain echo. *William Wordsworth*	147

LYRA MYSTICA

No one can describe the contact with Reality, which is rapture, yet everyone, I suppose, experiences it at some moment of his life. The most we can do is to put down a few inadequate words that report not the thing itself, but a memory of light and of more light.

E. YEATS-BROWN

DEATH IS BEFORE ME TODAY

Egyptian 3000 B.C.

Death is before me today
Like the recovery of a sick man,
Like going forth into a garden after sickness.

Death is before me today
Like the odour of myrrh,
Like sitting under the sail on a windy day. . . .

Death is before me today
Like the course of the freshet,
Like the return of a man from the war-galley to his
    house. . . .

Death is before me today
As a man longs to see his house
When he has spent years in captivity.

Anonymous

HYMN TO ATON

Egyptian Fourteenth Century B.C.

I shall breathe the sweet breath
Which comes forth from Thy mouth.
I shall behold Thy beauty every day.
It is my desire that I may hear Thy sweet voice,
Even the North wind, that my limbs may rejuvenate
    with life
Through love of Thee.

Give me Thy hands, holding Thy spirit,
That I may receive it and may live by it.
Call Thou upon my name throughout eternity
And it shall never fail.

Akhenaton (Amenhotep IV)

THE LORD IS MY SHEPHERD

Hebrew Tenth Century B.C.

The Lord is my shepherd;
I shall not want.

> He maketh me to lie down in green pastures:
> He leadeth me beside still waters.
> He restoreth my soul:
> He guideth me in paths of righteousness for his name's sake.
>
> Yea, though I walk through the valley of the shadow of death
> I will fear no evil;
> For thou art with me:
> Thy rod and thy staff, they comfort me.
>
> Thou preparest a table before me
> In the presence of mine enemies:
> Thou anointest my head with oil:
> My cup runneth over.

Surely goodness and mercy shall follow me all the days of my life:
And I will dwell in the house of the Lord forever.

David, King of Judah and Israel

Lyra Mystica

O LORD THOU HAST SEARCHED ME

Hebrew Tenth Century B.C.

O Lord, thou hast searched me and known me.
    Thou knowest my downsitting and mine uprising,
    Thou understandest my thought afar off.
Thou searchest out my path and my lying down,
    And art acquainted with all my ways.
For there is not a word in my tongue,
    But lo, O Lord, thou knowest it altogether.
Thou hast beset me behind and before,
    And laid thine hand upon me.
Such knowledge is too wonderful for me;
    It is high, I cannot attain unto it.
Whither shall I go from thy spirit?
    Or whither shall I flee from thy presence?
If I ascend up into heaven, thou art there:
    If I make my bed in Sheol, behold thou art there.
If I take the wings of the morning,
    And dwell in the uttermost parts of the sea;
Even there shall thy hand lead me,
    And thy right hand shall hold me.
If I say, Surely the darkness shall overwhelm me,
    And the light about me shall be night;
Even the darkness hideth not from thee,
    But the night shineth as the day:
        The darkness and the light are both alike to thee.
For thou hast possessed my reins:
    Thou hast covered me in my mother's womb.
I will give thanks unto thee; for I am fearfully and won-
        derfully made:

Wonderful are thy works;
> And that my soul knoweth right well.

My frame was not hidden from thee,
> When I was made in secret,
>> And curiously wrought in the lowest parts of the earth.

Thine eyes did see my unperfect substance,
> And in thy book were all my members written,

Which day by day were fashioned,
> When as yet there was none of them.

How precious also are thy thoughts unto me, O God!
> How great is the sum of them!

If I could count them they are more in number than the sand:
> When I awake I am still with thee.

Surely thou wilt slay the wicked, O God:
> Depart from me, therefore, ye bloodthirsty men.

For they speak against thee wickedly,
> And thine enemies take thy name in vain.

Do I not hate them that hate thee, O Lord?
> And am I not grieved with those that rise up against thee?

I hate them with a perfect hatred:
> I count them mine enemies,

Search me, O God, and know my heart:
> Try me and know my thoughts;

And see if there be any way of wickedness in me,
> And lead me in the way everlasting.

David, King of Judah and Israel

THIS I ASK THEE

Persian Tenth Century B.C.

This I ask Thee—tell it to me truly, Lord!
Who the Sire was, Father first of Holiness?
Who the pathway for the sun and stars ordained?
Who, through whom its moon doth wax and wane again?
This and much else do I long, O God, to know.

This I ask Thee—tell it to me truly, Lord!
Who set firmly earth below, and kept the sky
Sure from falling? Who the streams and trees did make?
Who their swiftness to the winds and clouds hath yoked?
Who, O Mazda, was the Founder of Good Thought?

This I ask Thee—tell it to me truly, Lord!
Who, benignant, made the darkness and the light?
Who, benignant, sleep and waking did create?
Who the morning, noon, and evening did decree
As reminders to the wise, of duty's call?

Zoroaster

HYMN TO ZEUS

Greek Fifth Century B.C.

Zeus,—by what name soe'er
    He glories being addressed,
Even by that holiest name
    I name the Highest and the Best.
On him I cast my troublous care,
    My only refuge from despair:

Weighing all else, in Him alone I find
Relief from this vain burden of the mind.

One erst appeared supreme,
  Bold with abounding might,
But like a darkling dream
  Vanished in long past night
Powerless to save; and he is gone
  Who flourished since, in turn to own
Him conqueror, to whom with soul on fire
Man crying aloud shall gain his soul's desire—,

Zeus who prepared for men
  The path of wisdom, binding fast
Learning to suffering. In their sleep
  The mind is visited again
With memory of affliction past.
  Without the will, reflection deep
Reads lesson that perforce shall last,
Thanks to the power that plies the sovran oar,
Resistless, toward the eternal shore.

Æschylus

LET US HASTEN, LET US FLY

Greek 455–375 B.C.

Let us hasten—let us fly—
Where the lovely meadows lie;
 Where the living waters flow;
 Where the roses bloom and blow.
Heirs of immortality,

Segregated, safe and pure,
Easy, sorrowless, secure;
Since our earthly course is run,
We behold a brighter sun.
Holy lives—a holy vow—
Such rewards await us now.

Aristophanes

BEAUTY

Greek 428–348 B.C.

For he who has been taught in things of love so far,
And who has learned to see the beautiful
In order and succession,
When he comes toward the end
Will suddenly perceive a world of beauty,—

. . . .

Not fair or foul, according to the point of view,
Or time, or place, but beauty absolute,
Apart; simple, and everlasting,
Without increase, decrease, or any change,
Imparted to the ever-growing
Changeful beauties of all other things;
He who, impelled by love, uprising thence,
Begins to see that beauty,
Nears the end.

The time process, of being led
To things of love, is this—
To use earth's beauty as the stair
Up which he mounts to other beauty,

Going from one to all fair forms,
And from fair forms
To actions fair, to fair ideas,
Until he comes to beauty absolute,
To beauty's essence.

This—to Socrates, the Mantineian stranger spoke—
Is the life a man should lead, above all others,
In contemplation of beauty absolute,
Which, if you once beheld,
You would perceive to be not measured,
As by gold, or garments, or fair bodies.

. . . .

But what if man had eyes to see
The beauty pure, divine and clear, and unalloyed,—
Not clogged with the pollutions of mortality,
And all the vanities and colors of this life—
Thither looking, holding converse with true beauty,
Divine and simple, bringing into being
And educating creations of virtue,
And not idols alone.

Do you not see that in this communion only
Beholding beauty with the mind,
He will be enabled to bring forth
Not images of beauty, but realities?
For he has hold of a reality;
He brings forth and educates true virtue;
To become the friend of God and be immortal,
If a mortal may,
Would that be an ignoble life?

Such, Phaedrus—and I speak not to you alone,
But to all men—
Were the words of Diotima,
And I am persuaded of their truth.

Plato

ALL THESE THINGS LIVE

Hebrew Second Century B.C.

All these things live and abide forever,
    And for every need all are obedient to Him.
All things are different, this from that,
    And He made not one of them superfluous.
One thing surpasseth another in its goodness,
    And who shall be satiated in beholding their beauty?

. . . .

For His own sake He maketh His work to prosper,
    And by His word He worketh His pleasure.
Yet more things like these we will not add,
    And the end of the matter is: He is all.
We will still magnify, though we cannot fathom,
    For greater is He than all His works.

From "The Wisdom of Ben-Sira"

INSPIRATION

Greek First Century B.C.

As the hand moves over the harp, and the strings speak,
So speaks in my members the Spirit of the Lord,
And I speak by His love.

For He destroys what is foreign, and everything that is bitter:
For thus it was from the beginning and will be to the end,
That nothing should be His adversary,
And nothing should stand up against Him.

The Lord hath multiplied the knowledge of Himself,
And is zealous that these things should be known,
Which by His grace have been given unto us.
And the praise of His name He gave us:
Our spirits praise His holy Spirit.

For there went forth a stream and became a river great and broad;
For it flooded and broke up everything and it brought (water) to the Temple:
And the restrainers of the children of men were not able to restrain it,
Nor the arts of those whose business it is to restrain water;
For it spread over the face of the whole earth, and filled everything:
And all the thirsty upon earth were given to drink of it;
And thirst was relieved and quenched: for from the Most High the draft was given.

Blessed then are the ministers of that draft who are entrusted with that water of His:
They have assuaged the dry lips, and the will that had fainted they have raised up;

And souls that were near departing they have brought
    back from death:
And limbs that had fallen they straightened and set up:
They gave strength for their feebleness and light to
    their eyes:
For everyone knew them in the Lord, and they lived
    by the water of life forever.

                                Hallelujah.
                        From Ode VI of Solomon

LOVE

Jewish-Roman First Century

I may speak with the tongues of men and of angels,
But if I have no love,
    I am a noisy gong or a clanging cymbal;
I may prophesy, fathom all mysteries and secret lore,
I may have such absolute faith that I can move hills
        from their place,
But if I have no love, I count for nothing;
I may distribute all I possess in charity,
I may give up my body to be burnt,
    But if I have no love,
    I make nothing of it.

Love is very patient, very kind.
Love knows no jealousy, love makes no parade,
Gives itself no airs, is never rude, never selfish, never
    irritated,
Never resentful; love is never glad when others go
    wrong,

Love is gladdened by goodness,
Always slow to expose, always eager to believe the best,
Always hopeful, always patient.

Love never disappears.
As for prophesying, it will be superseded;
As for tongues, they will cease;
As for knowledge, it will be outgrown.
For we know only in part, and prophesy in part;
But when the perfect comes, the imperfect passes
    away.

.   .   .   .

At present we see only baffling reflections in a mirror,
But then it will be face to face.
At present I am learning bit by bit,
But then I shall understand, as all along I have been
    understood.
Thus faith and hope and love last on,
But the greatest of all is love.

St. Paul

OVER ALL PRESIDES THE UNIVERSAL SOUL

Egyptian-Roman Third Century

Over all presides the Universal Soul.
Created things are born and die.
The Universal Soul is Being, pure,—
Ageless life which changes not.
To contemplate this Soul
We must be worthy by nobility;
We must release our minds from error,

Lyra Mystica

Immerse ourselves in meditation,
Withdraw our thoughts from things that fascinate the eye,
Subdue the agitations of the flesh,
Silence the tumult of the earth and air,
And let our souls stand in the presence of the Power
Which from all sides o'erflows the world,—
Which penetrates it intimately, lights it up
Even as the sun irradiates the darkness of a cloud.
Thus the Universal Soul, descending,
Redeems the world from death,
Imparting movement, life and immortality.
It is the Soul that holds the world, immense and manifold,
Within the bonds of universal unity.

Plotinus

WE ARE NOT CAST AWAY

Egyptian-Roman Third Century

We are not cast away, not separate;
What though the body-nature press us close?—
We breathe and hold our ground,
For the Supreme does not give and pass,
But abides forever.
Our being is the fuller for our turning toward God;
This is our peace, escape from evil, refuge from the wrong;
To hold aloof is loneliness and loss.
Here is living, since apart from God,
All life is but a shadow and a mimicry.

Life, in the consciousness of the Supreme,
In virtue of that converse, brings forth beauty, richness,—
Brings forth moral good.
The soul is pregnant that is filled with God.
From God the soul proceeds, its good lies there.
Life here, with things of earth, is but defeat—
A sinking, a failing of the wing.
Love for God is native to the soul;
We long to be at one with Him.
Even as a child, lured by a lower love, forgets a time
The ties that bind her to a noble sire,
But comes at length to hate her shame,
Returns at last to seek his face,
And in his presence finds her peace.

Plotinus

THE SOUL IS IN THE BODY AS THE PILOT IN THE SHIP

Egyptian-Roman Third Century

The soul is in the body as the pilot in the ship,—
Not as an idle passenger,
Nor even as an honored guest aboard,
But as an active, moving power;
It is as if the pilot were incarnate in the helm.
Or, let us rather say,
The soul is in the body as light is in the air.
The air escapes,—does not the light remain?

Plotinus

WE MAY ASCEND TO HIM

Egyptian-Roman Third Century

We may ascend to Him, and grasp Him.
But we shall find no terms
To mark His greatness.
When we shall see Him and resign
All effort to define the undefinable,
We shall proclaim that He exists,
Alone, above all being but His own.
Having found Him, still we may not say
"Lo, He is here!" His presence
Rises everywhere before the vision of the soul.
Whichever way the soul directs her sight
She sees Him,—unless, her thought diverted,
She obscures the vision of Divinity.

Plotinus

GREAT ART THOU, O LORD

Egyptian-Roman 354–430

Great art Thou, O Lord, and greatly to be praised;
Great is Thy power, and of Thy wisdom there is no end.
And man, being a part of Thy creation, desires to praise Thee,—
Man, who bears about with him his mortality,
The witness of his sin, even the witness that Thou "resistest the proud,"—
Yet man, this part of Thy creation, desires to praise Thee.

Thou movest us to delight in praising Thee;
For Thou hast formed us for Thyself,
And our hearts are restless till they find rest in Thee.
Lord, teach me to know and understand
Which of these should be first, to call on Thee, or to Praise Thee;
And likewise to know Thee, or to call upon Thee.
But who is there that calls upon Thee without knowing Thee?
For he that knows Thee not may call upon Thee as other than Thou art.
Or perhaps we call on Thee that we may know Thee.
"But how shall they call on Him in whom they have not believed? or how shall they believe without a preacher?"
And those who seek the Lord shall praise Him.
For those who seek shall find Him, and those who find Him shall praise Him.
Let me seek Thee, Lord, in calling on Thee,
And call on Thee in believing in Thee;
For Thou hast been preached unto us.
O Lord, my faith calls on Thee,—
And faith which Thou hast imparted to me,
Which Thou hast breathed into me through the incarnation of Thy Son,
Through the ministry of Thy preacher.

St. Augustine

Lyra Mystica

AND HOW SHALL I CALL UPON MY GOD?

Egyptian-Roman 354–430

And how shall I call upon my God—my God and my Lord?
For when I call on Him I ask Him to come into me.
And what place is there in me into which my God can come—
Into which God can come, even He who made heaven and earth?
Is there anything in me, O Lord my God, that can contain Thee?
Do indeed the very heaven and earth, which Thou hast made,
And in which Thou hast made me, contain Thee? Or, as nothing could exist without Thee,
Doth whatever exists contain Thee?
    indeed exist, and could not exist if Thou wert
Why, then, do I ask Thee to come into me, since I not in me?
Because I am not yet in hell, though Thou art even there; for "if I go down into hell Thou art there."
I could not therefore exist, could not exist at all,
O my God, unless Thou wert in me.
Or should I not rather say,
That I could not exist unless I were in Thee
From whom are all things, by whom are all things,
In whom are all things? Even so, Lord; even so.
Where do I call Thee to, since Thou art in me,
Or whence canst Thou come into me?

For where outside heaven and earth can I go
That from thence my God may come into me who has said,
"I fill heaven and earth"?

St. Augustine

HYMN OF SIVAITE PURITANS

East Indian Tenth Century

When once I knew the Lord,
What to me were the host
Of pagan deities,
Some fixed in temple shrine
Or carried in the crowd;
Some made of unbaked clay,
And some burnt hard with fire?
With all the lying tales
That fill the sacred books,
They've vanished from my mind.

How many flowers I gave
At famous temple-shrines!
How often told my Cede
And washed the idol's head!
And still with weary feet
Encircled Siva's shrines!
But now at last I know
Where dwells the King of Gods,
And never will adore
A temple made by hands.

But yet I have a shrine—
The mind within my breast.
An image too is there—
The soul that came from God.
I offer ash and flowers—
The praises of my heart.

Anonymous

INVOCATION

Jewish Eleventh Century

At the dawn I seek Thee,
Refuge, Rock Sublime:
Set my prayer before Thee in the morning
And my prayer at eventime.

I before Thy greatness
Stand and am afraid;
All my secret thoughts Thine eye beholdeth,
Deep within my bosom laid.

And withal what is it
Heart and tongue can do?
What is this my strength and what is even
This the Spirit in me too?

But indeed man's singing
May seem good to Thee,
So I praise Thee, singing, while there dwelleth
Yet the breath of God in me.

Ibn Gabirol

Lyra Mystica

QUATRAINS

Persian Eleventh Century

Let no one of Thy boundless Grace despair;
Thine own elect shall ever upward fare;
The mote, if once illumined by Thy sun,
The brightness of a thousand suns shall share.

O God, I crave Thy Grace for hapless me!
For hapless me enough Thy clemency!
Each some protector, some defender claims;
But I, poor friendless I, have none but Thee!

By whatsoever Path, blessed the feet
Which seek Thee; blessed He who strives to meet
Thy Beauty; blessed they who on it gaze,
And blessed every tongue which Thee doth greet!

Since first I was, ne'er far from Thee I've been;
My lucky star hath served me well, I ween;
Extinguished in Thine Essence, if extinct,
And if existent, by Thy light I'm seen.

Abu Sa'id Ibn Abi'l-Khayr

WHERE SHALL I FIND THEE?

Jewish-Spanish 1086–1140

O Lord, where shall I find Thee?
   All hidden and exalted is Thy place;
   And where shall I not find Thee?
Full of Thy glory is the infinite space.

Lyra Mystica

Found near-abiding ever,
He made the earth's ends, set their utmost bar;
  Unto the nigh a refuge,
Yea, and a trust to them who wait afar.
  Thou sittest throned between the Cherubim,
  Thou dwellest high above the cloud-rack dim.
Praised by Thine hosts and yet beyond their praises
    Forever far exalt;
The endless whirl of worlds may not contain Thee,
    How then one heaven's vault?

  And Thou, withal uplifted
O'er man, upon a mighty throne apart,
  Art yet forever near him,
Breath of his spirit, life-blood of his heart.
    His own mouth speaketh testimony true
    That Thou his Maker art alone; for who
Shall say he hath not seen Thee? Lo! the heavens
    And all their host aflame
With glory show Thy fear in speech unuttered,
    With silent voice proclaim.

  Longing I sought Thy presence,
Lord, with my whole heart did I call and pray,
    And going out toward Thee,
  I found Thee coming to me on the way;
  Yea, in Thy wonder's might as clear to see
  As when within the shrine I looked for Thee.
Who shall not fear Thee? Lo! upon their shoulders
    Thy yoke divinely dread!
Who shall forbear to cry to Thee, That givest
    To all their daily bread?

    And can the Lord God truly—
God the Most High—dwell here within man's breast?
    What shall he answer, pondering—
Man, whose foundations in the dust do rest?
      For Thou art holy, dwelling 'mid the praise
      Of them that waft Thee worship all their days.
Angels adoring, singing of Thy wonder,
    Stand upon Heaven's height;
And Thou, enthroned o'erhead, all things upholdest
    With everlasting might.

Jehudah Halevi

THE LORD IS MY PORTION

Jewish-Spanish 1086–1140

Servants of time, lo! these be slaves of slaves;
    But the Lord's servant hath his freedom whole.
Therefore when every man his portion craves,
    "The Lord is my portion," saith my soul.

Jehudah Halevi

I DIED

Persian Thirteenth Century

I died from mineral and plant became;
Died from the plant, and took a sentient frame;
Died from the beast, and donned a human dress;
When by my dying did I e'er grow less?
Another time from manhood I must die
To soar with angel pinions through the sky.
'Midst angels also I must lose my place,

Since "Everything shall perish save His Face."
Let me be Naught! The harp-strings tell me plain
That "unto Him do we return again"!

Jalal ud-Din Rumi

CANTICLE OF THE SUN

Italian Thirteenth Century

Oh, Most High, Almighty, Good Lord God, to Thee belong praise, glory, honor and all blessing.

Praised be my Lord God, with all His creatures, and especially our brother the Sun, who brings us the day and who brings us the light: fair is he, and he shines with a very great splendor.

O Lord, he signifies us to thee!

Praised be my Lord for our sister the Moon, and for the stars, the which He has set clear and lovely in the heaven.

Praised be my Lord for our brother the wind, and for air and clouds, calms and all weather, by which Thou upholdest life and all creatures.

Praised be my Lord for our sister water, who is very serviceable to us, and humble and precious and clean.

Praised be my Lord for our brother fire, through whom thou givest us light in the darkness; and he is bright and pleasant and very mighty and strong.

Praised be my Lord for our mother the earth, the which doth sustain us and keep us, and bringeth forth divers fruits and flowers of many colors, and grass.

Praised be my Lord for all those who pardon one
another for love's sake, and who endure weakness
and tribulation: blessed are they who peacefully
shall endure, for thou, O Most High, wilt give
them a crown.

Praised be my Lord for our sister, the death of the
body, from which no man escapeth. Woe to him
who dieth in mortal sin. Blessed are those who
die in thy most holy will, for the second death
shall have no power to do them harm.

Praise ye and bless the Lord, and give thanks to Him
and serve Him with great humility.

St. Francis of Assisi

INEFFABLE LOVE DIVINE

Italian 1228–1306

Ineffable Love Divine!
    Sweetness unformed, yet bright,
    Measureless, endless Light,
Flame in this heart of mine!

Well did I know Thee, meseemed,
    Thy visible semblance saw,
      Through intellect and through awe;
    Tasted Thy savour sweet:
And perfectly, so I deemed,
    I held Thee without a flaw,
      Close to Thy Heart could I draw,
    Love, timeless, measureless, great!
  Yet now, all seemeth a cheat:

Lyra Mystica

I hold Thee less and less;
I grasped, yet not possess
    Thee, Uttermost Verity.

O Inconceivable Light!
    Who can Thy secrets tell?
    Thou Who wast fain to dwell
In darkness deep and obscure!
No more is Thy lantern bright
    To guide the soul who would spell,
    Measure, and mark Thee well,
And seize on Thine Essence pure.
Virtue nor strength is sure;
    The night is turned to the day,
    No words, no language have they
        Thy splendour and light that see.

. . . .

When the mind's very being is gone,
    Sunk in a conscious sleep,
    In a rapture divine and deep,
Itself in the Godhead lost:—
It is conquered, ravished and won!
    Set in Eternity's sweep,
    Gazing back on the steep,
Knowing not how it was crossed—
    To a new world now is it tossed,
    Drawn from its former state,
    To another, measureless, great—
        Where Love is drowned in the Sea.

In the midst of this Ocean's tide

Whelmed for evermore
It cannot find a shore,
Gone is the solid ground:
Thought it hath laid aside,
Transformed to its inmost core
It knows not its own heart's lore;
New-clad the soul is found:
Its feeling is sunk and enwound
In the Good that is ultimate,
The beauty to contemplate
That is colourless, formless, free.

It welcometh any fate:
Transformed so wondrously
By union profound and free,
It whispereth "All is mine!"
Wide open standeth the gate—
The soul is joined to Thee,
Endlessly, utterly,
Possessing all that is Thine.
It feels that it cannot divine,
Sees what it may not discern,
Grasps more than Faith can learn,
Tastes God unknowingly.

It hath found the measureless way
Itself to lose and to spend,
And so it can comprehend,
The Immeasurable Height:
And purifying its clay
From all alloy or blend,
It drinks without pause or end

Ineffable Delight.
Loosing, yet holding tight,
    No longer the soul doth seek
    Power to tell and to speak,
      Transformed so utterly.

To lose, and yet to keep,
    To love, and in joy to wait,
    To gaze and to contemplate,
This is the True and the Real.
To possess in certainty deep;
    To float in that blessed state,
    Anchored, yet early and late,
Nearer, nearer to steal;
Deeper than woe or weal
    Is the Act of Heavenly Love,
    And the Light of Truth from above,
      Strong, eternal and free.

 .   .   .   .

If thou in images fair,
    In types and figures, wouldst see,
    And the Unconditioned, the Free,
Wouldst measure and mark and taste:
If thou thinkest, by searching and care,
    To encompass Infinity,
    To enclose and clasp It to thee,
Vain are thy hopes and thy haste!
Thy thoughts are error and waste!
    Thy faith, so strong and certain,
    Is but dissolving curtain,
      Hiding the Perfect from thee.

Lyra Mystica

When the Unknown takes thy hand,
    Let Him lead thee where He will;
    Perchance He may guide thee still
To the vision of His Truth.
Stript of thy self must thou stand,
    Vain are thy searchings until
    Vanity's cup thou spill;
It never can quench thy drouth.
Love Calm, that is tranquil and smooth,
    Beyond all feeling and deed;
    It will satisfy thy need,
        Sink thyself in that Sea!

Be happy in any place
    Where He pleaseth to set thy feet;
    'Tis in vain the bars to beat,
Effort and struggle are vain.
If He offer thee His embrace,
    Run His caress to meet!
    If not, His withholding is sweet,—
Reck not of loss nor of gain.
If thy love be pure from stain,
    Thou wilt be ever content,
    Thy longings only bent
        To shine more fearlessly.

. . . . . .

When thou lov'st thyself no longer,
    But only that Good and Fair,
    Utterly strive and dare
Therewith One Thing to be made.
Thine answer must aye be stronger

Lyra Mystica

To thy Lover's tender prayer,
Drawn into His Essence there,
Towards His Being swayed.
This One-head can never fade;
Division must strive in vain,
To make One Heart into twain,
So deep is this Unity.

If thou hast served Him well,
Given Him all that was thine,
Loved only the Divine,
He never will part from thee.
Wholly in Him shalt thou dwell,
Thy being with His combine:
If sin should sully that shrine,
Sharer in sin would He be!
From Himself how can He flee?
His light can never be quenched,
So thou, in that glory drenched,
Shalt he His to Eternity.

O loftiest Verity!
All, all is under Thy sway;
Thou art the End and the Way,
For all who can seek Thee and find.
O gentle Tranquillity!
Whose greatness endureth for aye,
Who knowest not change nor decay,
Whom naught can vary nor bind.
Thy Light with Thy Strength is twined;

Thy Infinite Essence and Soul
Can pass through all that is foul,
    Nor sully Its purity.

* * * * * * *

The battle is over now,
    The travail that drains the blood,
    The spirit's struggle for good,—
Peace hath ended the war,
With his helmet on his brow,
    Behold the spirit renewed,
    With tempered armour endued,
Wound cannot hurt him nor scar.
He looks on the radiance afar,
    Asks not for symbol nor sign;
    No tapers of sense may shine,
        On those heights of Eternity.

* * * * * * *

Faith no longer is here,
    For faith is lost in sight;
    Hope is changed to delight,
Grasping what once it sought,
Desire no more draws near,
    Nor force of will, nor affright
    Lest the Treasure should take to flight;
The soul by Love is taught:
All his beliefs and his thought
    Were foolish and poor and blind,
    Tumult and tempest and wind,
        Error and falsity.

High in that Empyrean,
    The soul finds treasure so great,
    No place it hath, and no date,
Nothing for tongue to tell,
And wonder groweth more keen,
    At the soul, thus re-create,
    In a new and stronger state,
Where images cannot dwell,
Where illusions melt and dispel;
    It cannot be lost in night,
    Darkness is turned to light,
        In a love so great and free.

As air becomes luminous,
    When filled with the light of day;
    As wax dissolveth away,
In the heat and glow of fire:
So the soul grows glorious,
    Fused in that Heavenly Ray;
    No action can it essay,
Gone are its Will and Desire.
The Height that is ever higher
    Absorbs its heart and its breath,
    It is living, yet lives in death,
        Is vanquished in victory.

For wine poured into the sea,
    A man may search in vain,
    There is left of it not a stain,
In the ocean waves that roll.
Itself no more can it be,

Nor doth it ask to regain
　　Its former essence again;
It must give its being in toll,
So Love hath drunk the Soul,
　　And Truth hath changed it so,
　　All that it was must go,
　　　　It giveth its self in fee.

It yearns, yet desireth not,
　　For its will is not its own;
　　It longs for naught that is known,
Except that Beauty so fair.
Its longings are all forgot,
　　It asks nor bread nor a stone;
　　Nothingness is its throne;
Sweet is its holding there.
This state, so lofty and rare,
　　On Nothingness is it built,
　　In the Lord is it noughted and split,
　　　　Formed and stablished to be.

O Noughting mysterious!
　　So strong thou art and so great,
　　Thou openest every gate,
That leads to the Infinite.
Thou art Very Truth for us,
　　We fear not death nor fate,
　　Thou guidest evil and hate,
Thou makest the darkness bright.
The heart of man thou canst plight

Lyra Mystica

    So close to the Heart Divine,
    There is left no dividing line,
      To trouble Love's ecstasy.

So subtle thy wisdom and deep,
    The world that passeth away
    Below thy sphere must stay,
  Imperfect, shadowy, vain.
So light, so swift canst thou leap
    To that unclouded day,
    Thou needst not stoop nor delay,
  To gaze upon guilt or stain.
  Forever that joyful strain
    Rings in concord and peace;
    All pain and sorrow shall cease,
      Uplifted to Verity.

.   .   .   .

Thou seekest not any reward,
    And yet reward thou dost find,—
    New gifts, new light for the mind,
  More than heart could demand.
What thou tak'st, thou dost safely guard,
    And fast to thy being bind:
    Give all, for more is behind,
Fresh joys for thine emptied hand.
Thou dost run, though thou canst not stand;
    Dost mount, although thou descend;
    Hast more, the more thou dost spend,
      Possessing the Deity.

Lyra Mystica

Possessed of Him, He is thine,
    In union so intimate,
    That nothing shall separate—
Nothing draw thee away.
Thou drink'st, and thou art the Wine;
    Transformed to that perfect state,
    So holy, so pure and great,
Nothing can lead thee astray.
Never His hand can delay,
    Never His gifts shall cease,
    Thou hast entered His central peace
Beloved and Lover to be.

Death thou hast left behind,
    The centre of life is here;
    No wounding needst thou fear
Nothing can hurt thee more.
Nothing can force thee nor bind,
    Thy Self is no longer near;
    No hostile voice canst thou hear,
Upon this infinite shore.
God, Who taught thee to soar,
    He only can understand
    Thee, the work of His hand;
Thy Maker and Lord is He.

· · · · · · ·

When all that was thine is lost
    The riches thou countedst o'er,
    Never was known before
So great and rare an exchange!
O Light that gives without cost

A Lack that shall be a store,
A Want that is able to pour
Power beyond action's range!
O Covenant new and strange!
Where life doth sicken and fade,
Yet in sickness is stronger made,
Mounts and falls like the sea!

So deep, so pure is thy light,
It turns a fault to a gain;
All that would hinder and pain,
Lieth defeated and dead.
Thy gifts are perfect and right,
All others are useless and vain,
The dead thou raisest again,
The sick to health thou hast led.
Thou hast skill, the healing to shed
In the poison's venomous bite;
Splendour to hide in the night,
And in ruin, constancy.

Thou art a garden in bloom,
Adorned with many a flower;
And there, thro' sun and thro' shower,
The Tree of Life shall be green.
Purged of shadows and gloom,
Thou art Light divine, and Power,
Firmness and strength are thy dower,
From maiming and taint made clean.
And since to the truth unseen

Lyra Mystica

> Eternally thou art wed,
>   Change cannot touch thee, nor dread,
>   Nor any diversity.

> Love cannot transform the soul,
>   How strong so ever He be,
>   Save hand in hand with thee,
>   To make it perfect and fair.
> To gain that ultimate goal,
>   Virtue and Intellect flee;
>   Love's face they never may see,
>   Save with thy shelter and care.
>   No gates shall be bolted there,
>   Against the touch of thy hand;
>   Thou art the lord of that land,
>   Reigning in majesty.

> Sweetheart of Christ wast thou,
>   To every saint thou wast dear;
>   Pure is thy Light and clear,
>   Great the gifts of thy reign.
> We plead with Our lady now,
>   Who dwelt in thy holy sphere,
>   Our singing and prayers to hear,
>   To grant us Love without stain,
>   Vision unveiled and plain
>   Of Truth, supreme and apart;—
>   And the Noughting of our own heart,
>   In uttermost Poverty.

Jacopone da Todi

Lyra Mystica

O SOUL OF MINE, HOW NOBLE WERT THOU MADE!

Italian 1228–1306

O Soul of mine, how noble wert thou made!
Be not afraid,
    Nor dream thy nature low:
    Thou art not so,
High is thy birth, and lordly thine estate.

If a poor man a gift to thee should bring,
Thy heart would cling
    To him, and there abide,
With love and gratitude unfaltering;
So slight a thing
    Would bind thee to his side.
    Thy Lord, thy Guide,
Makes pilgrimage for thee,
Treads painfully
    His toilsome path alone:
    O heart of stone!
    To stand thus obdurate.

The King of France might have a daughter fair,
His only Heir,
    His pride and his delight.
The fame of her would travel everywhere,
Gems would she wear
    And robes of spotless white.
    But should she plight

Her troth, in marriage base,
Her tender grace
    To infamy betray,
    What should men say
    Of bonds so profligate?

The thing that thou hast done is worse than this,
To clasp and kiss
    The treacherous world abhorred!
Thy body, that thy humble servant is,
Thou'st used amiss,
    Given him the ruler's sword.
    Ah, careless lord,
  To set a slave to reign!
  So doth he gain
    A lordship criminal:
    And to this thrall
    'Tis thou hast oped the gate.

Thy kingdom of five parts is composite;
Hearing and Sight,
    And Taste, and Touch, and Scent.
This Body, that the world hath ruled outright,
Resents her plight,
    Restless in discontent.
    Her gaze is bent
  To seek the Beautiful;
  Naught else can lull
    Her ear, nor feed her eye:
    Earth's fragments die,
    Her makeshifts come too late.

Lyra Mystica

This World sufficeth not thine Eye to feed,
Because her need
    Must still be measureless.
She of a thousand Worlds would take no heed,
So strange her greed,
    So deep her thirstiness.
    The World's caress
  Is turned to torment so:
  The mind must go
    Defrauded of her gain;
    Joy becomes pain,
    The heart to penetrate.

This World feeds not thy senses, nor thy mind,
Nor canst thou bind
    Thy heart in her control.
Joy for these vassals if thou strive to find,
That task will grind
    Thy struggling, suffering soul.
    Then seek thy goal
  There, where thy heart must be;
  Thy kingdoms three
    Now lie, though once so fair,
    All parched and bare,
    Famished and desolate.

So high and in such honour wert thou born,
Thy nature's morn
    Awaked in gentlehood.
Ponder the grace and beauty thou hast worn,

So shalt thou scorn
   All else, with fortitude.
   Naught here is good—
No creature fair enough;
No earthly stuff
      Deserves thy heart's desire;
      God is thy Sire,
      To Him be consecrate.

Look in thy mirror for a little space
And thou shalt trace
      Thy delicate beauty there.
Thou bear'st thy Father's image on thy face:
O joy! O grace!
      His likeness thus to wear!
      The Eternal Fair,
Poured in thy little cup,
Floats trembling up,
      There Earth and Heaven meet.
      O Vessel sweet!
      So spoiled, so desecrate!

Thou art not nourished by created things;
Thy nature's wings
      To other realms must fly.
Thou art God's heir,—towards Him thy being springs,
His largess brings
      Wealth to thy poverty;
      Pause not, nor sigh;
Swift on Love's journey start:

Give Him thy heart,
    And let the pact be fair;
    Thou art His heir,
    Lay hold on thine Estate.

O Love, thou givest all, and for Love's sake
All dost thou take,
    To have and hold for aye.
Ah, to thy God great honour dost thou make,
All to forsake,
    To find in Him thy Way!
    What should man say?
  E'en God were sure unwise,
  If when He buys
    This treasure fathomless,
    He should give less,
    Bargain or hesitate.

Jacopone da Todi

O LOVE DIVINE AND GREAT

Italian 1228–1306

O Love Divine and Great,
    Why dost thou still besiege my heart?
    Of me infatuate thou art,
    From me thou canst not rest!

My five engirdling battlements
    Are all besieged by Thee;
The Ear, the Eye, Taste, Smell, and Touch,
    By Love, mine Enemy:

If I come forth I cannot flee,
  Nor hide me from Thy quest.

If I come forth by way of Sight,
  Love, Love is all around;
In radiance painted on the skies,
  In colour on the ground:
They plead with me, in beauty drowned,
  To take Thee to my breast.

If I come forth by Hearing's gate,
  O what is this I hear?
What is this woven mist of sound
  That breaks upon mine ear?
  Here's no escape! Thy voice is clear,—
  'Tis Love, in music drest.

If I come forth by way of Taste,
  In savours Thou art set;
That Love Divine, Who craves for me,
  And snares me in His net,
  Prisons me close, and closer yet,
  To be His child and guest.

If I come forth by way of Smell,
  Thine odours sweet and fine
In every creature I perceive,
  And every one divine;
  Thy spears they are, to make me Thine,
  They wound at Thy behest.

Lyra Mystica

If I come forth by way of Touch,
   On every creature fair
In sacred awe I lay my hands,
   For Thou are sculptured there;
    'Twere madness, Love, this way to dare
   Escape Thy sweet conquest.

O Love, why do I flee from Thee?
   Why should I fear to yield?
Because Thou wouldst remake my heart,
   In fires of love annealed?
    No more myself, in Thee concealed,
   And by Thy love possessed.

I, if I see another moved
   The downward step to make,
I am made partner of his loss,
   I suffer for his sake:
    Whom, Love Unmeasured, dost *Thou* take
   To Thy compassion blest?

Lead me to Christ, Who died for me,
   Draw me from sea to shore:
And make me mourn in penitence
   The wounds and grief He bore:
    Why did He suffer pains so sore?
   That I might be at rest.

                              Jacopone da Todi

Lyra Mystica
O SPLENDOUR OF GOD!

Italian 1265–1321

O splendour of God! by means of which I saw
   The lofty triumph of the realm veracious,
   Give me the power to say how it I saw!
There is a light above, which visible
   Makes the Creator unto every creature,
   Who only in beholding Him has peace,
And it expands itself in circular form
   To such extent, that its circumference
   Would be too large a girdle for the sun.
The semblance of it is all made of rays
   Reflected from the top of Primal Motion,
   Which takes therefrom vitality and power
And as a hill in water at its base
   Mirrors itself, as if to see its beauty
   When affluent most in verdure and in flowers,
So, ranged aloft all round about the light,
   Mirrored I saw in more tanks than a thousand
   All who above there have from us returned.
And if the lowest row collect within it
   So great a light, how vast the amplitude
   Is of this Rose in its extremest leaves!
My vision in the vastness and the height
   Lost not itself, but comprehended all
   The quantity and quality of that gladness. . . .
In fashion then as if a snow-white rose
Displayed itself to me the saintly host, . . .
Their faces had they all of living flame,

And wings of gold, and all the rest so white
No snow unto that limit doth attain. . . .
This realm secure and full of gladsomeness,
   Crowded with ancient people and with modern,
   Unto one mark had all its look and love.

Dante

PASSIONATE, WITH LONGING IN MINE EYES

East Indian Fourteenth Century

Passionate, with longing in mine eyes,
   Searching wide, and seeking nights and days,
Lo! I beheld the Truthful One, the Wise,
   Here in mine own house to fill my gaze.

That was the day of my lucky star.
   Breathless, I held him my Guide to be.
So my Lamp of Knowledge blazed afar,
   Fanned by slow breath from the throat of me.

Then, my bright Soul to my Self revealed,
   Winnowed I abroad my inner Light;
And with darkness all around me sealed
   Did I garner Truth and hold him tight.

Lâlla

SONNET TO LAURA

Italian Fourteenth Century

Let be, O calling bird and rippling lake;
And, crystal cymbals of the running streams,
Cease your intolerable clash that seems

Her cries and laughter: for my soul's awake,
And all my helpless verse into the heart-break
Of song springs up. Nay, what is that? There gleams
A Silken Something where the wild rose teems,
I thought her in the clay, by some mistake,
Not understanding heaven; but rosy, tanned,
She's there—that movement—all the red and white:
"No tears! No tears! You do not understand
That, when I seemed to have closed my eyes that night,
I merely opened them upon a land
Like one great flower—Infinity—the Light."

Petrarch

THE GIFT OF INTELLIGENCE

Flemish Fourteenth Century

He who seeks that gift to light him
Must rise beyond his nature,
To the highest height of being.
Brightness without measure
There shall he perceive it
In primal purity.
Through his soul will flow
The light of heavenly truth,
And he in it shall vanish.
That universal radiance
Enlightens the pure-hearted
According to their merits.
Then can they behold
With gaze that knows no limit
The very face of joy.

Lyra Mystica

Forever shall we gaze on
That which we there enjoy,
And lose ourselves in vision.
Far off has gone the Lover;
We turn our eyes forever
Towards the blessed vision.
Yet has he reached the goal,
And the lover has the loved one
In the lonely realm of union.
So shall we thus remain
And ever strive to follow
To that wondrous depth divine.

Jan van Ruysbroeck

THE KNIGHT OF JESUS

German Fourteenth Century

"Oh, to be the Knight of Jesus!
  Scorning pain, and shame, and loss.
There, the Crown, the Joy, the Glory,
  Here, O Lord, Thy Cross."

Then I wept with bitter longing
  Thus the Knight of God to be,
And the Lord, Who saw me weeping
  Gave the Cross to me.

Bitter pain, and shame, and sorrow,
  Came upon me as a flood.
I forgot, it was the tourney
  Of the Knight of God.

Soon there spake the Voice beloved,
    Still and sweet, my heart within—
"It is thus, O Knight of Jesus,
    Thou the prize must win."

"O, my Lord, the fight is weary,
    Weary, and my heart is sore."
And He answered: "Fair the Guerdon,
    And for evermore."

"I have shamed Thee, craven-hearted,
    I have been Thy recreant Knight;
Own me yet, O Lord, albeit,
    Weeping as I fight."

"Nay!" He said: "Thou wilt not shame me,
    Wilt not shame thy knightly guise;
I would have my angels wonder
    At thy gladsome eyes."

"Need'st thou pity, Knight of Jesus!
    Pity for thy glorious hest;
On! Let God, and men, and angels,
    See that thou art blest."

Henry Suso

I WILL HEARKEN WHAT THE LORD GOD WILL SPEAK

German 1379–1471

I will hearken what the Lord God will speak in me.
Blessed is the soul which hears within the Lord speaking,

And receives from His mouth the Word of consolation.
Blessed are the ears which catch the breathings of the Divine whisper,
And pay no heed to the whispers of the world.
Blessed indeed are the ears which listen not for the voice
Which sounds from without, but to the inner voice of truth.
Blessed are the eyes which are closed to outward objects,
But intent upon inward.
Blessed are they who dive into things internal,

. . . .

To gain a deeper capacity for receiving heavenly secrets.
Blessed are they who are glad to devote their time to God,
And break away from all worldly blindness.
Consider these things, O my soul, and shut the doors of your senses,
That you may be able to hear what the Lord God speaks within you.
Thus your Beloved says—"I am your salvation, your peace, your life";
"Keep yourself with Me, and you shall find peace."
Dismiss all transitory things, and seek the things eternal.
What are all temporal things but seductive,
And what would be the good of all creatures,
If you were forsaken by the Creator?
Bid farewell then to all things, and become

A well-pleasing and faithful servant to your Creator,
So that you may be able to lay hold of true blessedness.

Thomas à Kempis

SPEAK, LORD, FOR THY SERVANT HEARETH

German 1379–1471

"Speak, Lord, for Thy servant heareth.
   I am Thy servant: give me understanding
That I may know Thy testimonies."
Incline my heart to the words of Thy mouth,
Let Thy speech drop as the dew.
The children of Israel of old said to Moses,
"Speak thou unto us, and we will hear;
Let not the Lord speak unto us, lest we die."
Not so, O Lord, not so, I pray Thee;
But rather with Samuel, the prophet, I humbly and
    earnestly entreat,
"Speak, Lord, for Thy servant heareth."

Let not Moses speak to me, nor any of the prophets,
But rather do Thou, O Lord God,—
Inspirer and Enlightener of all the prophets,—
Speak unto me; for Thou alone without them
Art able perfectly to instruct me,
But they without Thee are of no avail at all.
They can indeed sound forth words, but cannot convey
    the Spirit.
They speak most beautifully, yet, if Thou art silent,
Their words do not reach the heart.
They deliver the words,

But Thou openest the understanding.
They bring forth mysteries,
But Thou unfoldest the sense of what is signified.
They proclaim precepts,
But Thou helpest us to keep them.
They shew the way, but Thou strengthenest us to walk in it.
They act upon us only outwardly,
But Thou teachest and enlightenest the heart.
They water the surface,
But Thou vouchsafest the increase.
They cry aloud with words,
But Thou givest understanding to the hearers.
Let not Moses, then, speak to me,
But Thou, O Lord, my God, Eternal Truth,
Lest if I only hear with the outward ear,
And am not inwardly enkindled,
I die and become unfruitful;
Lest the Word, heard but not acted on,
Known but not loved, believed but not kept,
Be turned to my condemnation.
Therefore, "Speak, Lord, for Thy servant heareth";
For "Thou hast the words of eternal life."
Speak to me, that it may be for some comfort to my soul,
And for the amendment of my whole life,
And also for Thy eternal praise, glory, and honour.

Thomas à Kempis

Lyra Mystica

O SERVANT, WHERE DOST THOU SEEK ME?

East Indian Fifteenth Century

O servant, where dost thou seek Me?
Lo! I am beside thee.
I am neither in temple nor in mosque:
 I am neither in Kaaba nor in Kailash:
Neither am I in rites and ceremonies, nor in Yoga and renunciation.
If thou art a true seeker, thou shalt at once see Me: thou shalt meet Me in a moment of time.
Kabir says, "O Sadhu! God is the breath of all breath."

Kabir

MY LORD HIDES HIMSELF

East Indian Fifteenth Century

My Lord hides Himself, and my Lord wonderfully reveals himself:
My Lord has encompassed me with hardness, and my Lord has cast down my limitations.
My Lord brings to me words of sorrow and words of joy, and He Himself heals their strife.
I will offer my body and mind to my Lord: I will give up my life, but never can I forget my Lord!

Kabir

HE WHO IS MEEK AND CONTENTED

East Indian Fifteenth Century

He who is meek and contented, he who has an equal
  vision, whose mind is filled with the fullness of
  acceptance and of rest;
He who has seen Him and touched Him, he is freed
  from all fear and trouble.
To him the perpetual thought of God is like sandal
  paste smeared on the body, to him nothing else is
  delight:
His work and his rest are filled with music: he sheds
  abroad the radiance of love.
Kabir says: "Touch His feet, who is one and indivisible, immutable and peaceful; who fills all vessels
  to the brim with joy, and whose form is love."

Kabir

THE OBSCURE NIGHT OF THE SOUL

Spanish Sixteenth Century

Upon an obscure night
Fevered with love in love's anxiety,
(O hapless, happy plight!)
I went, none seeing me,
Forth from my house where all things quiet be.

By night, secure from sight,
And by the secret stair disguisedly,
(O hapless, happy plight!)
By night and privily,
Forth from my house where all things quiet be.

Blest night of wandering,
In secret, where by none might I be spied,
Nor I see anything;
Without a light or guide,
Save that which in my heart burnt in my side.

That light did lead me on,
More surely than the shining of noontide,
Where well I knew that One
Did for my coming bide;
Where he abode might none but he abide.

O night that didst lead thus,
O night more lovely than the dawn of light,
O night that broughtest us,
Lover to lover's sight,
Lover with loved in marriage of delight.

Upon my flowery breast,
Wholly for him, and save himself for none,
There did I give sweet rest
To my beloved one;
The fanning of the cedars breathed thereon.

When the first moving air
Blew from his tower, and waved his locks aside,
His hand with gentle care,
Did wound me in the side,
And in my body all my senses died.

All things I then forgot,
My cheek on him who for my coming came;

All ceased, and I was not,
Leaving my cares and shame
Among the lilies and forgetting them.
St. John of the Cross

LIVING FLAME OF LOVE

Spanish Sixteenth Century

O flame of living love
That dost eternally
Pierce through my soul with so consuming heat,
Since there's no help above,
Make thou an end of me,
And break the bond of this encounter sweet.

O burn that burns to heal!
O more than pleasant wound!
And O soft hand, O touch most delicate,
That dost new life reveal,
That dost in grace abound,
And slaying, dost from death to life translate.

O lamps of fire that shined
With so intense a light
That those dark caverns where the senses live,
Which were obscure and blind,
Now with strange glories bright,
Both heat and light to his belovèd give.

With how benign intent
Rememberest thou my breast

Where thou alone abidest secretly,
And in thy sweet ascent,
With glory and good possessed,
How delicately thou teachest love to me.

St. John of the Cross

LINES WRITTEN IN HER BREVIARY

Spanish Sixteenth Century

Let nothing disturb thee,
Nothing affright thee;
All things are passing;
God never changeth;
Patient endurance
Attaineth to all things;
Who God possesseth
In nothing is wanting;
Alone God sufficeth.

St. Teresa

IF, LORD, THY LOVE FOR ME IS STRONG

Spanish Sixteenth Century

If, Lord, Thy love for me is strong
As this which binds me unto Thee,
What holds me from Thee, Lord, so long,
What holds Thee, Lord, so long from me?

O soul, what then desirest thou?
—Lord, I would see, who thus choose Thee.

What fears can yet assail thee now?
—All that I fear is to lose Thee.

Love's whole possession I entreat,
Lord, make my soul Thine own abode,
And I will build a nest so sweet
It may not be too poor for God.

O soul in God hidden from sin,
What more desires for thee remain,
Save but to love, and love again,
And all on flame with love within,
Love on, and turn to love again?

St. Teresa

THE HEAVENLY LIFE

Spanish Sixteenth Century

Fair realm of radiant light,
O meadow of the blest, that neither hail
Nor lightning flash may blight,
Where pleasure without fail,
Springing from richest soil doth e'er prevail.

With purple flowers and white
His head is crowned as, onward journeying,
To pastures of delight,
With neither crook nor sling,
The Shepherd his loved flock in thee doth bring.

He goes, and after him
Follow his happy sheep: their pasturage

Are flowers that wax not dim
But their desire assuage,
And cropped, still suffer neither change nor age.

In the blest mountain's fold
He guides, and zealous for their welfare goes,
Bathes them in waters cold
And plenteous fare bestows
The Pastor-Pasture whence all blessing flows.

When in the highest sphere
The sun to the heaven's zenith doth attain,
His flock around him, here
Resting will he sustain
His sacred ear's delight with music's strain.

Immortal ecstasy
The soul drinks as he strikes the sounding lyre;
Gold is mere mockery
In this consuming fire
Of endless blessings that outrun desire.

O voice! O music! might
But some faint strain descend into my sense,
In transports of delight,
That my soul, journeying hence,
Might lose itself in thee, O love immense.

Ah, then would it indeed
Beloved, know thy noontide resting-place,
And win, from prison freed

Of suffering, to thy grace,
Nor ever from thy fold its steps retrace.
                                    Luis de León

A NIGHT OF STARS

Spanish Sixteenth Century

When I behold the sky
With stars innumerable spangled bright,
And then the earth descry,
Encompassèd with night,
Buried in sleep, oblivion infinite,

Sorrow and love arise
And with a burning fever fill my breast,
And ever from my eyes
The tears flow without rest
Till my tongue speaks at last, with grief oppressed:

O dwelling of great might,
Temple of lovely light incomparable,
My soul, that to thy height
At birth aspired, what spell
Doth in this dark, low prison-house compel?

What mortal folly thus
From truth's possession can remove our sense,
So that, oblivious
Of heavenly gifts, it thence
Strays into shadowy lands and vain pretence?

Man lives imprisoned
In sleep and recks not of his destiny,
While still with silent tread
At Heaven's swift decree
Hour after hour his life doth from him flee.

Ah, mortal men, awake
And turn your thoughts intent upon your loss!
Shall souls divine forsake
Such blessings for the cross
Of life unreal and dull delusion's dross?

O, skyward lift your eyes,
Upward to this eternal heavenly sphere,
And you will then despise
The vain delights that here
Beguile our life, its every hope and fear.

O, how may we compare
The fleeting span of this low earthly scene
With that great region where
In noblest forms are seen
What is and what shall be and what hath been.

Who sees the eternal fires
With fixed laws move on their heavenly way,
How each with each conspires,—
Uneven their array,
Yet varying they one ordered scheme obey;

How in the moon's clear train
As she her silver sphere doth onward move,

Lyra Mystica

Goes light of wisdom's rain,
And gleaming there above,
Follows, serenely fair, the star of love;

But blood-red angry Mars
Chooses unto himself another way,
While girt with myriad stars
Jove in his blest array
Benignly calms the heavens with steadfast ray;

And yonder in the height
Whirls Saturn, father of the Age of Gold,
And after him the bright
Stars in fair choir enroll'd
Their light and all their treasure still unfold;

Who may all this descry
And pleasure still in this vile earth retain?
Who will not groan and sigh
To rive the imprisoning chain
Wherein his soul exiled from heaven hath lain?

Lo, here lies sweet content,
Reigns peace, and on a rich and lofty throne
Sits holy love, and blent
Together in its zone
Delight and honor evermore at one.

Here beauty infinite
Unveils itself, and light, quintessence pure,
Transparent gleams: no night

Its radiance may obscure,
Spring's flowerèd splendor here is ever sure.

O fields of truth most fair!
O meadows ever fresh indeed and bright!
O mines of riches rare!
O fountain of delight,
Deep valleys with a thousand blessings dight!

Luis de León

OF THE BLESSED SACRAMENT OF THE AULTER

English Sixteenth Century

The angells' eyes, whome veyles cannot deceive,
   Might best disclose that best they do descerne;
Men must with sounde and silent faith receive
   More than they can by sence or reason lerne;
God's poure our proofes, His workes our witt exceede,
The doer's might is reason of His deede.

A body is endew'd with ghostly rightes;
   And Nature's worke from Nature's law is free;
In heavenly sunne lye hidd eternall lightes,
   Lightes cleere and neere, yet them no eye can see;
Dedd formes a never-dyinge life do shroude;
A boundless sea lyes in a little cloude.

The God of hoastes in slender hoste doth dwell,
   Yea, God and man with all to ether dewe,
That God that rules the heavens and rifled hell,
   That man whose death did us to life renewe:

That God and man that is the angells' blisse,
In forme of bredd and wyne our nurture is.

Whole may His body be in smallest breadd,
   Whole in the whole, yea whole in every crumme;
With which be one or be tenn thowsand fedd,
   All to ech one, to all but one doth cumme;
And though ech one as much as all receive,
Not one too much, nor all too little have.

One soule in man is all in everye part;
   One face at once in many mirrhors shynes;
One feareful noyse doth make a thowsand start;
   One eye at once of countlesse thinges defynes;
If proofes of one in many, Nature frame,
God may in straunger sort performe the same.

God present is at once in everye place,
   Yett God in every place is ever one;
So may there be by giftes of ghostly grace,
   One man in many roomes, yett filling none.
Sith angells may effects of bodyes shewe,
God angells' giftes on bodyes may bestowe.

Robert Southwell

THE BURNING BABE

English Sixteenth Century

As I in hoary winter's night
   Stood shivering in the snow,
Surprised I was with sudden heat
   Which made my heart to glow;

And lifting up a fearful eye
    To view what fire was near,
A pretty babe all burning bright
    Did in the air appear;
Who, scorched with excessive heat,
    Such floods of tears did shed,
As though His floods should quench His flames,
    Which with His tears were bred:
"Alas!" quoth He, "but newly born
    In fiery heats I fry,
Yet none approach to warm their hearts
    Or feel my fire but I!

"My faultless breast the furnace is;
    The fuel, wounding thorns;
Love is the fire, and sighs the smoke;
    The ashes, shames and scorns;
The fuel Justice layeth on,
    And Mercy blows the coals,
The metal in this furnace wrought
    Are men's defiled souls:
For which, as now on fire I am
    To work them to their good,
So will I melt into a bath
    To wash them in my blood,"
With this He vanish'd out of sight
    And swiftly shrunk away,
And straight I called unto mind
    That it was Christmas Day.

Robert Southwell

Lyra Mystica

From HYMN TO HEAVENLY BEAUTY

English Sixteenth Century

But whoso may, thrice happy man him hold
Of all on earth whom God so much doth grace
And lets His own Beloved to behold;
For in view of her celestial face
All joy, all bliss, all happiness have place;
Nought on earth can want unto the sight
Who of herself can win the wishful sight.

For she out of her secret treasury,
Plenty of riches forth on him will pour,
Even heavenly riches, where there hidden lie
Within the closet of her chastest bower,
The eternal portion of her precious dower,
Which mighty God hath given to her free,
And to all those which thereof worthy be.

None thereof worthy be but those whom she
Vouchsafeth to her presence to receive,
And letteth them her lovely face to see,
Whereof such wondrous pleasure they conceive,
And sweet contentment, that it doth bereave
Their soul of sense, through infinite delight,
And them transport from flesh into the spright.

In which they see such admirable things
As carries them into ecstasy,
And hear such heavenly notes and carollings
Of God's high praise, that fills the brazen sky;

And feel such joy and pleasure inwardly
That maketh them all worldly cares forget,
And only think on that before them set.

. . . .

Ah, then, my hungry soul! which long hast fed
On idle fancies of thy foolish thought,
And, with false beauties' flattering bait misled,
Hast after deceitful vain shadows sought,
Which all are fled, and now have left thee nought
But late repentance through thy folly's proof;
Ah! cease to gaze on matter of thy grief:

And look at last up to that sovereign Light,
From whose pure beams all perfect beauty springs,
That kindleth love in every godly spright,
Even the Love of God; which loathing brings
Of this vile world and these gay-seeming things;
With whose sweet pleasures being so possessed,
Thy straying thoughts henceforth forever rest.

Edmund Spenser

ICARUS

English circa *Sixteenth Century*

Love wing'd my Hopes and taught me how to fly
Far from base earth, but not to mount too high:
  For true pleasure
  Lives in measure,
   Which if men forsake,
Blinded they into folly run and grief for pleasure take.

But my vain Hopes, proud of their new-taught flight,
Enamour'd sought to woo the sun's fair light,
>   Whose rich brightness
>   Moved their lightness
>   To aspire so high
That all scorch'd and consumed with fire now drown'd
   in woe they lie.

And none but Love their woeful hap did rue,
For Love did know their desires were true;
>   Though fate frownèd,
>   And now drownèd
>   They in sorrow dwell,
It was the purest light of heav'n for whose fair love
   they fell.

Anonymous

From THE DIVINE LOVER

English 1580–1650

See, Lord, see, I am dead:
Tombed in myself, myself my grave.
   A drudge: so born, so bred:
Myself even to myself a slave.
Thou Freedom, Life: can life and Liberty
Love bondage, death? Thy freedom I: I tyed
   To loose thy bonds; be bound to me:
   My yoke shall ease, my bonds shall free.
Dead soul, thy spring of life, my dying side:
There dye with me to live: to live in thee I dyed.

Phineas Fletcher

Lyra Mystica

EV'N LIKE TWO LITTLE BANK-DIVIDING BROOKS

English 1592–1644

"My beloved is mine, and I am his;
He feedeth among the lilies."

Ev'n like two little bank-dividing brooks,
   That wash the pebbles with their wanton streams,
And having rang'd and search'd a thousand nooks,
   Meet both at length in silver-breasted Thames,
     Where in a greater current they conjoin:
So I my best-beloved's am; so he is mine.

Ev'n so we met; and after long pursuit,
   Ev'n so we joyn'd; we both became entire;
No need for either to renew a suit,
   For I was flax and he was flames of fire:
     Our firm-united souls did more than twine;
So I my best-beloved's am; so he is mine.

If all those glitt'ring Monarchs that command
   The servile quarters of this earthly ball,
Should tender, in exchange, their shares of land,
   I would not change my fortunes for them all:
     Their wealth is but a counter to my coin:
The world's but theirs; but my beloved's mine.

Nay, more; If the fair Thespian Ladies all
   Should heap together their diviner treasure:

That treasure should be deem'd a price too small
  To buy a minute's lease of half my pleasure;
    'Tis not the sacred wealth of all the Nine
Can buy my heart from him, or his, from being mine.

Nor Time, nor Place, nor Chance, nor Death can bow
  My least desires unto the least remove;
He's firmly mine by oath; I his by vow;
  He's mine by faith; and I am his by love;
    He's mine by water; I am his by wine,
Thus I my best-beloved's am; thus he is mine.

He is my Altar; I, his Holy Place;
  I am his guest; and he, my living food;
I'm his by penitence; he mine by grace;
  I'm his by purchase; he is mine, by blood;
    He's my supporting elm; and I his vine;
Thus I my best beloved's am; thus he is mine.

He gives me wealth; I give him all my vows:
  I give him songs; he gives me length of dayes;
With wreaths of grace he crowns my conqu'ring brows,
  And I his temples with a crown of Praise,
    Which he accepts as an everlasting signe,
That I my best-beloved's am; that he is mine.

Francis Quarles

THE ELIXIR

Welsh 1593–1633

Teach me, my God and King,
In all things Thee to see,

And what I do in any thing
  To do it as for Thee.

Not rudely, as a beast,
  To runne into an action;
But still to make Thee prepossest,
  And give it his perfection.

A man that looks on glasse,
  On it may stay his eye;
Or if he pleaseth, through it passe,
  And then the heav'n espie.

All may of Thee partake:
  Nothing can be so mean
Which with this tincture, "for Thy sake,"
  Will not grow bright and clean.

A servant with this clause
  Makes drudgerie divine;
Who sweeps a room as for Thy laws
  Makes that and th' action fine.

This is the famous stone
  That turneth all to gold;
For that which God doth touch and own
  Cannot for lesse be told.

George Herbert

LOVE BADE ME WELCOME

Welsh 1593–1633

Love bade me welcome; yet my soul drew back,
    Guilty of dust and sin.
But quick-eyed Love, observing me grow slack
    From my first entrance in,
Drew nearer to me, sweetly questioning
    If I lacked anything.
"A Guest," I answered, "worthy to be here."
    Love said: "You shall be he."
"I, the unkind, ungrateful? Ah, my dear,
    I cannot look on Thee."
Love took my hand, and smiling did reply,
    "Who made the eyes, but I?"
"Truth, Lord, but I have marred them; let my shame
    Go where it doth deserve."
"And know you not," saith Love, "who bore the blame?"
    "My dear, then I will serve."
"You must sit down," says Love, "and taste My meat."
    So I did sit and eat.

George Herbert

THE PULLEY

Welsh 1593–1633

    When God at first made man,
Having a glasse of blessings standing by,
"Let us," said He, "poure on him all we can;

Let the world's riches, which dispersed lie,
  Contract into a span."

So strength first made a way;
Then beautie flow'd, then wisdome, honour, pleasure;
When almost all was out, God made a stay,
Perceiving that, alone of all His treasure,
  Rest in the bottome lay.

"For if I should," said He,
"Bestow this jewell also on My creature,
He would adore My gifts in stead of Me,
And rest in Nature, not the God of Nature:
  So both should losers be.

"Yet let him keep the rest,
But keep them with repining restlesnesse;
Let him be rich and wearie, that at least,
If goodnesse leade him not, yet wearinesse
  May tosse him to My breast."

George Herbert

THOU ART OF ALL CREATED THINGS

Spanish Seventeenth Century

Thou art of all created things,
O Lord, the essence and the cause,
The source and center of all bliss;
What are those veils of woven light
Where sun and moon and stars unite,
The purple morn, the spangled night,

But curtains which thy mercy draws
Between the heavenly world and this?
The terrors of the sea and land—
When all the elements conspire,
The earth and water, storm and fire—
Are but the sketches of thy hand;
Do they not all in countless ways—
The lightning's flash, the howling storm,
The dread volcano's awful blaze—
Proclaim thy glory and thy praise?
Beneath the sunny summer showers
Thy love assumes a milder form,
And writes its angel name in flowers;
The wind that flies with winged feet
Around the grassy gladdened earth,
Seems but commissioned to repeat
In echo's accents—silvery sweet—
That Thou, O Lord, didst give it birth.
There is a tongue in every flame,
There is a tongue in every wave;
To these the bounteous Godhead gave
These organs but to praise his name!
      Pedro Calderón de la Barca

A LITTLE BIRD I AM

French Seventeenth Century

A little bird I am,
 Shut from the fields of air;
And in my cage I sit and sing
 To Him Who placed me there;

Well pleased a prisoner to be,
Because, my God, it pleases Thee.

Nought have I else to do:
  I sing the whole day long;
And He Whom most I love to please
  Doth listen to my song:
He caught and bound my wandering wing;
But still He bends to hear me sing.

Thou hast an ear to hear
  A heart to love and bless;
And though my notes were e'er so rude,
  Thou wouldst not hear the less;
Because Thou knowest as they fall,
That love, sweet love, inspires them all.

My cage confines me round;
  Abroad I cannot fly;
But though my wing is closely bound,
  My heart's at liberty.
My prison-walls cannot control
The flight, the freedom of the soul.

Oh! it is good to soar
  These bolts and bars above,
To Him Whose purpose I adore,
  Whose providence I love;
And in Thy mighty will to find
The joy, the freedom of the mind.

Jeanne Marie Guyon

Lyra Mystica

'TIS NOT THE SKILL OF HUMAN ART

French Seventeenth Century

'Tis not the skill of human art
  Which gives me power my God to know:
The sacred lessons of the heart
  Come not from instruments below.

Love is my teacher. He can tell
  The wonders that he learnt above;
No other master knows so well:—
  'Tis Love alone can tell of Love.

Oh! then of God if thou wouldst learn,
  His wisdom, goodness, glory see,
All human arts and knowledge spurn,
  Let Love alone thy teacher be.

Jeanne Marie Guyon

IN THINE OWN HEART

German Seventeenth Century

Though Christ a thousand times
  In Bethlehem be born,
If He's not born in thee
  Thy soul is still forlorn.
The cross on Golgotha
  Will never save thy soul,
The cross in thine own heart
  Alone can make thee whole.

Whate'er thou lovest, man,
  That too become thou must;
God if thou lovest God,
  Dust if thou lovest dust.
Go out, God will go in.
  Die thou, and let Him live.
Be not, and He will be.
  Wait, and He'll all things give.

To bring thee to thy God
  Love takes the shortest route;
The way which knowledge leads
  Is but a round-about.
Drive out from thee the world
  And then like God thou'lt be
A heaven within thyself
  In calm eternity.

Let but thy heart, oh man,
  Become a valley low,
And God shall rain on it
  Till it shall overflow.
Oh, shame—the silkworm works
  And spins till it can fly,
And thou, my soul wilt still
  On thine old earth-clod lie?

Man, if the time on earth
  Should seem too long for thee,
Then turn to God and live,
  Time-free, eternally.
        Angelus Silesius (Johann Scheffler)

SEEK NO MORE ABROAD, SAY I

English Seventeenth Century

Seek no more abroad, say I,
House and Home, but turn thine eye
Inward, and observe thy breast;
There alone dwells solid Rest.
Say not that this House is small,
Girt up in a narrow wall:
In a cleanly sober mind
Heaven itself full room doth find.
Here content makes thine abode
With thy self and with thy God.
Here in this sweet privacy
May'st thou with thyself agree,
And keep House in peace, tho' all
Th' universe's fabric fall.

Joseph Beaumont

THE NIGHT IS COME

English Seventeenth Century

The night is come, like to the day,
Depart not Thou, Great God, away.
Let not my sins black as the night
Eclipse the luster of Thy light.
Keep still in my Horizon, for to me
The Sun makes not the day, but Thee!

Sir Thomas Browne

Lyra Mystica

A SONG

English Seventeenth Century

Lord, when the sense of thy sweet grace
Sends up my soul to seek thy face.
Thy blessed eyes breed such desire,
I dy in love's delicious Fire.
    O love, I am thy Sacrifice.
Be still triumphant, blessed eyes.
Still shine on me, fair suns! that I
Still may behold, though still I dy.

Though still I dy, I live again;
Still longing so to be still slain,
So gainfull is such lose of breath.
I dy even in desire of death.
    Still live in me this loving strife
Of living Death and dying Life.
For while thou sweetly slayest me
Dead to my selfe, I live in Thee.

Richard Crashaw

ON SAINT TERESA

English Seventeenth Century

O heart, the equal poise of Love's both parts,
Big alike with wounds and darts,
Live in these conquering leaves, live still the same,
And walk through all tongues one triumphant flame!
Live here, great heart, and love and die and kill,
And bleed, and wound, and yield, and conquer still.

Lyra Mystica

Let this immortal life, where'er it comes,
Walk in a crowd of loves and martyrdoms.
Let mystic deaths wait on it, and wise souls be
The love-slain witnesses of this life of thee.
O sweet incendiary! show here thy art
Upon this carcase of a hard, cold heart;
Let all thy scattered shafts of light, that play
Among the leaves of thy large books of day,
Combined against this breast at once break in
And take away from me myself and sin;
This glorious robbery shall thy bounty be,
And my best fortunes such fair spoils of me.
O thou undaunted daughter of desires!
By all thy dower of lights and fires,
By all the eagle in thee, all the dove,
By all the lives and deaths of love,
By thy large draughts of intellectual day,
And by thy thirsts of love more large than they;
By all thy brim-fil'd bowls of fierce desire,
By thy last morning's draught of liquid fire,
By the full kingdom of that final kiss
That seized thy parting soul and seal'd thee His;
By all the heavens thou hast in Him,
Fair sister of the seraphim!
By all of Him we have in Thee,
Leave nothing of myself in me;
Let me so read thy life, that I
Unto all life of mine may die.

Richard Crashaw

Lyra Mystica

AMENDMENT

English Seventeenth Century

That all things should be mine,
This makes His bounty most divine.
But that they all more rich should be,
   And far more brightly shine,
     As used by me;
It ravishes my soul to see the end,
To which this work so wonderful doth tend.

That we should make the skies
More glorious far before Thine eyes
Than Thou didst make them, and even Thee
   Far more Thy works to prize,
     As used they be
Than as they're made, is a stupendous work,
Wherein Thy wisdom mightily doth lurk.

Thy greatness, and Thy love,
Thy power, in this, my joy doth move;
Thy goodness, and felicity
   In this exprest above
     All praise I see:
While Thy great Godhead over all doth reign,
And such an end in such a sort attain.

What bound may we assign,
O God, to any work of Thine!

Lyra Mystica

Their endlessness discovers Thee
   In all to be divine,
     A Deity,
That will for evermore exceed the end
Of all that creature's wit can comprehend.

   Am I a glorious spring
  Of joys and riches to my King?
Are men made Gods? And may they see
   So wonderful a thing
    As God in me?
And is my soul a mirror that must shine
Even like the sun and be far more divine?

   Thy Soul, O God, doth prize
  The seas, the earth, our souls, the skies;
As we return the same to Thee
   They more delight Thine eyes,
    And sweeter be
As unto Thee we offer up the same,
Than as to us from Thee at first they came.

   O how doth Sacred Love
  His gifts refine, exalt, improve!
Our love to creatures makes them be
   In Thine esteem above
    Themselves to Thee!
O here His goodness evermore admire!
He made our souls to make His creatures higher.

                       Thomas Traherne

Lyra Mystica

THE RAPTURE

English Seventeenth Century

Sweet Infancy!
O fire of heaven! O sacred Light
    How fair and bright,
    How great am I,
Whom all the world doth magnify!

    O Heavenly Joy!
O great and sacred blessedness
    Which I possess!
    So great a joy
Who did into my arms convey?

    From God above
Being sent, the Heavens me enflame:
    To praise his Name
    The stars do move!
The burning sun doth shew His love.

    O how divine
Am I! To all this sacred wealth,
    This life and health,
    Who raised? Who mine
Did make the same? What hand divine?

Thomas Traherne

THE VISION

English Seventeenth Century

Flight is but the preparative. The sigh
    Is deep and infinite,

Lyra Mystica

Ah me! 'tis all the glory, love, light, space,
    Joy, beauty and variety
That doth adorn the Godhead's dwelling-place;
    'Tis all that eye can see.
Even trades themselves seen in celestial light,
    And cares and sins and woes are bright.

Order the beauty even of beauty is,
    It is the rule of bliss,
The very life and form and cause of pleasure;
    Which if we do not understand,
Ten thousand heaps of vain confused treasure
    Will but oppress the land.
In blessedness itself we that shall miss
    Being blind, which is the cause of bliss.

First then behold the world as thine, and well
    Note that where thou dost dwell.
See all the beauty of the spacious case,
    Lift up thy pleas'd and ravisht eyes,
Admire the glory of the Heavenly place
    And all its blessings prize.
That sight well seen thy spirit shall prepare,
    The first makes all the other rare.

Men's woes shall be but foils unto thy bliss,
    Thou once enjoying this:
Trades shall adorn and beautify the earth,
    Their ignorance shall make thee bright;
Were not their griefs Democritus his mirth?
    Their faults shall keep thee right:

Lyra Mystica

All shall be thine, because they all conspire
    To feed and make thy glory higher.

To see a glorious fountain and an end,
    To see all creatures tend
To thy advancement, and so sweetly close
    In thy repose: to see them shine
In use, in worth, in service, and even foes
    Among the rest made thine:
To see all these unite at once in thee
    Is to behold felicity.

To see the fountain is a blessed thing,
    It is to see the King
Of Glory face to face: but yet the end,
    The glorious, wondrous end is more;
And yet the fountain there we comprehend,
    The spring we there adore:
For in the end the fountain best is shown,
    As by effects the cause is known.

From one, to one, in one to see all things,
    To see the King of Kings
But once in two; to see His endless treasures
    Made all mine own, myself the end
Of all his labours! 'Tis the life of pleasures!
    To see myself His friend!
Who all things finds conjoined in Him alone,
    Sees and enjoys the Holy One.

Thomas Traherne

Lyra Mystica
THE WORLD
Welsh Seventeenth Century

I saw Eternity the other night
Like a great *Ring* of pure and endless light,
    All calm, as it was bright,
And round beneath it, Time in hours, days, years,
    Driv'n by the spheres
Like a vast shadow mov'd, in which the world
    And all her train were hurl'd;
The doting Lover in his queintest strain
    Did there Complain,
Neer him, his Lute, his fancy, and his flights,
    Wits sour delights,
With gloves, and knots the silly snares of pleasure
    Yet his dear Treasure
All scatter'd lay, while he his eys did pour
    Upon a flowr.

The darksome States-man hung with weights and woe
Like a thick midnight-fog mov'd there so slow
    He did not stay, nor go;
Condemning thoughts (like sad Ecclipses) scowl
    Upon his soul,
And Clouds of crying witnesses without
    Pursued him with one shout.
Yet dig'd the Mole, and lest his ways be found
    Workt under ground,
Where he did Clutch his prey, but one did see
    That policie,

Churches and altars fed him, Perjuries
    Were gnats and flies,
It rain'd about him bloud and tears, but he
    Drank them as free.

The fearfull miser on a heap of rust
Sate pining all his life there, did scarce trust
    His own hands with the dust,
Yet would not place one peece above, but lives
    In feare of theeves.
Thousands there were as frantick as himself
    And hug'd each one his pelf,
The down-right Epicure plac'd heav'n in sense
    And scornd pretence
While others slipt into a wide Excesse
    Said little lesse;
The weaker sort slight, triviall wares Inslave
    Who think them brave,
And poor, despised truth sate Counting by
    Their victory.

Yet some, who all this while did weep and sing,
And sing, and weep, soar'd up into the *Ring*,
    But most would use no wing.
O fools (said I), thus to prefer dark night
    Before true light,
To live in grots, and caves, and hate the day
    Because it shews the way,
The way which from this dead and dark abode
    Leads up to God,

Lyra Mystica

A way where you might tread the Sun, and be
    More bright than he.
But as I did their madness so discusse
    One whisper'd thus,
This Ring the Bride-groome did for none provide
    But for his bride.

Henry Vaughan

THE RETREATE

Welsh Seventeenth Century

Happy those early dayes! when I
Shin'd in my Angell-infancy.
Before I understood this place
Appointed for my second race,
Or taught my soul to fancy ought
But a white, Celestial thought;
When yet I had not walkt above
A mile, or two, from my first love,
And looking back (at that short space),
Could see a glimpse of his bright face;
When on some *gilded Cloud*, or *flowre*
My gazing soul would dwell an houre,
And in those weaker glories spy
Some shadows of eternity;
Before I taught my tonge to wound
My Conscience with a sinfull sound,
Or had the black art to dispence
A sev'rall sinne to ev'ry sence,
But felt through all this fleshly dresse

Bright *shootes* of everlastingnesse.
    O how I long to travell back
And tread again that ancient track!
That I might once more reach that plaine,
Where first I left my glorious traine,
From whence th' Inlightned spirit sees
That shady City of Palme trees;
But (ah!) my soul with too much stay
Is drunk, and staggers in the way.
Some men a forward motion love,
But I by backward steps would move,
And when this dust falls to the urn
In that state I came return.

Henry Vaughan

THE DWELLING-PLACE

Welsh Seventeenth Century

What happy, secret fountain,
Fair shade, or mountain,
Whose undiscover'd virgin glory
Boasts it this day, though not in story,
Was then thy dwelling? did some cloud
Fix'd to a Tent, descend and shrowd
My distrest Lord? or did a star,
Becken'd by thee, though high and far,
In sparkling smiles haste gladly down
To lodge light, and increase her own?
My dear, dear God! I do not know
What lodgd thee then, nor where, nor how;
But I am sure, thou dost now come

Oft to a narrow, homely room,
Where thou too hast but the least part,
My God, I mean *my sinful heart*.

Henry Vaughan

THEY ARE ALL GONE INTO THE WORLD OF LIGHT

Welsh Seventeenth Century

They are all gone into the world of light!
    And I alone sit ling'ring here.
Their very memory is fair and bright,
    And my sad thoughts doth clear.

It glows and glitters in my cloudy breast
    Like stars upon some gloomy grove,
Or those faint beams in which this hill is drest
    After the Sun's remove.

I see them walking in an air of glory,
    Whose light doth trample on my days;
My days, which are at best but dull and hoary,
    Mere glimmering and decays.

O holy Hope! and high Humility!
    High as the heavens above:
These are your walks, and you have shew'd them me
    To kindle my cold love.

Henry Vaughan

Lyra Mystica

GOD MAKES A PATH

Anglo-American Seventeenth Century

God makes a path, provides a guide,
  And feeds a wilderness;
His glorious name, while breath remains,
  O that I may confess.

Lost many a time, I had no guide,
  No house but a hollow tree;
In stormy winter night no fire,
  No food, no company;

In Him I found a house, a bed,
  A table, company;
No cup so bitter but's made sweet
  Where God shall sweetening be.

Roger Williams

ODE TO GOD

Russian Eighteenth Century

O Thou Eternal One! whose presence bright
All space doth occupy, all motions guide;
Unchanged through time's all-devastating flight;
Thou only God! There is no God beside!
Being of all beings! Mighty One!
Whom none could comprehend and none explore;
Who fillst existence with Thyself alone:
Embracing all, supporting, ruling o'er,—
Being whom we call God, and know no more!

Lyra Mystica

In its sublime research philosophy
May measure out the ocean deeps, may count
The sands or the sun's rays; but God! for thee
There is no weight nor measure: none can mount
Up to thy mysteries. Reason's brightest spark,
Though kindled by thy light, in vain would try
To trace thy counsels, infinite and dark;
And thought is lost ere thought can soar so high,
Even like past moments in eternity.

Thou from primeval nothingness didst call
First chaos, then existence: Lord, on thee
Eternity had its foundation; all
Sprung from thee,—of light, joy, harmony,
Sole origin: all life, all beauty thine.
Thy word created all and doth create;
Thy splendor fills all space with rays divine.
Thou wert and art and shalt be! Glorious! Great!
Light-giving, life-sustaining Potentate!
Thy chains the unmeasured universe surround,
Upheld by thee, by thee inspired with breath!
Thou the beginning with the end hast bound,
And beautifully mingled life and death!
As sparks mount upward from the fiery blaze,
So suns are born, so worlds spring forth from thee,
And as the spangles in the sunny rays
Shine round the silver snow, the pageantry
Of heaven's bright army glitters in thy praise.

A million torches lighted by thy hand
Wander unwearied through the blue abyss:

Lyra Mystica

They own thy power, accomplish thy command,
All gay with life, all eloquent with bliss.
What shall we call them? Piles of crystal light,
A glorious company of golden streams,
Lamps of celestial ether burning bright,
Suns lighting systems with their joyous beams?
But thou to these art as the noon to night.

Yes! As a drop of water in the sea,
All this magnificence in thee is lost:
What are ten thousand worlds compared to thee?
What am I, then? Heaven's unnumbered host,
Though multiplied by myriads, and arrayed
In all the glory of sublimest thought,
Is but an atom in the balance, weighed
Against thy greatness, is a cipher brought
Against infinity! Oh, what am I, then? Nought!

Nought, yet the effulgence of thy light,
Pervading worlds, hath reached my bosom, too;
Yes! In my spirit doth thy spirit shine,
As shines the sunbeam in a drop of dew.
Nought! Yet I live, and on hope's pinions fly
Eager toward thy presence; for in thee
I live and breathe and dwell; aspiring high,
Even to the throne of thy divinity.
I am, O God! and surely Thou must be!

Thou art! directing, guiding all, thou art!
Direct my understanding, then, to thee;

Control my spirit, guide my wandering heart:
Though but an atom midst immensity,
Still, I am something fashioned by Thy hand!
I hold a middle rank 'twixt heaven and earth
On the last verge of mortal being stand,
Close to the realm where angels have their birth,
Just on the boundaries of the spirit land!

The chain of being is complete in me;
In me is matter's last gradation lost,
And the next step is spirit—Deity!
I can command the lightning and am dust!
A monarch and a slave; a worm, a god!
Whence came I here? and how so marvellously
Constructed and conceived? Unknown! This clod
Lives surely through some higher energy;
For from itself alone it could not be!

Creator! yes, thy wisdom and thy word
Created me! Thou Source of life and good!
Thou Spirit of my Spirit, and my Lord!
Thy light, thy love, in their bright plenitude
Filled me with an immortal soul, to spring
Over the abyss of death, and bade it wear
The garments of eternal day, and wing
Its heavenly flight beyond this little sphere,
Even to its source—to thee—its Author there.

O thoughts ineffable! O visions blest!
Though worthless our conceptions all of thee,

Yet shall thy shadowed image fill our breast,
And waft its homage to thy Deity.
God! thus alone my lonely thoughts can soar;
Thus seek thy presence, Being wise and good!
Midst thy vast works admire, obey, adore;
And when the tongue is eloquent no more,
The soul shall speak in tears of gratitude!
Gavrila Románovich Derzhávin

From THE SEASONS

English Eighteenth Century

Should Fate command me to the farthest verge
Of the green earth, to distant barbarous climes,
Rivers unknown to song . . . 'tis nought to me,
Since God is ever present, ever felt,
In the void waste as in the city full,
And where he vital spreads there must be joy.
When even at last the solemn Hour shall come,
And wing my mystic flight to future worlds,
I cheerful will obey; there, with new powers,
With rising wonders sing: I cannot go
Where Universal Love not smiles around,
Sustaining all yon orbs, and all their sons;
From seeming Evil still educing Good,
And better thence again, and better still,
In infinite progression.— But I lose
Myself in Him, in Light ineffable. . . .
James Thomson

Lyra Mystica

ALL ARE BUT PARTS

English Eighteenth Century

All are but parts of one stupendous whole,
Whose body Nature is, and God the soul;
That, changed through all, and yet in all the same,
Great in the earth, as in th'ethereal frame,
Warms in the sun, refreshes in the breeze,
Glows in the stars and blossoms in the trees,
Lives through all life, extends through all extent,
Spreads undivided, operates unspent:
Breathes in our soul, informs our mortal part;
As full, as perfect, in a hair as heart;
As full, as perfect, in vile man that mourns
As the rapt Seraphim, that sings and burns:
To him, no high, no low, no great, no small—
He fills, he bounds, connects and equals all . . .
All nature is but art, unknown to thee:
All chance, direction, which thou canst not see:
All discord, harmony not understood;
All partial evil, universal good.

Alexander Pope

THE UNIVERSAL PRAYER

English Eighteenth Century

Father of all! In every age,
    In every clime adored,
By saint, by savage, and by sage,
    Jehovah, Jove, or Lord!

Lyra Mystica

Thou First great Cause, least understood,
    Who all my sense confined
To know but this, that thou art good,
    And that myself am blind!

Yet gave me, in this dark estate,
    To see the good from ill;
And, binding nature fast in fate,
    Left free the human will.

What conscience dictates to be done,
    Or warns me not to do,
This teach me more than hell to shun,
    That more than heaven pursue.

What blessings thy free bounty gives,
    Let me not cast away;
For God is paid when man receives;
    To enjoy is to obey.

Save me alike from foolish pride,
    And impious discontent,
At aught thy wisdom has denied,
    Or aught thy goodness lent.

Teach me to feel another's woe,
    To hide the fault I see;
That mercy I to others show,
    That mercy show to me.

Mean though I am, not wholly so,
    Since quickened by thy breath;

Oh, lead me wheresoe'er I go,
  Through this day's life or death.

This day be bread and peace my lot;
  All else beneath the sun
Thou knowest if best bestowed or not,
  And let thy will be done.

To thee, whose temple is all space,—
  Whose altar, earth, sea, skies,—
One chorus let all beings raise!
  All Nature's incense rise!

Alexander Pope

From MILTON

English 1757–1827

And did those feet in ancient time
  Walk upon England's mountains green?
And was the holy Lamb of God
  On England's pleasant pastures seen?

And did the Countenance Divine
  Shine forth upon our clouded hills?
And was Jerusalem builded here
  Among these dark Satanic Mills?

Bring me my bow of burning gold!
  Bring me my arrows of desire!
Bring me my spear! O clouds, unfold!
  Bring me my chariot of fire!

I will not cease from mental fight,
  Nor shall my sword sleep in my hand,
Till we have built Jerusalem
  In England's green and pleasant land.

William Blake

THE DIVINE IMAGE

English 1757–1827

To Mercy, Pity, Peace, and Love
All pray in their distress;
And to these virtues of delight
Return their thankfulness.

For Mercy, Pity, Peace, and Love
Is God, our Father dear,
And Mercy, Pity, Peace, and Love
Is man, His child and care.

For Mercy has a human heart,
Pity a human face,
And Love, the human form divine,
And Peace, the human dress.

Then every man, of every clime,
That prays in his distress,
Prays to the human form divine,
Love, Mercy, Pity, Peace.

And all must love the human form,
In heathen, Turk, or Jew;

Lyra Mystica

Where Mercy, Love, and Pity dwell
There God is dwelling too.

William Blake

AUGURIES OF INNOCENCE

English 1757–1827

To see a World in a grain of sand,
And a Heaven in a wild flower,
Hold Infinity in the palm of your hand,
And Eternity in an hour. . . .

The bat that flits at close of eve
Has left the brain that won't believe.
The owl that calls upon the night
Speaks the unbeliever's fright. . . .

Joy and woe are woven fine,
A clothing for the soul divine;
Under every grief and pine
Runs a joy with silken twine. . . .

Every tear from every eye
Becomes a babe in Eternity. . . .

The bleat, the bark, bellow, and roar
Are waves that beat on Heaven's shore. . . .

He who doubts from what he sees
Will ne'er believe, do what you please.
If the Sun and Moon should doubt,
They'd immediately go out. . . .

God appears, and God is Light,
To those poor souls who dwell in Night;
But does a Human Form display
To those who dwell in realms of Day.

William Blake

THERE IS ONE MIND

English 1772–1834

I

There is one Mind, one omnipresent Mind,
Omnific. His most holy name is Love.
Truth of subliming import! with the which
Who feeds and saturates his constant soul,
He from his small particular orbit flies
With blest outstarting! From himself he flies,
Stands in the sun, and with no partial gaze
Views all creation; and he loves it all,
And blesses it, and calls it very good!
This is indeed to dwell with the Most High!
Cherubs and rapture-trembling Seraphim
Can press no nearer to the Almighty's throne.
But that we roam unconscious, or with hearts
Unfeeling of our universal Sire,
And that in His vast family no Cain
Injures uninjured (in her best-aimed blow
Victorious Murder a blind Suicide)
Haply for this some younger Angel now
Looks down on Human Nature; and, behold!
A sea of blood bestrewed with wrecks, where mad
Embattling Interests on each other rush

With unhelmed rage!
                'Tis the sublime of man,
Our noontide Majesty, to know ourselves
Parts and proportions of one wondrous whole!
This fraternizes man, this constitutes
Our charities and bearings. But 'tis God
Diffused through all, that doth make all one whole;
This the worst superstition, him except
Aught to desire, Supreme Reality!
The plenitude and permanence of bliss!

2

        Toy-bewitched,
Made blind by lusts, disherited of soul,
No common centre Man, no common sire
Knoweth! A sordid solitary thing,
Mid countless brethren with a lonely heart
Through courts and cities the smooth savage roams
Feeling himself, his own low self the whole;
When he by sacred sympathy might make
The whole one Self! Self, that no alien knows!
Self, far diffused as Fancy's wing can travel!
Self, spreading still! Oblivious of its own,
Yet all of all possessing! This is Faith!
This the Messiah's destined victory!

Samuel Taylor Coleridge

HE IS MADE ONE WITH NATURE

English 1792–1822

He is made one with Nature: there is heard
His voice in all her music, from the moan

Of thunder, to the song of night's sweet bird;
He is a presence to be felt and known
In darkness and in light, from herb and stone,
Spreading itself where'er that Power may move
Which has withdrawn his being to its own;
Which wields the world with never-wearied love,
Sustains it from beneath, and kindles it above.

He is a portion of the loveliness
Which once he made more lovely: he doth bear
His part, while the one Spirit's plastic stress
Sweeps through the dull dense world, compelling there,
All new successions to the forms they wear;
Torturing th' unwilling dross that checks its flight
To its own likeness, as each mass may bear;
And bursting in its beauty and its might
From trees and beasts and men into the Heaven's light.

The splendours of the firmament of time
May be eclipsed, but are extinguished not;
Like stars to their appointed height they climb
And death is a low mist which cannot blot
The brightness it may veil. When lofty thought
Lifts a young heart above its mortal lair,
And love and life contend in it, for what
Shall be its earthly doom, the dead live there
And move like winds of light on dark and stormy air.

The One remains, the many change and pass;
Heaven's light forever shines, Earth's shadows fly;

Lyra Mystica

Life, like a dome of many-coloured glass,
Stains the white radiance of Eternity,
Until Death tramples it to fragments,—Die,
If thou wouldst be with that which thou dost seek!
Follow where all is fled!—Rome's azure sky,
Flowers, ruins, statues, music, words, are weak
The glory they transfuse with fitting truth to speak.

Why linger, why turn back, why shrink, my Heart?
Thy hopes are gone before: from all things here
They have departed; thou shouldst now depart!
A light is passed from the revolving year,
And man, and woman; and what still is dear
Attracts to crush, repels to make thee wither.
The soft sky smiles,—the low wind whispers near:
"Tis Adonais calls." Oh, hasten thither,
No more let Life divide what Death can join together.

That light whose smile kindles the Universe,
That Beauty in which all things work and move,
That benediction which the eclipsing Curse
Of birth can quench not, that sustaining Love
Which through the web of being blindly wove
By man and beast and air and earth and sea,
Burns bright or dim, as each are mirrors of
The fire for which all thirst; now beams on me,
Consuming the last clouds of cold mortality.

The breath whose might I have involved in song
Descends on me; my spirit's bark is driven,
Far from the shore, far from the trembling throng

Whose sails were never to the tempest given;
The massy earth and sphered skies are riven!
I am borne darkly, fearfully, afar;
Whilst, burning through the inmost veil of Heaven,
The soul of Adonais, like a star,
Beacons from the abode where the Eternal are.

Percy Bysshe Shelley

HYMN TO INTELLECTUAL BEAUTY

English 1792–1822

The awful shadow of some unseen Power
    Floats though unseen among us,—visiting
    This various world with an inconstant wing
As summer winds that creep from flower to flower,—
Like moonbeams that behind some piny mountain shower,
    It visits with inconstant glance
    Each human heart and countenance;
Like hues and harmonies of evening,—
    Like clouds in starlight widely spread,—
    Like memory of music fled,—
    Like aught that for its grace may be
Dear, and yet dearer for its mystery.

Spirit of Beauty, that dost consecrate
    With thine own hues all thou dost shine upon
    Of human thought or form,—where art thou gone?
Why dost thou pass away and leave our state,

This dim vast vale of tears, vacant and desolate?
    Ask why the sunlight not for ever
    Weaves rainbows o'er yon mountain-river,
Why aught should fail and fade that once is shown,
    Why fear and dream and death and birth
    Cast on the daylight of this earth
    Such gloom,—why man has such a scope
For love and hate, despondency and hope?

No voice from some sublimer world hath ever
    To sage or poet these responses given—
    Therefore the names of Demon, Ghost, and Heaven,
Remain the records of their vain endeavour,
Frail spells—whose uttered charm might not avail to sever,
    From all we hear and all we see,
    Doubt, chance, and mutability.
Thy light alone—like mist o'er mountains driven,
    Or music by the night-wind sent
    Through strings of some still instrument,
    Or moonlight on a midnight stream,
Gives grace and truth to life's unquiet dream.

Love, Hope, and Self-esteem, like clouds depart
    And come, for some uncertain moments lent.
    Man were immortal, and omnipotent,
Didst thou, unknown and awful as thou art,
Keep with thy glorious train firm state within his heart.
    Thou messenger of sympathies,
    That wax and wane in lovers' eyes—

Thou—that to human thought art nourishment,
  Like darkness to a dying flame!
  Depart not as thy shadow came,
  Depart not—lest the grave should be,
Like life and fear, a dark reality.

While yet a boy I sought for ghosts, and sped
  Through many a listening chamber, cave and ruin,
  And starlight wood, with fearful steps pursuing
Hopes of high talk with the departed dead.
I called on poisonous names with which our youth is fed;
  I was not heard—I saw them not—
  When musing deeply on the lot
Of life, at that sweet time when winds are wooing
  All vital things that wake to bring
  News of birds and blossoming,—
  Sudden, thy shadow fell on me;
I shrieked, and clasped my hands in ecstasy!

I vowed that I would dedicate my powers
  To thee and thine—have I not kept the vow?
  With beating heart and streaming eyes, even now
I call the phantoms of a thousand hours
Each from his voiceless grave: they have in visioned bowers
  Of studious zeal or love's delight
  Outwatched with me the envious night—
They know that never joy illumed my brow
  Unlinked with hope that thou wouldst free

This world from its dark slavery,
That thou—O awful Loveliness,
Wouldst give whate'er these words cannot express.

The day becomes more solemn and serene
    When noon is past—there is a harmony
    In autumn, and a lustre in its sky,
Which through the summer is not heard or seen,
As if it could not be, as if it had not been!
    Thus let thy power, which like the truth
    Of nature on my passive youth
Descended, to my onward life supply
    Its calm—to one who worships thee,
    And every form containing thee,
    Whom, Spirit fair, thy spells did bind
To fear himself, and love all human kind.

Percy Bysshe Shelley

NOW THAT I HAVE GROWN TO MANHOOD

German-Jewish 1797–1856

Now that I have grown to manhood,
Read and journeyed more than most,
Swells my heart in truth believing,
Steadfast, in the Holy Ghost.

He who wrought the greatest wonders,
Greater still can do. He broke
Strongholds of the robber barons,
Shattering the servile yoke.

Mortal wounds for ever healing,
He renews each ancient right,
Men are equal born before Him,
All are noble in His sight.

He has banished clouds of sorrow,
Every phantom as it gloomed,
All that hindered love and gladness,
Day and night that held us doomed.

Knights in thousands, nobly weaponed,
Did the Spirit set apart,
And, that they might do His pleasure,
Put His courage in their heart.

Bright their precious swords are gleaming,
High their lordly banners wave,
Gladly wouldst thou see, my darling,
See these glorious knights and brave.

Kiss me and look boldly, darling,
One is standing in thy sight,
For I rode behind His banner,
I, the Holy Spirit's Knight!

Heinrich Heine

PEACE

German-Jewish, 1797–1856

High in heaven stood the sun,
With white clouds sailing round him;

The sea was still,
And by the helm I lay thinking,
Dreamily thinking; and half in waking
And half in slumber these eyes beheld Him,
The Saviour of men.
Arrayed in a waving white vesture
He walked in His mighty stature
Over land and sea.
His head reached up to the heavens,
His hands were held out in blessing
Over land and sea;
And as a heart in His bosom
Wore He the sun,
The red and flaming sun;
And the red and flaming sun-heart
Poured abroad its gracious life-beams,
Its tender and gladdening radiance,
Enlightening and warming,
Over land and sea.

Near us floated the music of church bells,
And like swans those clear notes were drawing
The ship by a cable of roses,
And they drew it in play to the green shore
Where men dwell, in the many-steepled
And high-roofed town.

O marvel of peace! How quiet the town lay!
Hushed was the sullen hum
Of the chattering, stifling workshops,
And along the clean, echoing streets

White-robed people were walking,
Each carrying a palm-branch;
And when one met another,
Their glance told the secret,
And trembling, in love and sweet self-denial
They kissed a friend on the forehead
And their gaze sought the heaven,
Where the Saviour's sun-heart was beaming,
And red drops from it were falling
For man in joyous atonement;
And the blest ones—thrice blest ones—were saying
"May Jesus Christ be praised!"

Heinrich Heine

L'INFINITO

Italian 1798–1837

I always loved this solitary hill,
This hedge as well, which takes so large a share
Of the far-flung horizon from my view;
But seated here, in contemplation lost,
My thought discovers vaster space beyond
Supernal silence and unfathomed peace;
Almost I am afraid; then, since I hear
The murmur of the wind among the leaves,
I match that infinite calm unto this sound
And with my mind embrace eternity,
The vivid, speaking present and dead past;
In such immensity my spirit drowns,
And sweet to me is shipwreck in this sea.

Giacomo Leopardi

Lyra Mystica
THE PROPHET
Russian 1799–1837

Athirst in spirit, through the gloom
Of an unpeopled waste I blundered,
And saw a six-winged Seraph loom
Where the two pathways met and sundered.
He laid his fingers on my eyes:
His touch lay soft as slumber lies,—
And like an eagle's, his crag shaken,
Did my prophetic eyes awaken.
Upon my ears his fingers fell
And sound rose,—stormy swell on swell:
I heard the spheres revolving, chiming,
The angels in their soaring sweep,
The monsters moving in the deep,
The green vine in the valley climbing.
And from my mouth the Seraph wrung
Forth by its roots my sinful tongue;
The evil things and vain it babbled
His hand drew forth and so effaced,
And the wise serpent's tongue he placed
Between my lips with hand blood-dabbled;
And with a sword he clove my breast,
Plucked out the heart he made beat higher,
And in my stricken bosom pressed
Instead a coal of living fire.
Upon the wastes, a lifeless clod,
I lay, and heard the voice of God:
"Arise, oh, prophet, watch and hearken,
And with my Will thy soul engird,

Roam the gray seas, the roads that darken,
And burn men's hearts with this, my Word."
Alexander Sergeyevich Pushkin

CONFESSION

French Nineteenth Century

O my God, thou hast wounded me with love,
Behold the wound that is still vibrating,
O my God, thou hast wounded me with love.

O my God, thy fear hath fallen upon me,
Behold the burn is there, and it throbs aloud.
O my God, thy fear hath fallen upon me.

O my God, I have known all that is vile,
And thy glory hath stationed itself in me,
O my God, I have known all that is vile.

Drown my soul in floods, floods of thy wine,
Mingle my life with the body of thy bread.
Drown my soul in floods, floods of thy wine.

Take my blood that I have not poured out,
Take my flesh unworthy of thy suffering,
Take my blood that I have not poured out.

Take my brow that has only learned to blush,
To be the footstool of thine adorable feet,
Take my brow that has only learned to blush.

Lyra Mystica

Take my hands because they have labored not,
For coals of fire and for rare frankincense,
Take my hands because they have labored not.

Take my heart that has beaten for vain things,
To throb under the thorns of Calvary,
Take my heart that has beaten for vain things.

Take my feet, frivolous travellers,
That they may run to the crying of thy grace,
Take my feet, foolish travellers.

Take my voice, a harsh and lying noise,
For the reproaches of thy penitence,
Take my voice, a harsh and lying noise.

Take mine eyes, luminaries of deceit,
That they may be extinguished in the tears of prayer,
Take mine eyes, luminaries of deceit.

Ah, thou God of pardon and promises,
What is the pit of mine ingratitude!
Ah, thou God of pardon and promises.

God of terror and God of holiness,
Alas, my sinfulness is a black abyss,
God of terror and holiness.

Thou God of peace, of joy and delight,
All my tears, all my ignorances,
Thou God of peace, of joy and delight.

Thou, O God, knowest all this, all this,
How poor I am, poorer than any man,
Thou, O God, knowest all this, all this.

And what I have, my God, I give to thee.
Paul Verlaine

IN GOD MY SOUL REPOSES

German Nineteenth Century

In God my soul reposes;
  I live by God alone:
All life revolves about Him,
I cannot do without Him,
  He cannot me disown.

In God my soul reposes,
  It dies at last, you say;
But, I no fear will cherish,
The soul can never perish,
  Who lives in Him today.

In God my soul reposes,
  The bond of souls is He,
This secret comprehended,
Faith, Hope and Love descended
  From Heaven to dwell with me.

In God my soul reposes,
  How small a thing am I!
How fruitless my endeavour,

Mourn not, O Soul, forever,
  Salvation draweth nigh.

In God my soul reposes,
  God shall my plan fulfill;
His purpose bounds existence
In spite of my resistance,
  He brings to pass His will.

Theodore Fechner

EVENING SONG

Danish Nineteenth Century

The sun in beauty left the hill.
Now rise the stars' bright legions,
Lamps of a world more glorious still,
Charting the darker regions.

Night is a vast cathedral hung
Between the arching spaces,
The world, a hidden leaf among
A forest's secret places.

The smallest leaf in deepest wood
Where creatures live securely;
Each fashioned in the mind of God,
Blessed and remembered surely.

That mind, that hand, where great and small
Are one, shall always cherish

The hidden soul whose leaf may fall
Away, but shall not perish.

B. S. Ingeman

SHADOWS

Russian Nineteenth Century

Dear friend, seest thou not
    that whatever we look on here
Is but an image, shadows only
    of a beauty hid from our eyes?

Dear friend, hear'st thou not
    this jarring tumult of life
Is but a far discordant echo
    of heaven's triumphant harmonies?

Dear friend, know'st thou not
    that the only truth in the world
Is what one heart telleth another
    in speechless greetings of love?

Vladimir Solovev

EAST LONDON

English Nineteenth Century

'Twas August, and the fierce sun overhead
Smote on the squalid streets of Bethnal Green,
And the pale weaver, through his windows seen
In Spitalfields, look'd thrice dispirited.

I met a preacher there I knew, and said:
"Ill and o'erworked, how fare you in this scene?"
"Bravely!" said he; "for I of late have been
Much cheer'd by thoughts of Christ, *the living bread*."

O human soul! so long as thou canst so
Set up a mark of everlasting light,
Above the howling senses' ebb and flow,
To cheer thee, and to right thee if thou roam—
Not with lost toil thou laborest through the night!
Thou mak'st the heaven thou hopest indeed thy home.

Matthew Arnold

CALM SOUL OF ALL THINGS

English Nineteenth Century

Calm soul of all things! make it mine
To feel, amid the city's jar,
That there abides a peace of thine,
Man did not make, and cannot mar!

The will to neither strive nor cry,
The power to feel with others give!
Calm, calm me more! nor let me die
Before I have begun to live.

Matthew Arnold

DOMINUS ILLUMINATIO MEA

English Nineteenth Century

In the hour of death, after this life's whim,
When the heart beats low, and the eyes grow dim,

And pain has exhausted every limb—
  The lover of the Lord shall trust in Him.

When the will has forgotton the lifelong aim,
  And the mind can only disgrace its fame,
And a man is uncertain of his own name—
  The power of the Lord shall fill this frame.

When the last sigh is heaved, and the last tear shed,
  And the coffin is waiting beside the bed,
And the widow and child forsake the dead—
  The angel of the Lord shall lift this head.

For even the purest delight may pall,
  And power must fail, and the pride must fall,
And the love of the dearest friends grow small—
  But the glory of the Lord is all in all.

R. D. Blackmore

THE VISIONARY

English Nineteenth Century

Silent is the house: all are laid asleep:
One alone looks out o'er the snow-wreaths deep,
Watching every cloud, dreading every breeze
That whirls the wildering drift, and bends the groaning trees.

Cheerful is the hearth, soft the matted floor;
Not one shivering gust creeps through pane or door;
The little lamp burns straight, its rays shoot strong and far:
I trim it well, to be a wanderer's guiding-star.

Frown, my haughty sire! chide, my angry dame!
Set your slaves to spy; threaten me with shame:
But neither sire nor dame nor prying serf shall know
What angel nightly tracks that waste of frozen snow.

What I love shall come like visitant of air,
Safe in secret power from lurking human snare;
What loves me, no word of mine shall e'er betray,
Though for faith unstained my life must forfeit pay.

Burn, then, little lamp; glimmer straight and clear—
Hush! a rustling wing stirs, methinks, the air:
He for whom I wait, thus ever comes to me;
Strange Power! I trust thy might; trust thou my constancy.

Emily Brontë

LAST LINES

English Nineteenth Century

No coward soul is mine,
No trembler in the world's storm-troubled sphere:
    I see Heaven's glories shine,
And faith shines equal, arming me from fear.

    O God within my breast,
Almighty, ever-present Deity!
    Life—that in me has rest,
As I undying Life—have power in Thee!

    Vain are the thousand creeds
That move men's hearts: unutterably vain;

Worthless as withered weeds,
Or idlest froth amid the boundless main,

To waken doubt in one
Holding so fast by thine infinity;
  So surely anchor'd on
The steadfast rock of immortality.

With wide-embracing love
Thy Spirit animates eternal years,
  Pervades and broods above,
Changes, sustains, dissolves, creates, and rears.

Though earth and man were gone,
And suns and universes ceased to be,
  And Thou were left alone,
Every existence would exist in Thee.

There is not room for Death,
Nor atom that his might could render void:
  Thou—THOU art Being and Breath,
And what THOU art may never be destroy'd.

Emily Brontë

From THE SOUL'S TRAVELLING

English Nineteenth Century

God, God!
With a child's voice I cry,
Weak, sad, confidingly—
  God, God!

Lyra Mystica

Thou knowest, eyelids, raised not always up
Unto Thy love (as none of ours are), droop
    As ours, o'er many a tear!
Thou knowest, though Thy universe is broad,
Two little tears suffice to cover all:
Thou knowest, Thou, who art so prodigal
Of beauty, we are oft but stricken deer
Expiring in the woods—that care for none
Of those delightsome flowers they die upon.

O blissful Mouth which breathed the mournful breath
We name our souls, self-spoilt!—by that strong passion
Which paled Thee once with sighs,—by that strong death
Which made Thee once unbreathing—from the wrack
Themselves have called around them, call them back,
Back to Thee in continuous aspiration!
    For here, O Lord,
For here they travel vainly,—vainly pass
From city-pavement to untrodden sward,
Where the lark finds her deep nest in the grass
Cold with the earth's last dew. Yea, very vain
The greatest speed of all these souls of men
Unless they travel upward to the throne
Where sittest THOU, the satisfying ONE,
With help for sins and holy perfectings
For all requirements—while the archangel, raising
Unto Thy face his full ecstatic gazing,
Forgets the rush and rapture of his wings.

Elizabeth Barrett Browning

PROSPICE

English Nineteenth Century

Fear death?—to feel the fog in my throat
    The mist in my face,
When the snows begin, and the blasts denote
    I am nearing the place,
The power of the night, the press of the storm,
    The post of the foe;
Where he stands, the Arch-Fear in a visible form,
    And the strong man must go:
For the journey is done, and the summit attained,
    And the barriers fall,
Though a battle's to fight ere the guerdon be gained,
    The reward of it all.
I was ever a fighter, so—one fight more,
    The best and the last!
I would hate that death bandaged my eyes and forbore,
    And bade me creep past.
No, let me taste the whole of it, fare like my peers,
    The heroes of old,
Bear the brunt, in a minute pay glad life's arrears
    Of pain, darkness and cold.
For sudden the worst turns the best to the brave,
    The black minute's at end,
And the elements rage, the fiend-voices that rave,
    Shall dwindle, shall blend,
Shall change, shall become first a peace out of pain,
    Then a light, then thy breast,
O thou soul of my soul! I shall clasp thee again,
    And with God be the rest!

Robert Browning

Lyra Mystica

THEREFORE TO WHOM TURN I BUT TO THEE?

English Nineteenth Century

Therefore to whom turn I but to thee, the ineffable Name?
    Builder and maker, thou, of houses not made with hands!
What, have fear of change from thee who art ever the same?
    Doubt that thy power can fill the heart that thy power expands?
There shall never be one lost good! What was, shall live as before;
    The evil is null, is naught, is silence implying sound;
What was good shall be good, with, for evil, so much good more;
    On the earth the broken arcs; in the heaven a perfect round.

All we have willed, or hoped or dreamed of good shall exist;
    Not its semblance, but itself; no beauty, nor good, nor power
Whose voice has gone forth, but each survives for the melodist
    When eternity affirms the conception of an hour.
The high that proved too high, the heroic for earth too hard,

> The passion that left the ground to lose itself in the sky,
> Are music sent up to God by the lover and the bard;
> Enough that he heard it once: we shall hear it by and by.
>
> And what is our failure here but a triumph's evidence
> For the fulness of the days? Have we withered or agonized?
> Why else was the pause prolonged but that singing might issue thence?
> Why rushed the discords in, but that harmony should be prized?
> Sorrow is hard to bear, and doubt is slow to clear,
> Each sufferer says his say, his scheme of the weal and woe:
> But God has a few of us whom he whispers in the ear;
> The rest may reason and welcome: 'tis we musicians know.
> Well, it is earth with me; silence resumes her reign:
> I will be patient and proud, and soberly acquiesce.
> Give me the keys. I feel for the common chord again,
> Sliding by semitones till I sink to the minor,—yes,
> And I blunt it into a ninth, and I stand on alien ground,
> Surveying awhile the heights I rolled from into the deep;
> Which, hark, I have dared and done, for my resting-place is found,
> The C Major of this life: so, now I will try to sleep.

Robert Browning

Lyra Mystica

WITH WHOM IS NO VARIABLENESS, NEITHER SHADOW OF TURNING

English Nineteenth Century

It fortifies my soul to know
That though I perish, truth is so;
That, howsoe'er I stray and range,
Whate'er I do, Thou dost not change.
I steadier step when I recall
That, if I slip, Thou dost not fall.
Arthur Hugh Clough

From THE THOUGHTS OF GOD

English Nineteenth Century

They say there is a hollow, safe and still,
A point of coolness and repose
Within the centre of a flame, where life might dwell
Unharmed and unconsumed, as in a luminous shell,
   Which the bright walls of fire enclose
In breachless splendour, barrier that no foes
    Could pass at will.

   There is a point of rest
At the great centre of the cyclone's force,
  A silence at its secret source;—
A little child might slumber undistressed,
Without the ruffle of one fairy curl,
In that strange central calm amid the mighty whirl.

So in the centre of these thoughts of God,
Cyclones of power, consuming glory-fire,—
　　As we fall o'erawed
Upon our faces, and are lifted higher
By His great gentleness, and carried nigher
Than unredeemed angels, till we stand
　　Even in the hollow of His hand,—
　　Nay more! we lean upon His breast—
There, there we find a point of perfect rest
　　And glorious safety. There we see
　　His thoughts to us-ward, thoughts of peace
That stoop to tenderest love; that still increase
With increase of our need; that never change,
That never fail, or falter, or forget.
　　O pity infinite!
　　O royal mercy free!
O gentle climax of the depth and height
Of God's most precious thoughts, most wonderful,
　　most strange!
"For I am poor and needy, yet
The Lord Himself, Jehovah, *thinketh upon me!*"
　　　　　　　　　　　　Frances Ridley Havergal

THICK IS THE DARKNESS

English Nineteenth Century

Thick is the darkness—
　　Sunward, O, Sunward!
Rough is the highway—
　　Onward, still onward!

Lyra Mystica

Dawn harbors surely
    East of the shadows.
Facing us somewhere
    Spread the sweet meadows.

Upward and forward!
    Time will restore us:
Light is above us,
    Rest is before us.
William Ernest Henley

I WENT TO SLEEP; AND NOW I AM REFRESHED

English Nineteenth Century

I went to sleep; and now I am refreshed,
A strange refreshment: for I feel in me
An inexpressible lightness, and a sense
Of freedom, as I were at length myself,
And ne'er had been before. How still it is!
I hear no more the busy beat of time,
No, nor my fluttering breath, nor struggling pulse;
Nor does one moment differ from the next. . . .
Another marvel: some one has me fast
Within his ample palm; 'tis not a grasp
Such as they use on earth, but all around
Over the surface of my subtle being,
As though I were a sphere and capable
To be accosted thus, a uniform
And gentle pressure tells me I am not
Self-moving, but borne forward on my way.

And hark! I hear a singing; yet in sooth
I cannot of that music rightly say
Whether I hear or touch or taste the tones.
Oh, what a heart-subduing melody! . . .
Now know I surely that I am at length
Out of the body: had I part with earth,
I never could have drunk those accents in,
And not have worshipped as a God that voice
That was so musical; but now I am
So whole of heart, so calm, so self-possessed,
With such a full content, and with a sense
So apprehensive and discriminate,
As no temptation can intoxicate.
Nor have I even terror at the thought
That I am clasped by such a saintliness.
John Henry Newman

From THE ANCIENT SAGE

English Nineteenth Century

If thou would'st hear the Nameless, and wilt dive
Into the Temple-cave of thine own self,
There, brooding by the central altar, thou
May'st haply learn the Nameless hath a voice,
By which thou wilt abide, if thou be wise,
As if thou knewest, tho' thou canst not know;
For Knowledge is the swallow on the lake
That sees and stirs the surface-shadow there
But never yet hath dipt into the abysm,
The Abysm of all Abysms, beneath, within
The blue of sky and sea, the green of earth,

Lyra Mystica

And in the million-millionth of a grain
Which cleft and cleft again for evermore,
And ever vanishing, never vanishes,
To me, my son, more mystic than myself,
Or even than the Nameless is to me.

    And when thou sendest thy free soul thro' heaven,
Nor understandest bound nor boundlessness,
Thou seest the Nameless of the hundred names.

    And if the Nameless should withdraw from all
Thy frailty counts most real, all thy world
Might vanish like thy shadow in the dark.

"And since— from when this earth began—
    The Nameless never came
Among us, never spake with man,
    And never named the Name"—

Thou canst not prove the Nameless, O my son,
Nor canst thou prove the world thou movest in,
Thou canst not prove that thou art body alone,
Nor canst thou prove that thou art spirit alone,
Nor canst thou prove that thou art both in one;
Thou canst not prove thou art immortal, no
Nor yet that thou art mortal—nay my son,
Thou canst not prove that I, who speak with thee,
Am not thyself in converse with thyself,
For nothing worthy proving can be proven,
Nor yet disproven: wherefore thou be wise,
Cleave ever to the sunnier side of doubt,
And cling to Faith beyond the forms of Faith.
She reels not in the storm of warring words,

Lyra Mystica

She brightens at the clash of "Yes" and "No,"
She sees the Best that glimmers thro' the Worst,
She feels the Sun is hid but for a night,
She spies the summer thro' the winter bud,
She tastes the fruit before the blossom falls,
She hears the lark within the songless egg,
She finds the fountain where they wail'd "Mirage"!

Alfred, Lord Tennyson

THE HIGHER PANTHEISM

English Nineteenth Century

The sun, the moon, the stars, the seas, the hills and the plains—
Are not these, O Soul, the Vision of Him who reigns?

Is not the Vision He? tho' He be not that which He seems?
Dreams are true while they last, and do we not live in dreams?

Earth, these solid stars, this weight of body and limb,
Are they not sign and symbol of thy division from Him?

Dark is the world to thee: thyself art the reason why;
For is He not all but thou, that hast power to feel "I and I"?

Glory about thee, without thee; and thou fulfillest thy doom,

Making Him broken gleams, and a stifled splendour and gloom.

Speak to Him thou for He hears, and Spirit with Spirit can meet—
Closer is He than breathing, and nearer than hands and feet.

God is law, say the wise; O Soul, and let us rejoice,
For if He thunder by law the thunder is yet His voice.

Law is God, say some: no God at all, says the fool;
For all we have power to see is a straight staff bent in a pool;

And the ear of man cannot hear, and the eye of man cannot see;
But if we could see and hear, this Vision—were it not He?

Alfred, Lord Tennyson

THE HUMAN CRY

English Nineteenth Century

Hallowed be Thy name—Halleluiah!—
　　Infinite Ideality!
　　Inmeasurable Reality!
　　Infinite Personality!
Hallowed be Thy name—Halleluiah!

We feel we are nothing—for all is Thou and in
    Thee;
We feel we are something—*that* also has come from
    Thee;
We know we are nothing—but Thou wilt help us to
    be.
Hallowed be Thy name—Halleluiah!

Alfred, Lord Tennyson

CROSSING THE BAR

English Nineteenth Century

Sunset and evening star,
    And one clear call for me!
And may there be no moaning of the bar
    When I put out to sea,

But such a tide as moving seems asleep,
    Too full for sound or foam,
When that which drew from out the boundless deep
    Turns again home.

Twilight and evening bell,
    And after that, the dark!
And may there be no sadness of farewell,
    When I embark;

For though from out our bourne of Time and Place
    The flood may bear me far,
I hope to see my Pilot face to face,
    When I have crossed the bar.

Alfred, Lord Tennyson

Lyra Mystica

PRAYER

English Nineteenth Century

O living well that shall endure
   When all that seems shall suffer shock,
   Rise in the spiritual rock,
Flow through our deeds and make them pure,

That we may lift from out the dust
   A voice as unto him that hears,
   A cry above the conquered years
To one that with us works, and trust

With faith that comes from self-control,
   The truths that never can be proved
   Until we close with all we loved,
And all we flow from, soul in soul.
Alfred, Lord Tennyson

FLOWER IN THE CRANNIED WALL

English Nineteenth Century

Flower in the crannied wall,
I pluck you out of the crannies;—
Hold you here, root and all, in my hand,
Little flower—but if I could understand
What you are, root and all, and all in all,
I should know what God and man is.
Alfred, Lord Tennyson

Lyra Mystica

IF THERE HAD ANYWHERE APPEARED

English Nineteenth Century

If there had anywhere appeared in space
   Another place of refuge, where to flee,
Our hearts had taken refuge in that place,
      And not with Thee.

For we against creation's bars had beat
   Like prisoned eagles, through great worlds had sought
Though but a foot of ground to plant our feet,
      Where Thou wert not.

And only when we found in earth and air,
   In heaven or hell, that such might nowhere be—
That we could not flee from Thee anywhere,
      We fled to Thee.

Richard Chenevix Trench

ADVENTANTE DEO

English Nineteenth Century

Lift up your heads, gates of my heart, unfold
   Your portals to salute the King of kings!
   Behold Him come, borne on cherubic wings
Engrained with crimson eyes and grail of gold!
Before His path the thunder-clouds withhold
   Their stormy pinions, and the desert sings:
   He from His lips divine and forehead flings
Sunlight of peace unfathomed, bliss untold.

O soul, faint soul, disquieted how long!
    Lift up thine eyes, for lo, thy Lord is near,
    Lord of all loveliness and strength and song,
The Lord who brings heart-sadness better cheer,
    Scattering those midnight dreams that dote on wrong,
    Purging with heaven's pure rays love's atmosphere!
John Addington Symonds

AN INVOCATION

English Nineteenth Century

To God, the everlasting, who abides,
One Life within things infinite that die:
To Him whose unity no thought divides:
Whose breath is breathed through immensity.

Him neither eye hath seen, nor ear hath heard;
Nor reason, seated in the souls of men,
Though pondering oft on the mysterious word,
Hath e'er revealed His Being to mortal ken.

Earth changes, and the starry wheels roll round;
The seasons come and go, moons wax and wane;
The nations rise and fall, and fill the ground,
Storing the sure results of joy and pain:

Slow knowledge widens toward a perfect whole,
From that first man who named the name of heaven,
To him who weighs the planets as they roll,
And knows what laws to every life are given.

Yet He appears not. Round the extreme sphere
Of science still thin ether floats unseen:
Darkness still wraps Him round; and ignorant fear
Remains of what we are, and what have been.

Only we feel Him; and in aching dreams,
Swift intuitions, pangs of keen delight,
The sudden vision of His glory seems
To sear our souls, dividing the dull night:

And we yearn toward Him, Beauty, Goodness, Truth;
These three are one; one life, one thought, one being;
One source of still rejuvenescent youth;
One light for endless and unclouded seeing.

Mere symbols we perceive—the dying beauty,
The partial truth that few can comprehend,
The vacillating faith, the painful duty,
The virtue labouring to a dubious end.

O God, unknown, invisible, secure,
Whose being by dim resemblances we guess,
Who in man's fear and love abidest sure,
Whose power we feel in darkness and confess!

Without Thee nothing is, and Thou art nought
When on Thy substance we gaze curiously:
By Thee impalpable, named Force and Thought,
The solid world still ceases not to be.

Lead Thou me, God, Law, Reason, Duty, Life!
All names for Thee alike are vain and hollow—

Lead me, for I will follow without strife;
Or, if I strive, still must I blindly follow.
John Addington Symonds

THE PRISM OF LIFE

English Nineteenth Century

All that began with God, in God must end:
   All lives are garnered in His final bliss:
   All wills hereafter shall be one with His,
   When in the sea we sought, our spirits blend.
Rays of pure light, which one frail prism may rend
   Into conflicting colours, meet and kiss
   With manifold attraction, yet still miss
   Contentment, while their kindred hues contend.
Break but that three-edged glass:—inviolate
   The sundered beams resume their primal state,
   Weaving pure light in flawless harmony.
Thus decomposed, subject to love and strife,
   God's thought, made conscious through man's mortal life,
   Resumes through death the eternal unity.
John Addington Symonds

SPONSA DEI

English Nineteenth Century

What is this maiden fair,
The laughing of whose eye
Is in man's heart renew'd virginity;
Who yet sick longing breeds

For marriage which exceeds
The inventive guess of Love to satisfy
With hope of utter binding, and of loosing endless dear despair?
What gleams about her shine,
More transient than delight and more divine!
If she does something but a little sweet,
As gaze towards the glass to set her hair,
See how his soul falls humbled at her feet!
Her gentle step, to go or come,
Gains her more merit than a martyrdom;
And, if she dance, it doth such grace confer
As opes the heaven of heavens to more than her,
And makes a rival of her worshipper.
To die unknown for her were little cost!
So is she without guile,
Her mere refused smile
Makes up the sum of that which may be lost!
Who is this Fair
Whom each hath seen,
The darkest once in this bewailed dell,
Be he not destin'd for the gloom of hell?
Whom each hath seen
And known, with sharp remorse and sweet, as Queen
And tear-glad Mistress of his hopes of bliss,
Too fair for man to kiss?
Who is this only happy She,
Whom, by a frantic flight of courtesy,
Born of despair
Of better lodging for his Spirit fair,
He adores as Margaret, Maude, or Cecily?

And what this sigh,
That each one heaves for Earth's last lowlihead
And the Heaven high
Ineffably lock'd in dateless bridal-bed?
Are all, then, mad, or is it prophecy?
"Sons now we are of God," as we have heard,
"But what we shall be hath not yet appear'd."
O, Heart, remember thee,
That Man is none,
Save One.

  What if this Lady be thy Soul, and He
Who claims to enjoy her sacred beauty be,
Not thou, but God; and thy sick fire
A female vanity,
Such as a Bride, viewing her mirror'd charms,
Feels when she sighs, "All these are for his arms!"
A reflex heat
Flash'd on thy cheek from His immense desire,
Which waits to crown, beyond thy brain's conceit,
Thy nameless, secret, hopeless longing sweet,
Not by and by, but now,
Unless deny Him thou!

Coventry Kersey Dighton Patmore

THE CITY OF GOD

English Nineteenth Century

O Thou not made with hands,
Not throned above the skies,
Nor wall'd with shining walls,

Lyra Mystica

Nor framed with stones of price,
 More bright than gold or gem,
 God's own Jerusalem!

Where'er the gentle heart
Finds courage from above;
Where'er the heart forsook
Warms with the breath of love;
 Where faith bids fear depart,
 City of God! thou art.

Thou art where'er the proud
In humbleness melts down;
Where self itself yields up;
Where martyrs win their crown;
 Where faithful souls possess
 Themselves in perfect peace.

Where life's common ways
With cheerful feet we go;
When in His steps we tread
Who trod the way of woe;
 Where He is in the heart,
 City of God! thou art.

Not throned above the skies,
Nor golden-wall'd afar,
But where Christ's two or three
In His name gather'd are,
 Be in the midst of them,
 God's own Jerusalem!

Francis Turner Palgrave

Lyra Mystica

THE GOAL IN SIGHT

English Nineteenth Century

The goal in sight! Look up and sing,
   Set faces full against the light,
Welcome with rapturous welcoming
   The goal in sight.

Let be the left, let be the right,
   Straight forward! make your footsteps ring
A loud alarum through the night.

Death hunts you, yea, but reft of sting,
   Your bed is green, your shroud is white.
Hail! Life and Death, and all that brings
   The goal in sight.

Christina Rossetti

UP-HILL

English Nineteenth Century

Does the road wind up-hill all the way?
   Yes, to the very end.
Will the day's journey take the whole long day?
   From morn to night, my friend.

But is there for the night a resting-place?
   A roof for when the slow dark hours begin.
May not the darkness hide it from my face?
   You cannot miss that inn.

Shall I meet other wayfarers at night?
Those who have gone before.
Then must I knock or call when just in sight?
They will not keep you standing at the door.

Shall I find comfort, travel-sore and weak?
Of labour you shall find the sum.
Will there be beds for me and all who seek?
Yea, beds for all who come.

Christina Rossetti

From ODE: INTIMATIONS OF IMMORTALITY

English Nineteenth Century

O joy! that in our embers
Is something that doth live,
That nature yet remembers
What was so fugitive!
The thought of our past years in me doth breed
Perpetual benediction: not indeed
For that which is most worthy to be blest;
Delight and liberty, the simple creed
Of Childhood, whether busy or at rest,
With new-fledged hope still fluttering in his breast:—
 Not for these I raise
 The song of thanks and praise;
 But for those obstinate questionings
 Of sense and outward things,
 Fallings from us, vanishings;
 Blank misgivings of a Creature
Moving about in worlds not realized,

High instincts before which our mortal Nature
Did tremble like a guilty Thing surprised:
       But for those first affections,
       Those shadowy recollections,
   Which, be they what they may,
Are yet the fountain-light of all our day,
Are yet a master-light of all our seeing:
   Uphold us, cherish, and have power to make
Our noisy years seem moments in the being
Of the eternal Silence: truths that wake,
       To perish never:
Which neither listlessness, nor mad endeavour,
       Nor Man nor Boy,
Nor all that is at enmity with joy,
Can utterly abolish or destroy!
       Hence in a season of calm weather
       Though inland far we be,
Our Souls have sight of that immortal sea
       Which brought us higher,
       Can in a moment travel thither,
And see the Children sport upon the shore,
And hear the mighty waters rolling evermore.

Then sing, ye Birds, sing, sing a joyous song!
       And let the young Lambs bound
       As to the tabor's sound!
We in thought will join your throng,
       Ye that pipe and ye that play,
       Ye that through your hearts to-day
       Feel the gladness of the May!
What though the radiance which was once so bright

Be now for ever taken from my sight,
>   Though nothing can bring back the hour
Of splendour in the grass, of glory in the flower;
>   We will grieve not, rather find
>   Strength in what remains behind;
>   In the primal sympathy
>   Which having been must ever be;
>   In the soothing thoughts that spring
>   Out of human suffering;
>   In the faith that looks through death,
In years that bring the philosophic mind.

And O, ye Fountains, Meadows, Hills, and Groves,
Forebode not any severing of our loves!
Yet in my heart of hearts I feel your might;
I only have relinquished one delight
To live beneath your more habitual sway.
I love the Brooks which down their channels fret,
Even more than when I tripped lightly as they;
The innocent brightness of a new-born Day
>   Is lovely yet;
The Clouds that gather round the setting sun
Do take a sober colouring from an eye
That hath kept watch o'er man's mortality;
Another race hath been, and other palms are won.
Thanks to the human heart by which we live,
Thanks to its tenderness, its joys, and fears,
To me the meanest flower that blows can give
Thoughts that do often lie too deep for tears.
>   *William Wordsworth*

Lyra Mystica

From THE EXCURSION

English Nineteenth Century

              I have seen
A curious child, who dwelt upon a tract
Of inland ground, applying to his ear
The convolution of a smooth-lipped shell;
To which, in silence hushed, his very soul
Listened intensely; and his countenance soon
Brightened with joy; for from within were heard
Murmurings, whereby the monitor expressed
Mysterious union with its native sea.
Even such a shell the universe itself
Is to the ear of Faith; and there are times,
I doubt not, when to you it doth impart
Authentic tidings of invisible things;
Of ebb and flow, and ever-during power;
And central peace, subsisting at the heart
Of endless agitation.

To every Form of being is assigned
An *active* Principle:—howe'er removed
From sense and observation, it subsists
In all things, in all natures; in the stars
Of azure heaven, the unenduring clouds,
In flower and tree, in every pebbly stone
That paves the brooks, the stationary rocks,
The moving waters, and the invisible air.
Whate'er exists hath properties that spread
Beyond itself, communicating good,
A simple blessing, or with evil mixed;

Spirit that knows no insulated spot,
No chasm, no solitude; from link to link
It circulates, the Soul of all the worlds.
This is the freedom of the universe;
Unfolded still the more, more visible,
The more we know; and yet is reverenced least,
And least respected in the human Mind,
Its most apparent home.

William Wordsworth

FOR I HAVE LEARNED TO LOOK ON NATURE

English Nineteenth Century

For I have learned
To look on nature, not as in the hour
Of thoughtless youth; but hearing oftentimes
The still, sad music of humanity,
Nor harsh nor grating, though of ample power
To chasten and subdue. And I have felt
A presence that disturbs me with the joy
Of elevated thoughts; a sense sublime
Of something far more deeply interfused,
Whose dwelling is the light of setting suns,
And the round ocean and the living air,
And the blue sky, and in the mind of man:
A motion and a spirit, that impels
All thinking things, all objects of all thought,
And rolls through all things. Therefore am I still
A lover of the meadows and the woods,
And mountains; and of all that we behold
From this green earth; of all the mighty world

Of eye, and ear,—both what they half create,
And what perceive; well pleased to recognize
In nature and the language of the sense,
The anchor of my purest thoughts, the nurse,
The guide, the guardian of my heart, and soul
Of all my moral being.

William Wordsworth

YES, IT WAS THE MOUNTAIN ECHO

English Nineteenth Century

Yes, it was the mountain Echo,
Solitary, clear, profound,
Answering to the shouting Cuckoo,
Giving to her sound for sound!

Unsolicited reply
To a babbling wanderer sent:
Like her ordinary cry,
Like—but oh, how different!

Hears not also mortal Life? we, unthinking
    Creatures!
Slaves of folly, love, or strife—
Voices of two different natures?

Have not we too?—yes, we have
Answers, and we know not whence;
Echoes from beyond the grave,
Recognized intelligence!

Such rebounds our inward ear
Catches sometimes from afar—
Listen, ponder, hold them dear;
For of God,—of God they are.

William Wordsworth

I GAZE ALOOF

English Nineteenth Century

I gaze aloof at the tissued roof,
Where time and space are the warp and woof
Which the King of Kings, like a curtain flings
O'er the dreadfulness of eternal things.

But if I could see as in truth they be
The glories that encircle me,
I should lightly hold this tissued fold
With its marvelous curtain of blue and gold.

For soon the whole, like a parchèd scroll
Shall before my amazèd eyes unroll,
And without a screen, at one burst be seen
The Presence in which I have always been.

Thomas Whytehead

THE CIRCUIT OF BEING

Nineteenth Century

The snowflake that glistens at morn on Kailasa,
   Dissolved by the sunbeams, descends to the plain;
Then, mingling with Gunga, it floats to the ocean,
   And lost in its waters returns not again.

On the roseleaf at sunrise bright glistens the dewdrop
    That in vapor exhaled falls in nourishing rain;
Then in rills back to Gunga through green fields meanders,
Till onward it flows to the ocean again.

A snowflake still whitens the peak of Kailasa,
    But the snowflake of yesterday flows to the main;
At dawning a dewdrop still hangs on the roseleaf,
    But the dewdrop of yesterday comes not again.

The soul that is freed from the bondage of nature
    Escapes from illusions of joy and of pain;
And, pure as the flame that is lost in the sunbeams,
    Ascends unto God, and returns not again.
It comes not and goes not, it comes not again.

Anonymous

I HAVE A LIFE WITH CHRIST TO LIVE

Scottish Nineteenth Century

I have a life with Christ to live,
    But, ere I live it, must I wait
Till learning can clear answer give
    Of this and that book's date?

I have a life in Christ to live,
    I have a death in Christ to die;—
And must I wait, till science give
    All doubts a full reply?

Nay rather, while the sea of doubt
Is raging wildly round about,

Lyra Mystica

Questioning of life and death and sin,
  Let me but creep within
Thy fold, O Christ, and at Thy feet
  Take but the lowest seat,
And hear Thine awful voice repeat
In gentlest accents, heavenly sweet,
  Come unto Me, and rest:
  Believe Me, and be blest.

John Campbell Shairp

From THE CITY OF DREAM

Scottish Nineteenth Century

The Woof that I weave not
  Thou wearest and weavest,
The Thought I conceive not
  Thou darkly conceivest;
The wind and the rain,
  The night and the morrow,
The rapture of pain
  Fading slowly to sorrow,
The dream and the deed,
  The calm and the storm,
The flower and the seed,
  Are thy Thought and thy Form.
I die, yet depart not,
  I am bound, yet soar free,
Thou art and thou art not,
  And ever shalt be!

Robert Buchanan

Lyra Mystica

From THE CITY OF DREAM

Scottish Nineteenth Century

The Man

Yonder the veil'd Musician sits, His feet
Upon the pedals of dark formless suns,
His fingers on the radiant spheric keys,
His face, that it is death to look upon,
Misted with incense rising nebulous
Out of abysmal chaos and cohering
Into the golden flames of Life and Being!
And underneath his touch Music itself
Grows living, heard as far as thought can creep
Or dream can soar; or that Creation stirs,
And drinks the sound, and sings!—So far away
He sits, the Mystery, wrapt for ever round
With brightness and with awe and melody;
Yet even here, on these low-lying shores,
Lower than is the footstool of His throne,
We hear Him and adore Him, nay, can feel
His breath as vapour round our mouths, inhaling
That soul within the soul whereby we live
From that divine for-ever-beating Heart
Which thrills the universe with Light and Love!

The Pilgrim

So far away He dwells, my soul indeed
Scarcely discerns Him, and in sooth I seek
A gentler presence and a nearer Friend.

Lyra Mystica

The Man

So far? O blind, He broods beside thee now
Here in this silence, with His eyes on thine!
O deaf, His voice is whispering in thine ears
Soft as the breathing of the slumberous seas!

The Pilgrim

I see not and I hear not; but I see
Thine eyes burn dimly, like a corpse-light seen
Flickering amidst the tempest; and I hear
Only the elemental grief and pain
Out of whose shadow I would creep for ever.

The Man

Thou canst not, brother; for these, too, are God!

The Pilgrim

How? Is my God, then, as a homeless ghost
Blown this way, that way, with the elements?

The Man

He is without thee, and within thee too;
Thy living breath, and that which drinks thy breath;
Thy being, and the bliss beyond thy being.

Lyra Mystica

The Pilgrim

So near, so far? He shapes the farthest sun
New-glimmering on the farthest fringe of space,
Yet stoops and with a leaf-light finger-touch
Reaches my heart and makes it come and go!

The Man

Yea; and He is thy heart within thy heart,
And thou a portion of His Heart Divine!
Robert Buchanan

ALL THINGS ARE FULL OF GOD

Scottish Nineteenth Century

All things are full of God. Thus spoke
   Wise Thales in the days
When subtle Greece to thought awoke
   And soared in lofty ways.
And now what wisdom have we more?
   No sage divining-rod
Hath taught than this a deeper lore,
   All things are full of God.

The Light that gloweth in the sky
   And shimmers in the sea,
That quivers in the painted fly
   And gems the pictured lea,
The million hues of Heaven above
   And Earth below are one,

And every lightful eye doth love
  The primal light, the Sun.

Even so, all vital virtue flows
  From life's first fountain, God;
And he who feels, and he who knows,
  Doth feel and know from God.
As fishes swim in briny sea,
  As fowl do float in air,
From Thy embrace we cannot flee;
  We breathe, and Thou art there.

Go, take thy glass, astronomer,
  And all the girth survey
Of sphere harmonious linked to sphere
  In endless bright array.
All that far-reaching Science there
  Can measure with her rod,
All powers, all laws, are but the fair
  Embodied thoughts of God.

John Stuart Blackie

GOD'S GRANDEUR

Irish Nineteenth Century

The world is charged with the grandeur of God.
  It will flame out, like shining from shook foil,
  It gathers to a greatness like the ooze of oil
Crushed. Why do men then now not reck His rod?
Generations have trod, have trod, have trod;
  And all is seared with trade; bleared, smeared with toil;

And bears man's smudge, and shares man's smell;
    the soil
Is bare now, nor can foot feel being shod.
And for all this, nature is never spent;
    There lives the dearest freshness deep down
        things;
And though the last lights from the black west went,
    Oh, morning at the brown brink eastwards
        springs—
Because the Holy Ghost over the bent
    World broods with warm breast, and with, ah,
        bright wings.

Gerard Manley Hopkins

THE WRECK OF THE DEUTSCHLAND

Irish Nineteenth Century

1

Thou mastering me
God! giver of breath and bread;
World's strand, sway of the sea;
Lord of living and dead;
Thou hast bound bones and veins in me, fastened
    me flesh,
And after it almost unmade, what with dread,
    Thy doing: and dost thou touch me afresh?
Over again I feel thy finger and find thee.

2

I did say yes
O at lightning and lashed rod;

Thou heardst me truer than tongue confess
　　Thy terror, O Christ, O God;
Thou knowest the walls, altar and hour and night:
The swoon of a heart that the sweep and the hurl of thee trod
　　Hard down with a horror of height;
And the midriff astrain with leaning of, laced with fire of stress.

3
The frown of his face
　　Before me, the hurtle of hell
Behind, where, where was a, where was a place?
　　I whirled out wings that spell
And fled with a fling of the heart to the heart of the Host.
My heart, but you were dovewinged, I can tell,
　　Carrier-witted, I am bold to boast,
To flash from the flame to the flame then, tower from the grace to the grace.

4
I am soft sift
　　In an hourglass—at the wall
Fast, but mined with a motion, a drift,
　　And it crowds and it combs to the fall;
I steady as a water in a well, to a poise, to a pane,
But roped with, always, all the way down from the tall
　　Fells or flanks of the voel, a vein

Lyra Mystica

Of the gospel proffer, a pressure, a principle, Christ's gift.

5

I kiss my hand
To the stars, lovely-asunder
Starlight, wafting him out of it; and
Glow, glory in thunder;
Kiss my hand to the dappled-with-damson west:
Since, tho' he is under the world's splendour and wonder,
His mystery must be instressed, stressed;
For I greet him the days I meet him, and bless when I understand.

6

Not out of his bliss
Springs the stress felt
Nor first from heaven (and few know this)
Swings the stroke dealt—
Stroke and a stress that stars and storms deliver,
That guilt is hushed by, hearts are flushed by and melt—
But it rides time like riding a river
(And here the faithful waver, the faithless fable and miss).

7

It dates from day
Of his going in Galilee;
Warm-laid grave of a womb-life grey;
Manger, maiden's knee;

The dense and the driven Passion, and frightful sweat;
Thence the discharge of it, there its swelling to be,
Though felt before, though in high flood yet—
What none would have known of, only the heart, being hard at bay,

8
Is out with it! Oh,
We lash with the best or worst
Word last! How a lush-kept plush-capped sloe
Will, mouthed to flesh-burst,
Gush!—flush the man, the being with it, sour or sweet,
Brim, in a flash, full!—Hither then, last or first,
To hero of Calvary, Christ's feet—
Never ask if meaning it, wanting it, warned of it—men go.

9
Be adored among men,
God, three-numbered form;
Wring thy rebel, dogged in den,
Man's malice, with wrecking and storm,
Beyond saying sweet, past telling of tongue,
Thou art lightning and love, I found it, a winter and warm;
Father and fondler of heart thou hast wrung:
Hast thy dark descending and most art merciful then.

Lyra Mystica

10
With an anvile-ding
And with fire in him forge thy will
Or rather, rather then, stealing as Spring
Through him, melt him but master him still:
Whether at once, as once at a crash Paul,
Or as Austin, a lingering-out sweet skill,
Make mercy in all of us, out of us all
Mastery, but be adored, but be adored King.

Gerard Manley Hopkins

PIED BEAUTY

Irish Nineteenth Century

Glory be to God for dappled things—
For skies of couple-colour as a brindled cow;
For rose-moles all in stipple upon trout that swim;
Fresh-firecoal chestnut-falls; finches' wings;
Landscape plotted and pieced—fold, fallow, and plough;
And all trades, their gear and tackle and trim.

All things counter, original, spare, strange;
Whatever is fickle, freckled (who knows how?)
With swift, slow; sweet, sour; adazzle, dim;
He fathers-forth whose beauty is past change:
Praise him.

Gerard Manley Hopkins

Lyra Mystica

THE QUEST

Irish Nineteenth Century

They said: "She dwelleth in some place apart,
   Immortal Truth, within whose eyes
    Who looks may find the secret of the skies
And healing for life's smart!"

I sought Her in loud caverns underground,—
   On heights where lightnings flashed and fell;
    I scaled high Heaven; I stormed the gates of Hell,
But Her I never found

Till thro' the tumults of my Quest I caught
   A whisper: "Here, within thy heart,
    I dwell; for I am thou: behold, thou art
The Seeker—and the Sought."

                                James H. Cousins

ADRIFT

Irish Nineteenth Century

Unto my faith as to a spar, I bind
   My love—and Faith and Love adrift I cast
    On a dim sea. I know not if at last
They the eternal shore of God shall find.

I know that neither waves nor wind
   Can sunder them, the cords are tied so fast
    That faith shall never—doubts and dangers past—
Come safe to land and Love be left behind.

                                Mrs. Edward Dowden

Lyra Mystica
LAND, HO!

Manx Nineteenth Century

I know 'tis but a loom of land,
Yet is it land, and so I will rejoice,
I cannot hear His voice
   Upon the shore, nor see Him stand;
   Yet is it land, ho! land.

The land! the land! the lovely land!
"Far off," dost say? *Far off*—ah, blessed home!
Farewell! farewell! thou salt sea-foam!
   Ah, keel upon the silver sand—
   Land, ho! land.

You cannot see the land, my land,
You cannot see, and yet the land is there—
My land, my land, through murky air—
   I did not say 'twas close at hand—
   But—land, ho! land.

Dost hear the bells of my sweet land,
Dost hear the kine, dost hear the merry birds?
No voice, 'tis true, no spoken words,
   No tongue that thou may'st understand—
   Yet is it land, ho! land.

It's clad in purple mist, my land,
In regal robe it is apparellèd,
A crown is set upon its head,
   And on its breast a golden band—
   Land, ho! land.

Dost wonder that I long for land?
My land is not a land as others are—
Upon its crest there beams a star,
  And lilies grow upon the strand—
  Land, ho! land.

Give me the helm! there is the land!
Ha! lusty mariners, she takes the breeze!
And what my spirit sees it sees—
  Leap, bark, as leaps the thunderbrand—
  Land, ho! land.

Thomas Edward Brown

SPECULA

Manx Nineteenth Century

When He appoints to meet thee, go thou forth—
  It matters not
If south or north,
  Bleak waste or sunny plot.
Nor think, if haply He thou seek'st be late,
  He does thee wrong.
To stile or gate
  Lean thou thy head, and long!
It may be that to spy thee He is mounting
  Upon a tower,
Or in thy counting
  Thou has mista'en the hour.
But, if he come not, neither do thou go
  Till Vesper chime.

Belike thou then shalt know
> He hath been with thee all the time.
>> *Thomas Edward Brown*

MY GARDEN

Manx Nineteenth Century

A garden is a lovesome thing, God wot!
Rose plot,
  Fringed pool,
Fern'd grot—
  The veriest school
  Of peace; and yet the fool
Contends that God is not—
Not God! in gardens! when the eve is cool?
  Nay, but I have a sign;
  'Tis very sure God walks in mine.
>> *Thomas Edward Brown*

WHERE IS GOD?

Anglo-American Nineteenth Century

"Oh! where is the sea?" the fishes cried,
As they swam the crystal clearness through;
"We've heard from of old of the ocean's tide,
And we long to look on the waters blue.
The wise ones speak of the infinite sea,
Oh! who can tell us if such there be?"

The lark flew up in the morning bright,
And sang and balanced on sunny wings;

And this was its song: "I see the light,
I look o'er the world of beautiful things;
But flying and singing everywhere,
In vain have I searched to find the air."

Robert Collyer

THE WORD

Anglo-American Nineteenth Century

O Earth! Thou hast not any wind that blows
Which is not music; every weed of thine
Pressed rightly flows in aromatic wine;
And humble hedge-row flower that grows,
And every little brown bird that doth sing,
Hath something greater than itself, and bears
A living word to every living thing,
Albeit holds the message unawares.
All shapes and sounds have something which is not
Of them: a spirit broods amid the grass;
Vague outlines of the Everlasting Thought
Lie in the melting shadows as they pass;
The touch of an eternal presence thrills
The fringes of the sunsets and the hills.

Richard Realf

DE MORTUIS NIL NISI BONUM

Anglo-American Nineteenth Century

De mortuis nil nisi bonum. When
For me the end has come and I am dead,

Lyra Mystica

And little, voluble, chattering daws of men
  Peck at me curiously, let it then be said
By some one brave enough to speak the truth,
  Here lies a great soul killed by cruel wrong.
Down all the balmy days of his fresh youth
  To his bleak, desolate noon, with sword and song,
And speech that rushed up hotly from the heart,
  He wrought for liberty; till his own wound,
(He had been stabbed) concealed with painful art
  Through wasting years, mastered him and he swooned,
And sank there where you see him lying now,
With that word Failure written on his brow.

But say that he succeeded. If he missed
  World's honors and world's plaudits, and the wage
Of the world's deft lackeys, still his lips were kissed
  Daily by those high angels who assuage
The thirstings of the poets—for he was
  Born unto singing—and a burden lay
Mightily on him, and he moaned because
  He could not rightly utter to his day
What God taught in the night. Sometimes, natheless
  Power fell upon him, and bright tongues of flame
And blessings reached him from poor souls in stress;
  And benedictions from black pits of shame;
And little children's love; and old men's prayers;
And a Great Hand that led him unawares.

So he died rich. And if his eyes were blurred
  With thick films—silence, for he is in his grave.

Greatly he suffered; greatly, too, he erred;
    Yet broke his heart in trying to be brave.
Nor did he wait till Freedom had become
    The popular shibboleth of courtiers' lips;
But smote for her when God himself seemed dumb,
    And all his arching skies were in eclipse.
    He was aweary, but he fought his fight,
    And stood for simple manhood; and was joyed
To see the august broadening of the light,
    And new earths heaving heavenward from the void.
He loved his fellows, and their love was sweet—
Plant daisies at his head and at his feet.

Richard Realf

HIDDEN LIFE

American Nineteenth Century

Since Eden it keeps the secret!
    Not a flower beside it knows
To distill from the day the fragrance
    And beauty that flood the rose.

Silently speeds the secret
    From the loving eye of the sun
To the willing heart of the flower:
    The life of the twain is one.

Folded within my being,
    A wonder to me is taught,
Too deep for curious seeing,
    Or fathom of sounding thought.

Of all sweet mysteries holiest!
    Faded are rose and sun!
The Highest hides in the lowliest:
    My Father and I are one.

Charles G. Ames

GO NOT AWAY

American Nineteenth Century

Go not away, Lord! Leave us not
Amid the mystery of our lot,
Life's baffling problem half unwrought—
Nor haunting doubt, nor halting thought
Can work the far solution out;
Thy love alone can make it plain
Why high resolve in us is slain,
Why dear to us the tempter's call,
And why we falter till we fall;
Thou, who rememberest we are dust,
Who gave our little day in trust,
Knowest the meaning of it all.
Go not away! We travel on;
And every hour that rest is won
We feel we need Thy love anew—
To save us from the deed we'd do,
To strengthen for the deed undone,
To help the aching feet to run
With patience all the tiresome road;
To lighten some the weary load
That every life must bear alone,
Save Thou dost make its weight Thine own.

Lyra Mystica

<blockquote>
The spirit's cry
Is all for Thee, O love unseen,
To fill the need that hath not been
By any human passion filled,
By any human giving stilled;
For Thee—for only Thee—its cry,
O love supreme, to satisfy!
</blockquote>

Mary Clemmer Ames

NO DISTANT LORD

American Nineteenth Century

No distant Lord have I
Loving afar to be;
Made flesh for me, He cannot rest
Until He rests in me.

Brother in joy and pain,
Bone of my bone was He,
Now,—intimacy closer still,
He dwells Himself in me.

I need not journey far
This dearest friend to see,
Companionship is always mine,
He makes His home with me.

Maltbie D. Babcock

LORD, I HAVE SHUT MY DOOR

American Nineteenth Century

Lord, I have shut my door,—
Shut out life's busy cares and fretting noise:

Here in this silence they intrude no more.
  Speak thou, and heavenly joys
Shall fill my heart with music sweet and calm,—
    A holy psalm.

Yes, I have shut my door
Even on all the beauty of thine earth,—
To its blue ceiling from its emerald floor,
  Filled with spring's bloom and mirth:
From these thy works I turn, thyself I seek
    To thee I speak.

And I have shut my door
On earthly passion,—all its yearning love,
Its tender friendships, all the priceless store
  Of human ties. Above
All these my heart aspires, O Heart divine!
    Stoop thou to mine.

Lord, I have shut my door!
Come thou and visit me: I am alone!
Come, as when doors were shut thou cam'st of yore,
  And visitedst thine own.
My Lord! I kneel with reverent love and fear
  For thou art here!

Mary E. Atkinson

TO A WATERFOWL

American Nineteenth Century

Whither, midst falling dew,
While glow the heavens with the last steps of day,

Far, through their rosy depths, dost thou pursue
Thy solitary way?

Vainly the fowler's eye
Might mark thy distant flight to do thee wrong,
As, darkly painted on the crimson sky,
Thy figure floats along.

Seek'st thou the plashy brink
Of weedy lake, or marge of river wide,
Or where the rocking billows rise and sink
On the chafed ocean-side?

There is a Power whose care
Teaches thy way along that pathless coast—
The desert and illimitable air—
Lone wandering, but not lost.

All day thy wings have fanned,
At that far height, the cold, thin atmosphere,
Yet stoop not, weary, to the welcome land,
Though the dark night is near.

And soon that toil shall end;
Soon shalt thou find a summer home, and rest,
And scream among thy fellows; reeds shall bend,
Soon o'er thy sheltered nest.

Thou'rt gone, the abyss of heaven
Hath swallowed up thy form; yet, on my heart
Deeply has sunk the lesson thou hast given,
And shall not soon depart.

> He who, from zone to zone,
> Guides through the boundless sky thy certain flight,
> In the long way that I must tread alone,
> Will lead my steps aright.
>
> William Cullen Bryant

YEA EVERY DAY HE COMES

American Nineteenth Century

Yea every day he comes!
Not in the earthly form that once he bore,
Not in the glorious shape which now he wears;
In mean attire, and toil-worn, painful guise
He stands and calls beside our path, our door;
Weary and spent he comes, his wound he bares,
And bends on us his deep, appealing eyes,
Which voiceless, find a voice and speak and say,
" 'Tis I who call thee, child; wilt thou obey?"

Susan Coolidge

DEATH

American Nineteenth Century

I am a stranger in the land
    Where my forefathers trod;
A stranger I unto each heart,
    But not unto my God!

I pass along the crowded streets,
    Unrecognized my name;

This thought will come amid regrets,
    My God is still the same!

I seek with joy my childhood's home,
    But strangers claim the sod;
Not knowing where my kindred roam,
    Still present is my God!

They tell me that my friends all sleep
    Beneath the valley clod;
Oh, is not faith submissive sweet!
    I have no friend save God!

Anonymous

ETERNITY, I'M COMING

American Nineteenth Century

A wife at daybreak I shall be,
Sunrise, thou hast a flag for me?
At midnight I am yet a maid—
How short it takes to make it bride!
Then, Midnight, I have passed from thee
Unto the East and Victory.

Midnight, "Good night"
I hear thee call.
The angels bustle in the hall,
Softly my Future climbs the stair,
I fumble at my childhood's prayer—
So soon to be a child no more!
Eternity, I'm coming, sir—
Master, I've seen that face before.

Emily Dickinson

Lyra Mystica

DOST THOU REMEMBER ME?

American Nineteenth Century

Saviour, I've no one else to tell
And so I trouble Thee,
I am the one forgot Thee so.
Dost Thou remember me?

Not for myself I came so far,
That were the little load—
I brought Thee the imperial heart
I had not strength to hold.

The heart I carried in my own,
Till mine too heavy be,
Yet strangest—heavier
Since it went—
Is it too large for Thee?

Emily Dickinson

MY FAITH IS LARGER THAN THE HILLS

American Nineteenth Century

My faith is larger than the hills,
So when the hills decay,
My faith must take the purple wheel
To show the Sun the way.

'Tis first he steps upon the vane
And then upon the hill;

And then abroad the world he goes
To do his golden will.

And if his yellow feet should miss,
The birds would not arise,
The flowers would slumber on their stems—
No bells have Paradise.

How dare I therefore stint a faith
On which so vast depends,
Lest Firmament should fail for me—
The rivet in the bands.

Emily Dickinson

CHARTLESS

American Nineteenth Century

I never saw a moor,
I never saw the sea;
Yet now I know how the heather looks
And what a wave must be.

I never spoke with God
Nor visited in Heaven;
Yet certain am I of the spot
As if the chart were given.

Emily Dickinson

From THRENODY

American Nineteenth Century

Wilt thou not ope thy heart to know
What rainbows teach, and sunsets show?

Verdict which accumulates
From lengthening scroll of human fates
Voice of earth to earth returned,
Prayers of saints that inly burned,—
Saying, *What is excellent,*
As God lives, is permanent;
Hearts are dust, hearts' loves remain;
Heart's love will meet thee again.
Revere the Maker; fetch thine eye
Up to His style, and manners of the sky.
Not of adamant and gold
Built He heaven stark and cold;
No, but a nest of bending reeds,
Flowering grass and scented weeds;
Or like a traveler's fleeing tent,
Or bow above the tempest bent;
Built of tears and sacred flames,
And virtue reaching to its aims;
Built of furtherance and pursuing,
Not of spent deeds, but of doing.
Silent rushes the swift Lord
Through ruined systems still restored,
Broadsowing, bleak and void to bless,
Plants with worlds the wilderness;
Waters with tears of ancient sorrow
Apples of Eden ripe to-morrow.
House and tenant go to ground,
Lost in God, in Godhead found.

Ralph Waldo Emerson

Lyra Mystica

THE PROBLEM

American Nineteenth Century

Out from the heart of nature rolled
The burdens of the Bible old;
The litanies of nations came
Like the volcano's tongue of flame
Up from the burning core below—
The canticles of love and woe.

The word unto the prophets spoken
Was writ on tablets yet unbroken;
Still floats upon the morning wind,
Still whispers to the willing mind;
One accent of the Holy Ghost
The heedless world has never lost.

Ralph Waldo Emerson

THE MESSENGER

American Nineteenth Century

Strong angel of the peace of God,
   Not wholly undivined thy mien;
Along the weary path I trod,
   Thou hast been with me, the unseen.

My hopes have been a mad turmoil,
   A clutch and conflict all my life,
The very craft I loved a toil,
   And love itself a seed of strife.

And sometimes in a sudden hour
  I have been great with Godlike calm,
As if thy tranquil world of power
  Flowed in about me like a psalm.

And peace has fallen on my face,
  And stillness on my struggling breath;
And, living, I have known a space
  The hush and mastery of death.

Stretch out thy hand upon me, thou
  Who comest as the still night comes!
I have not flinched at buffets: now
  Let strife go by, with all his drums.

Richard Hovey

DOUBT

American Nineteenth Century

They bade me cast the thing away,
They pointed to my hands all bleeding,
They listened not to all my pleading;
  The thing I meant I could not say:
  I knew that I should rue the day
  If once I cast that thing away.

I grasped it firm, and bore the pain;
The thorny husks I stripped and scattered;
If I could reach its heart, what mattered
  If other men saw not my gain,
  Or even if I should be slain?
  I knew the risks; I chose the pain.

Oh, had I cast that thing away,
I had not found what most I cherish,
A faith without which I should perish,
   The faith which, like a kernel, lay
   Hid in the husks which on that day
   My instinct would not throw away!

Helen Hunt Jackson

THE GUEST

American Nineteenth Century

Speechless sorrow sat with me;
I was sighing wearily.
Lamp and fire were out; the rain
Beat wildly on the window pane.
In the dark we heard a knock,
And a hand was on the lock;
One in waiting spake to me,
   Saying sweetly,
"I am come to sup with thee."

All my room was dark and damp;
"Sorrow," said I, "trim the lamp
Light the fire and cheer thy face,
Set the guest-chair in its place."
And again I heard the knock;
In the dark I found the lock,—
"Enter, I have turned the key,—
   Enter, stranger,
Who art come to sup with me."

Lyra Mystica

Opening wide the door, he came,
But I could not speak his name;
In the guest-chair took his place,
But I could not see his face.
When my cheerful fire was beaming,
And my little lamp was gleaming,
And the feast was spread for three,
     Lo! my Master
Was the guest that supped with me!

Harriet M. Kimball

From FLORIDA SUNDAY

American Nineteenth Century

All riches, goods and braveries never told
Of earth, sun, air and heaven—now I hold
Your being in my being; I am ye,
   And ye myself; yea, lastly, Thee,
God, whom my roads all reach, howe'er they run,
My Father, Friend, Beloved, dear All-One,
Thee in my soul, my soul in Thee, I feel,
Self of my self. Lo, through my sense doth steal
Clear cognizance of all selves and qualities,
Of all existence that hath been or is,
Of all strange haps that men miscall of chance,
And all the works of tireless circumstance:
Each borders each, like mutual sea and shore,
Nor aught misfits his neighbor that's before,
Nor him that's after—nay, through this still air,
Out of the North come quarrels, and keen blare
Of challenge by the hot-breath'd parties blown;

Yet break they not this peace with alien tone,
Fray not my heart, nor fright me for my land,
　—I hear from all-wards, allwise understand,
The great bird Purpose bears me 'twixt her wings,
And I am one with all the kinsmen things
That e'er my Father fathered. Oh, to me
All questions solve in this tranquillity:
E'en this dark matter, once so dim, so drear,
Now shines upon my spirit heavenly-clear:
Thou, Father, without logic, tellest me
How this divine denial true may be,
　—How *All's in each, yet every one of all
Maintains his Self complete and several.*
Sidney Lanier

From THE MARSHES OF GLYNN

American Nineteenth Century

Oh, what is abroad in the marsh and the terminal sea?
　Somehow my soul seems suddenly free
From the weighing of fate and the sad discussion of sin,
By the length and the breadth and the sweep of the marshes of Glynn.

Ye marshes, how candid and simple and nothing-withholding and free
Ye publish yourselves to the sky and offer yourselves to the sea!
Tolerant plains, that suffer the sea and the rains and the sun,

Ye spread and span like the catholic man who hath
    mightily won
God out of knowledge and good out of infinite pain
And sight out of blindness and purity out of a stain.

As the marsh-hen secretly builds on the watery sod,
Behold I will build me a nest on the greatness of God:
I will fly in the greatness of God as the marsh-hen flies
In the freedom that fills all the space 'twixt the marsh
    and the skies:
By so many roots as the marsh-grass sends in the sod
I will heartily lay me a-hold on the greatness of God:
Oh, like to the greatness of God is the greatness within
The range of the marshes, the liberal marshes of
    Glynn.

And the sea lends large, as the marsh: lo, out of his
    plenty the sea
Pours fast: full soon the time of the flood-tide must be:
Look how the grace of the sea doth go
About and about through the intricate channels that
    flow
  Here and there,
        Everywhere,
Till his waters have flooded the uttermost creeks and
    the low-lying lanes,
And the marsh is meshed with a million veins,
That like as with rosy and silvery essences flow
  In the rose-and-silver evening glow.
        Farewell, my lord Sun!
The creeks overflow: a thousand rivulets run

'Twixt the roots of the sod; the blades of the marsh-
grass stir;
Passeth a hurrying sound of wings that westward whirr;
Passeth, and all is still; and the currents cease to run;
And the sea and the marsh are one.

How still the plains of the waters be!
The tide is in his ecstasy.
The tide is at his highest height:
    And it is night.
And now from the Vast of the Lord will the waters of
sleep
Roll in on the souls of men,
But who will reveal to our waking ken
The forms that swim and the shapes that creep
    Under the waters of sleep?
And I would I could know what swimmeth below
when the tide comes in
On the length and the breadth of the marvellous
marshes of Glynn.

Sidney Lanier

A SONG OF THE FUTURE

American Nineteenth Century

    Sail fast, sail fast,
Ark of my hopes, Ark of my dreams;
Sweep lordly o'er the drowned Past,
  Fly glittering through the sun's strange beams,
    Sail fast, sail fast.
Breaths of new buds from off some drying lea
With news about the Future scent the sea;

My brain is beating like the heart of Haste:
I'll loose me a bird upon this Present waste;
    Go, trembling song,
And stay not long; oh, stay not long:
Thou'rt only a gray and sober dove,
But thine eye is faith and thy wing is love.
Sidney Lanier

OUR CHRIST

American Nineteenth Century

In Christ I feel the heart of God
    Throbbing from heaven through earth.
Life stirs again within the clod,
    Renewed in beauteous birth.
The soul springs up, a flower of prayer,
Breathing His breath out on the air.

In Christ I touch the hand of God,
    From His pure heights reached down,
By blessed ways before untrod,
    To lift us to our crown;
Victory that only perfect is
Through loving sacrifice like His,

Holding His hand my steadied feet
    May walk the air, the seas;
On life and death His smile falls sweet,
    Lights up all mysteries;
Stranger nor exile can I be
In new worlds where He leadeth me.

Not my Christ only; He is ours:
  Humanity's close bond;
Key to its vast unopened powers,
  Dream of our dreams beyond,
What yet we shall be none can tell;
Now we are His, and all is well.

Lucy Larcom

IMMORTAL

American Nineteenth Century

Into the heaven of Thy heart, O God,
  I lift up my life, like a flower;
Thy light is deep, and Thy love is broad,
  And I am not the child of an hour.

The throb of Thy infinite life I feel
  In every beat of my heart;
Upon me hast Thou set eternity's seal;
  Forever alive as Thou art.

I know not Thy mystery, O my God,
  Nor yet what my own life means,
That feels after Thee, through the mould and the sod
  And the darkness that intervenes.

But I know that I live, since I hate the wrong,
  The glory of truth can see;
Can cling to the right with a purpose strong,
  Can love and can will with Thee.

Lucy Larcom

Lyra Mystica

THE WORLD WE LIVE IN

American Nineteenth Century

The world we live in wholly is redeemed,
Not man alone, but all that man holds dear,
His orchard and his maize.
Forget-me-nots and heartsease in his garden,
And all the wild aerial blossoms of his untamed wood,
That make its savagery so home-like,—
All these have felt Christ's sweet love
Watering their roots.
There are no Gentile oaks, no Pagan pines,
The grass beneath our feet is Christian grass,
The Wayside weed is sacred unto God.

Lucy Larcom

LONGING

American Nineteenth Century

Of all the myriad moods of mind
   That through the soul come thronging,
Which one was e'er so dear, so kind,
   So beautiful as Longing?
The thing we long for, that we are
   For one transcendent moment,
Before the Present poor and bare
   Can make its sneering comment.

Still, through our paltry stir and strife,
   Glows down the wished Ideal,

Lyra Mystica

And Longing moulds in clay what Life
    Carves in the marble Real;
To let the new life in, we know,
    Desire must ope the portal;—
Perhaps the longing to be so
    Helps make the soul immortal.

Longing is God's fresh heavenward will
    With our poor earthward striving;
We quench it that we may be still
    Content with merely living;
But, would we learn that heart's full scope
    Which we are hourly wronging,
Our lives must climb from hope to hope
    And realize our longing.

Ah! let us hope that to our praise
    Good God not only reckons
The moments when we tread His ways,
    But when the spirit beckons,—
That some slight good is also wrought
    Beyond self-satisfaction,
When we are simply good in thought,
    Howe'er we fall in action.

James Russell Lowell

GOD IS NOT DUMB

American Nineteenth Century

God is not dumb, that he should speak no more;
If thou hast wanderings in the wilderness

And find'st not Sinai, 'tis thy soul is poor;
  There towers the mountain of the Voice no less,
Which whoso seeks shall find; but he who bends
Intent on manna still, and mortal ends,
  Sees it not, neither hears its thundered lore.

Slowly the Bible of the race is writ,
  And not on paper leaves, nor leaves of stone;
Each age, each kindred, adds a verse to it,
  Texts of despair or hope, of joy or moan.
While swings the sea, while mists the mountains shroud,
While thunder's surges burst on cliffs of cloud,
  Still at the prophets' feet the nations sit.

James Russell Lowell

EVENTIDE

American Nineteenth Century

At cool of day, with God I walk
  My garden's grateful shade;
I hear His voice among the trees,
  And I am not afraid.

He speaks to me in every wind,
  He smiles from every star;
He is not deaf to me, nor blind,
  Nor absent, nor afar.

His hand that shuts the flowers to sleep,
  Each in its dewy fold,
Is strong my feeble life to keep,
  And competent to hold.

The powers below and powers above,
   Are subject to His care—
I cannot wander from His love
   Who loves me everywhere.

Thus dowered, and guarded thus, with Him
   I walk this peaceful shade;
I hear His voice among the trees,
   And I am not afraid.

Caroline Atherton Mason

THE GODDESS' SONG from AL AARAAF

American Nineteenth Century

Spirit! that dwellest where,
   In the deep sky,
The terrible and fair,
   In beauty vie!
Beyond the line of blue—
   The boundary of the star
Which turneth at the view
   Of thy barrier and thy bar—
Of the barrier overgone
   By the comets who were cast
From their pride and from their throne
   To be drudges till the last—
To be carriers of fire
   (The red fire of their heart)
With speed that may not tire
   And with pain that shall not part—

Who livest—*that* we know—
  In Eternity—we feel—
But the shadow of whose brow
  What spirit shall reveal?
Though the beings whom thy Nesace,
  Thy messenger hath known,
Have dreamed for thy Infinity
  A model of their own—
Thy will is done, O God!
  The star hath ridden high
Through many a tempest, but she rode
  Beneath thy burning eye;
And here, in thought, to thee—
  In thought that can alone
Ascend thy empire, and so be
  A partner of thy throne—
By winged Fantasy,
  My embassy is given,
Till secrecy shall knowledge be
  In the environs of Heaven.

Edgar Allan Poe

LIFE AND DEATH

American Nineteenth Century

I dreamed I saw two angels hand in hand,
  And very like they were, and very fair.
One wore about his head a golden band;
  A thorn-wreath crowned the other's matted hair.

The one was fair, and tall, and white of brow;
  A radiant spirit smile of wondrous grace

Shed, like an inner altar-lamp, a glow
  Upon his beautiful uplifted face.

The other's face, like marble-carvèd Grief,
  Had placid brows laid whitely o'er with pain,
With lips that never knew a smile's relief,
  And eyes like violets long drenched in rain.

Then spake the fair sweet one, and gently said:
  "Between us—Life and Death—choose thou thy lot.
By him thou lovest best thou shalt be led;
  Choose thou between us, soul, and fear thou not."

I pondered long. "O Life," at last I cried,
  "Perchance 'twere wiser Death to choose; and yet
My soul with thee were better satisfied!"
  The angel's radiant face smiled swift regret.

Within his brother's hand he placed my hand;
  "Thou didst mistake," he said in underbreath,
"And choosing Life, didst fail to understand.
  He with the thorns is Life, and I am Death."

Laura Spencer Porter

LIGHT

American Nineteenth Century

Thou one all perfect Light,
  Our lamps are lit at Thine;
And into darkness, as of night,
  We go, to prove they shine.

M. Elizabeth Crouse

Lyra Mystica

THE SEEN AND THE UNSEEN

American Nineteenth Century

Nature is but the outward vestibule
Which God has placed before an unseen shrine;
The Visible is but a fair, bright vale
That winds around the great Invisible;
The Finite—it is nothing but a smile
That flashes from the face of Infinite;
A smile with shadows on it—and 'tis sad
Men bask beneath the smile, but oft forget
The loving Face that very smile conceals.
The Changeable is but the broidered robe
Enwrapped about the great Unchangeable;
The Audible is but an echo, faint,
Low whispered from the far Inaudible;
This earth is but an humble acolyte
A-kneeling on the lowest altar-step
Of this creation's temple, at the Mass
Of Supernature, just to ring the bell
At Sanctus! Sanctus! Sanctus! while the world
Prepares its heart for consecration's hour.
Nature is but the ever-rustling veil
Which God is wearing, like the Carmelite
Who hides her face behind her virgin-veil
To keep it all unseen from mortal eyes,
Yet by her vigils and her holy prayer,
And ceaseless sacrifices night and day,
Shields souls from sin—and many hearts from harm.

God hides in nature as a thought doth hide
In humbly-sounding words; and as the thought

Lyra Mystica

Beats through the lowly word like pulse of heart
That giveth life and keepeth life alive,
So God, thro' nature, works on ev'ry soul;
For nature is His word so strangely writ
In heav'n, in all the letters of the stars,
Beneath the stars in alphabets of clouds,
And on the seas in syllables of waves,
And in the earth, on all the leaves of flowers,
And on the grasses and the stately trees,
And on the rivers and the mournful rocks
The word is clearly written; blest are they
Who read the word aright—and understand.

For God is everywhere—and He doth find
In every atom which His hand hath made
A shrine to hide His presence, and reveal
His name, love, power, to those who kneel
In holy faith upon this bright below
And lift their eyes, thro' all this mystery,
To catch the vision of the great beyond.
Yea! nature is His shadow, and how bright
Must that face be which such a shadow casts?
We walk within it, for "we live and move
And have our being" in His ev'rywhere.
Why is God shy? Why doth He hide Himself?
The tiniest grain of sand on ocean's shore
Entemples Him; the fragrance of the rose
Folds Him around as blessed incense folds
The altars of His Christ: yet some will walk
Along the temple's wondrous vestibule
And look on and admire—yet enter not

Lyra Mystica

To find within the Presence, and the Light
Which sheds its rays on all that is without.

And nature is His voice; who list may hear
His name low-murmured every—everywhere.
In song of birds, in rustle of the flowers,
In swaying of the trees, and on the seas
The blue lips of the wavelets tell the ships
That come and go, His holy, holy name.
The winds, or still or stormy, breathe the same;
And some have ears and yet they will not hear
The soundless voice re-echoed everywhere;
And some have hearts that never are enthrilled
By all the grand Hosannahs nature sings.
List! Sanctus! Sanctus! Sanctus! without pause
Sounds sweetly out of all creation's heart,
That hearts with power to love may echo back
Their Sanctus! Sanctus! Sanctus! to the hymn.
Abram J. Ryan

THE STARRY HOST

American Nineteenth Century

The countless stars, which to our human eye
  Are fixed and steadfast, each in proper place,
  Forever bound to changeless points in space,
Rush with our sun and planets through the sky,
And like a flock of birds still onward fly;
  Returning never whence began their race.
  They speed their ceaseless way with gleaming face
As though God bade them win infinity.

Ah, whither, whither is their forward flight
  Through endless time and limitless expanse?
What Power with unimaginable might
  First hurled them forth to spin in tireless dance?
What Beauty lures them on through primal night,
  So that, for them, to be is to advance?

John Lancaster Spalding

From THE FINAL THOUGHT

American Nineteenth Century

Which way are my feet set?
Through infinite changes yet
Shall I go on,
Nearer and nearer drawn
To Thee,
God of eternity?
How shall the human grow,
By changes fine and slow,
To thy perfection from the life-dawn sought:
What is the highest thought?

. . . . . .

Love! Faith is born of it!
Death is the scorn of it!
It fills the earth and thrills the heavens above:
And God is love,
And life is love, and though we heed it not,
Love is the final thought.

Maurice Thompson

Lyra Mystica

From PRAYER OF COLUMBUS

American Nineteenth Century

My terminus near,
The clouds already closing in upon me,
The voyage balk'd, the course disputed, lost,
I yield my ships to Thee.

My hands, my limbs grow nerveless,
My brain feels rack'd, bewildered,
Let the old timbers part, I will not part,
I will cling fast to Thee, O God, though the waves buffet me,
Thee, Thee, at least I know.

Walt Whitman

From PASSAGE TO INDIA

American Nineteenth Century

Greater than stars or suns,
Bounding O soul thou journeyest forth;
What love than thine and ours could wider amplify?
What aspiration, wishes, outvie thine and ours, O soul?
What dreams of the ideal? what plans of purity, perfection, strength?
What cheerful willingness for others' sake to give up all?
For others' sake to suffer all?

Reckoning ahead O soul, when thou, the time achiev'd,
The seas all cross'd, weather'd the capes, the voyage done,

Lyra Mystica

Surrounded, copest, frontest God, yieldest, the aim attain'd,
As fill'd with friendship, love complete, the Elder Brother found,
The Younger melts in fondness in his arms.

Passage to more than India!
Are thy wings plumed indeed for such far flights?
O soul, voyagest thou indeed on voyages like those?
Disportest thou on waters such as those?
Soundest below the Sanscrit and the Vedas?
Then have thy bent unleash'd.

Passage to you, your shores, ye aged fierce enigmas!
Passage to you, to mastership of you, ye strangling problem!
You, strew'd with the wrecks of skeletons, that, living, never reach'd you.

Passage to more than India!
O secret of the earth and sky!
Of you O waters of the sea! O winding creeks and rivers!
Of you O woods and fields! of you strong mountains of my land!
Of you O prairies! of you gray rocks!
O morning red! O clouds! O rain and snows!
O day and night, passage to you!

O sun and moon and all you stars! Sirius and Jupiter!
Passage to you!

Passage, immediate passage! the blood burns in my veins!
Away O soul! hoist instantly the anchor!
Cut the hawsers—haul out—shake out every sail!
Have we not stood here like trees in the ground long
    enough?
Have we not grovel'd here long enough, eating and
    drinking like mere brutes?
Have we not darken'd and dazed ourselves with books
    long enough?

Sail forth—steer for the deep waters only,
Reckless, O soul, exploring, I with thee, and thou with
    me,
For we are bound where mariner has not yet dared to go,
And we will risk the ship, ourselves and all.
O my brave soul!
O farther farther sail!
O daring joy, but safe! are they not all the seas of
    God?
O farther, farther, farther sail!

Walt Whitman

THE ETERNAL GOODNESS

American Nineteenth Century

O friends! with whom my feet have trod
    The quiet aisles of prayer,
Glad witness to your zeal for God
    And love of man I bear.

I trace your lines of argument;
    Your logic linked and strong

I weigh as one who dreads dissent,
    And fears a doubt as wrong.

But still my human hands are weak
    To hold your iron creeds;
Against the words ye bid me speak
    My heart within me pleads.

Who fathoms the Eternal Thought?
    Who talks of scheme and plan?
The Lord is God! He needeth not
    The poor device of man.

I walk with bare, hushed feet the ground
    Ye tread with boldness shod;
I dare not fix with mete and bound
    The love and power of God.

Ye praise His justice; even such
    His pitying love I deem:
Ye seek a king; I fain would touch
    The robe that hath no seam.

Ye see the curse that overbroods
    A world of pain and loss;
I hear our Lord's beatitudes
    And prayer upon the cross.

· · · · · · · ·

I see the wrong that round me lies,
    I feel the guilt within;
I hear, with groan and travail-cries,
    The world confess its sin.

Yet, in the maddening maze of things,
    And tossed by storm and flood,
To one fixed trust my spirit clings;
    I know that God is good!

. . . .

And so beside the Silent Sea
    I wait the muffled oar;
No harm from Him can come to me
    On ocean or on shore.

I know not where His islands lift
    Their fronded palms in air;
I only know I cannot drift
    Beyond His love and care.

O brothers! if my faith is vain,
    If hopes like these betray,
Pray for me that my feet may gain
    The sure and safer way.

And Thou, O Lord! by whom are seen
    Thy creatures as they be,
Forgive me if too close I lean
    My human heart on Thee!

              John Greenleaf Whittier

A DANCE CHANT

American Indian Iroquois

Hail! Hail! Hail!
Listen, O Creator, with an open ear to the words of
    thy people as they ascend to thy dwelling!

Give to the keepers of Thy faith wisdom rightly to do thy commands.
Give to our warriors and to our mothers strength to perform the sacred ceremonies appointed.
We thank Thee that thou hast kept them pure unto this day.
Listen to us still!
We thank Thee that Thou hast spared the lives of so many of Thy children to take part in these exercises.
We thank Thee for the increase of the earth,
For the rivers and streams,
For the sun and moon,
For the winds that banish disease,
For the herbs and plants that cure the sick,
For all things that minister to good and happiness.
We pray for a prosperous year to come.
Lastly, we give thee thanks, our Creator and Ruler!
In Thee are embodied all things!
We believe that Thou canst do no evil;
We believe that Thou dost all things for our good and for our happiness.
Should Thy people disobey Thy commands, deal not harshly with them!
Be kind to us, as Thou hast been to our fathers in times long gone by,
Hearken to our words as they ascend—
May they be pleasing to Thee, our Creator!
Preserver of all things visible and invisible!

Anonymous

Lyra Mystica
IMPLICIT FAITH
Irish 1814–1902

Of all great Nature's tones that sweep
  Earth's resonant bosom, far or near,
Low-breathed or loudest, shrill or deep,
  How few are grasped by mortal ear.

Ten octaves close our scale of sound:
  Its myriad grades, distinct or twined,
Transcend our hearing's petty bound,
  To us as colours to the blind.

In Sound's unmeasured empire thus
  The heights, the depths alike we miss;
Ah, but in measured sound to us
  A compensating spell there is!

In holy music's golden speech
  Remotest notes to notes respond:
Each octave is a world; yet each
  Vibrates to worlds its own beyond.

Our narrow pale the vast resumes;
  Our sea-shell whispers of the sea:
Echoes are ours of angel-plumes
  That winnow far infinity!

—Clasp thou of Truth the central core!
  Hold fast that centre's central sense!
An atom there shall fill thee more
  Than realms on Truth's circumference.

That cradled Saviour, mute and small,
    Was God—is God while worlds endure!
Who holds Truth truly holds it all
    In essence, or in miniature.

Know what thou know'st! He knoweth much
    Who knows not many things: and he
Knows most whose knowledge hath a touch
    Of God's divine simplicity.

Aubrey Thomas de Vere

I CANNOT FIND THEE

American 1821–1896

I cannot find Thee! Still on restless pinion
My spirit beats the void where Thou dost dwell;
I wander lost through all Thy vast dominion,
And shrink beneath Thy light ineffable.

I cannot find Thee! Even when most adoring
Before Thy shrine I bend in lowliest prayer,
Beyond these bounds of thought, my thought upsoaring,
From furthest quest comes back: Thou are not there.

Yet high above the limits of my seeing,
And folded far within the inmost heart,
And deep below the deeps of conscious being,
Thy splendor shineth; there, O God, Thou art.

I cannot lose Thee! Still in Thee abiding
The end is clear, how wide so e'er I roam;

Lyra Mystica

The Law that holds the worlds my steps is guiding,
And I must rest at last in Thee, my home.

Eliza Scudder

THE CLIFF

Scottish Modern

Come in the glory of Thine excellence;
Rive the dense gloom with wedges of clear light;
And let the shimmer of Thy chariot wheels
Burn through the cracks of night.—So slowly, Lord,
To lift myself to Thee with hands of toil,
Climbing the slippery cliffs of unheard prayer!
Lift up a hand among my idle days—
One beckoning finger. I will cast aside
The clogs of earthly circumstance, and run
Up the broad highways where the countless worlds
Sit ripening in the summer of Thy love.

Eric Ericson

A PRAYER FOR THE PAST

Scottish 1824–1905

All sights and sounds of day and year,
All groups and forms, each leaf and gem,
Are thine, O God, nor will I fear
To talk to Thee of them.

Too great Thy heart is to despise,
Whose day girds centuries about;
From things which we name small, Thine eyes
See great things looking out.

Therefore the prayerful song I sing
May come to Thee in ordered words:
Though lowly born, it needs not cling
In terror to its chords.

I think that nothing made is lost;
That not a moon has ever shone,
That not a cloud my eyes hath crossed
But to my soul is gone.

That all the lost years garnered lie
In this Thy casket, my dim soul;
And Thou wilt, once, the key apply,
And show the shining whole.

But were they dead in me, they live
In Thee, Whose Parable is—Time,
And Worlds, and Forms—all things that give
Me thoughts, and this my rime.

. . . . . .

Father, in joy our knees we bow:
This earth is not a place of tombs:
We are but in the nursery now;
They in the upper rooms.

For are we not at home in Thee,
And all this world a visioned show;
That, knowing what Abroad is, we
What Home is too may know?

George MacDonald

Lyra Mystica

OBEDIENCE

Scottish 1824–1905

I said: "Let me walk in the fields."
   He said: "No, walk in the town."
I said: "There are no flowers there."
   He said: "No flowers, but a crown."

I said: "But the skies are black;
   There is nothing but noise and din."
And He wept as He sent me back—
   "There is mire," He said; "there is sin."

I said: "But the air is thick,
   And fogs are veiling the sun."
He answered: "Yet souls are sick,
   And souls in the dark undone!"

I said: "I shall miss the light,
   And friends will miss me, they say."
He answered: "Choose tonight
   If I am to miss you or they."

I pleaded for time to be given.
   He said: "It is hard to decide?
It will not seem so hard in heaven
   To have followed the steps of your Guide."

I cast one look at the fields,
   Then set my face to the town;
He said, "My child, do you yield?
   Will you leave the flowers for the crown?"

Lyra Mystica

>Then into His hand went mine;
>   And into my heart came He;
>And I walk in a light divine,
>   The path I had feared to see.
>
>   *George MacDonald*

LOST AND FOUND

Scottish 1824–1905

>I missed him when the sun began to bend;
>I found him not when I had lost his rim;
>With many tears I went in search of him,
>Climbing high mountains which did still ascend,
>And gave me echoes when I called my friend;
>Through cities vast and charnel-houses grim,
>And high cathedrals where the light was dim,
>Through books and arts and works without an end,
>But found him not—the friend whom I had lost.
>And yet I found him—as I found the lark,
>A sound in fields I heard but could not mark;
>I found him nearest when I missed him most;
>I found him in my heart, a life in frost,
>A light I knew not till my soul was dark.
>
>   *George MacDonald*

TRANSFIGURATION

American 1831–1912

>The harp is ever singing to itself
>   In soft and soullike sounds we cannot hear;

The stars of morning sing, and soundless words
  Make God's commands run swift from sphere to
    sphere.

Each flower is always sending incense up
  As if in act of holy worshiping,
Till fragrant earth is one great altar, like
  To heaven where saints their prayer-filled censers
    swing.

The stars send out a thousand rays, writ full
  Of mysteries we cannot read nor see,
Of histories so long and going forth,
  So vast, the volumes fill infinity.

Celestial presences have walked with man,
  Alluring him to Nebo's lofty height;
Transfigured forms in tender light, too oft
  Invisible to our low range of sight.

O Source Divine of things so fine and high,
  Touch all thy children's souls with power to see
That vibrant earth and air and boundless sky
  Still throb with immanent divinity.

Henry W. Warren

A HEATHEN HYMN

Welsh 1833–1907

O Lord, the Giver of my days,
My heart is ready, my heart is ready;

I dare not hold my peace, nor pause,
For I am fain to sing Thy praise.

I praise Thee not, with impious pride,
For that Thy partial hand has given
Bounties of wealth or form or brain,
Good gifts to other men denied.

Nor weary Thee with blind request,
For fancied goods Thy hand withholds;
I know not what to fear or hope,
Nor aught but that Thy will is best.

Not whence I come, nor whither I go,
Nor wherefore I am here, I know;
Nor if my life's tale ends on earth,
Or mounts to bliss, or sinks to woe.

Nor know I aught of Thee, O Lord;
Behind the veil Thy face is hidden:
We faint, and yet Thy face is hidden;
We cry,—Thou answerest not a word.

But this I know, O Lord, Thou art,
And by Thee I too love and am;
We stand together, face to face,
Thou the great whole, and I the part.

We stand together, soul to soul,
Alone amidst Thy waste of worlds;
Unchanged, though all creation fade,
And Thy swift suns forget to roll.

Wherefore, because my life is Thine,
Because, without Thee I were not;
Because, as doth the sea, the sun,
My nature gives back the Divine.

Because my being with ceaseless flow
Sets to Thee as the brook to the sea;
Turns to Thee, as the flower to the sun,
And seeks what it may never know.

Because, without me Thou hadst been
For ever, seated midst Thy suns,
Marking the soulless cycles turn,
Yet wert Thyself unknown, unseen.

I praise Thee, everlasting Lord,
In life and death, in heaven and hell:
What care I, since indeed Thou art,
And I the creature of Thy word.

Only if such a thing may be:
When all Thy infinite will is done,
Take back the soul Thy breath has given,
And let me lose myself in Thee.

Sir Lewis Morris

I VEX ME NOT

American 1836–1907

I vex me not with brooding on the years
That were ere I drew breath: why should I then

Distrust the darkness that may fall again
When life is done? Perchance in other spheres—
Dead planets—I once tasted mortal tears,
And walked as now amid a throng of men,
Pondering things that lay beyond my ken,
Questioning death, and solacing my fears.
Ofttimes indeed strange sense have I of this,
Vague memories that hold me with a spell,
Touches of unseen lips upon my brow,
Breathing some incommunicable bliss!
In years foregone, O Soul, was all not well?
Still lovelier life awaits thee. Fear not thou!

Thomas Bailey Aldrich

THEY LIST FOR ME THE THINGS I MAY NOT KNOW

They list for me the things I may not know:
Whence came the world? Whose hand flung out the light
Of yonder stars? How could a God of Right
Ordain for earth an ebbless tide of woe?

Their word is right; I would not scorn their doubt
Who press their questions of the how and why.
But this I know: that from that star-strewn sky
There comes to me a peace that puts to rout
All brooding thoughts of dread, abiding death;
And, too, I know with every fragrant dawn
That Life is Lord, that, with the Winter gone,
There cometh Spring, a great reviving breath.

It is enough that Life means this to me.
What Death shall mean, some sunny morn shall see.
Anonymous

A BALLADE OF THE CENTRE

When all the shores of knowledge fade
   Beyond the realms of night and day,
When the quick stir of thought is stayed
   And, as a dream of yesterday,
   The bonds of striving fall away:
There dawns sometimes a point of fire
   Burning the utter dark, that may
Fulfil our desperate desire.

Into the darkness, unafraid,
   Wherein soft hands of silence lay
Their veil of peace upon the blade
   Of too bright thought, we take our way.
   In changing of desire we pay
Whatever price the gods require,
   Knowing the end is theirs—and they
Fulfil our desperate desire.

Upon the stillness we have made
   Between our working and our play
A deeper stillness yet is laid.
   Like some white bird above the sway
   Of summer waves within the bay
Peace lights upon us ere we tire,
   And does (yet how, we cannot say)
Fulfil our desperate desire.

Lyra Mystica

Envoi

God of the world, to Whom we pray,
  Thou Inmost God to Whom aspire
All hopes that Thou wilt not betray—
  Fulfil our desperate desire!

Anonymous

OFF SHORE

English 1837–1909

As my soul has been dutiful
  Only to thee,
  O God most beautiful
  Lighten thou me
As I swim thro the long dim rollers, with eyelids
      uplift from the sea.

Be praised and adored of us
  All in accord,
  Father and lord of us,
  Always adored,
The slayer and the stayer and the harper, the
      light of us all and our lord.

At the sound of thy lyre,
  At the touch of thy rod,
  Air quickens to fire,
  By the foot of thee trod,
The savior and healer and singer, the living
      and visible God.

The years are before thee,
  As shadows of thee,
  As men that adore thee,
  As cloudlets that flee:
But thou art the God, and thy kingdom is heaven, and
        thy shrine is the sea."
Algernon Charles Swinburne

WAITING

American 1837–1921

Serene, I fold my hands and wait,
  Nor care for wind, nor tide, nor sea;
I rave no more 'gainst time or fate,
  For, lo! mine own shall come to me.

I stay my haste, I make delays,
  For what avails this eager pace?
I stand amid the eternal ways,
  And what is mine shall know my face.

Asleep, awake, by night or day,
  The friends I seek are seeking me;
No wind can drive my bark astray,
  Nor change the tide of destiny.

What matter if I stand alone?
  I wait with joy the coming years;
My heart shall reap what it has sown,
  And garner up its fruit of tears.

The waters know their own, and draw
    The brook that springs in yonder heights,
So flows the good with equal law
    Unto the soul of pure delights.

The stars come nightly to the sky;
    The tidal wave comes to the sea;
Nor time, nor space, nor deep, nor high,
    Can keep my own away from me.

John Burroughs

THE TWO MYSTERIES

American 1838–1905

[At the funeral of a friend, Walt Whitman held a little child upon his knees. The old poet was heard to say to the child, "You do not know what it means, dear, do you? No, neither do we."]

"We know not what it is, dear, this sleep so deep and still;
The folded hands, the awful calm, the cheek so pale and chill;
The lids that will not lift again, though we may call and call;
The strange white solitude of peace that settles over all.

"We know not what it means, dear, this desolate heart-pain;
This dread to take our daily way, and walk in it again.

Lyra Mystica

We know not to what other sphere the loved who leave
us go,
Nor why we're left to wander still, nor why we do
not know.

"But this we know: Our loved and dead, if they should
come this day,
Should ask us, 'What is life?' not one of us could say.
Life is a mystery as deep as ever death can be,
Yet oh! how sweet it is to us, this life we live and see.

"They might say, these vanished ones—and blessed is
the thought:
'So death is sweet, to us, beloved! though we may tell
you naught;
We may not tell it to the quick, this mystery of death;
Ye may not tell us, if ye would, the mystery of breath.'

"The child who enters life comes not with knowledge
or intent;
So those who enter death must go as little children
sent.
Nothing is known! But I believe that God is overhead;
And as life is to the living, so death is to the dead."

Mary Mapes Dodge

THE SPECTRUM

1840–1901

How many colors do we see set,
Like rings upon God's finger? Some say three,

Some four, some six, some seven. All agree
To left of red, to right of violet,
Waits darkness deep as night and black as jet.
And so we know what Noah saw we see,
Nor less nor more—of God's emblazonry
A shred—a sign of glory known not yet.
If red can glide to yellow, green to blue,
What joys may yet await our wider eyes
When we rewake upon a wider shore!
What deep pulsations exquisite and new!
What keener, swifter raptures may surprise
Men born to see the rainbow and no more!

Cosmo Monkhouse

From OUT OF THE SILENCE

American 1841-1923

Lo! in the vigils of the night, ere sped
The first bright arrows from the Orient shed,
The heart of Silence trembled into sound,
And out of Vastness came a Voice, which said:

I *am* alone; thou only art in Me:
I am the stream of Life that flows through thee:
I comprehend all substance, fill all space:
I am pure Being, by whom all things be.

I am thy Dawn, from darkness to release:
I am the Deep, wherein thy sorrows cease:
Be still! be still! and know that I am God:
Acquaint thyself with Me, and be at peace!

Lyra Mystica

I am the Silence that is more than sound:
If therewithin thou lose thee, thou art found:
The stormless, shoreless Ocean, which is I—
Thou canst not breathe, but in its bosom drowned.

I am all Love: there is naught else but I:
I am all power: the rest is phantasy:
Evil, and anguish, sorrow, death, and hell—
These are the fear-flung shadows of a lie.

Arraign not Mine Omnipotence, to say
That aught beside in earth or heaven hath sway!
The powers of darkness are not: that which is
Abideth: these but vaunt them for a day.

Know thou thyself: as thou hast learned of Me,
I made thee three in one, and one in three—
Spirit and Mind and Form, immortal Whole,
Divine and undivided Trinity.

Seek not to break the triple bond assigned:
Mind sees by Spirit: Body moves by Mind:
Divorced from Spirit, both way-wildered fall—
Leader and led, the blindfold and the blind.

Look not without thee: thou hast that within,
Makes whole thy sickness, impotent thy sin:
Survey thy forces, rally to thyself:
That which thou would'st not hath no power to win.

I, God, enfold thee like an atmosphere:
Thou to thyself wert never yet more near:

Think not to shun Me: whither would's thou fly?
Nor go not hence to seek Me: I am here.

James Rhoades

A COSMIC OUTLOOK

English 1843–1901

Backward!—beyond this momentary woe!—
    Thine was the world's dim dawn, the prime emprize;
    Eternal æons gaze thro' these sad eyes,
And all the empyreal sphere hath shaped thee so.
Nay! all is living, all is plain to know!
    This rock has drunk the ray from ancient skies;
    Strike! and the sheen of that remote sunrise
Gleams in the marble's unforgetful glow.
    Thus hath the cosmic light endured the same
        Ere first that ray from Sun to Sirius flew;
    Aye, and in heaven I heard the mystic Name
        Sound, and a breathing of the Spirit blew;
    Lit the long Past, bade shine the slumbering flame
        And all the Cosmorama blaze anew.

Onward! thro' baffled hope, thro' bootless prayer,
    With strength that sinks, with high task half begun,
    Things great desired, things lamentable done,
Vows writ in water, blows that beat the air.
On! I have guessed the end; the end is fair.
    Not with these weak limbs is thy last race run;
    Not all thy vision sets with this low sun;
Not all thy spirit swoons in this despair.

Look how thine own soul, throned where all is well,
    Smiles to regard thy days disconsolate;
Yea; since herself she wove the worldly spell,
    Doomed thee for lofty gain to low estate;—
Sown with thy fall a seed of glory fell;
    Thy heaven is in thee, and thy will thy fate.

Inward! aye, deeper far than love or scorn,
    Deeper than bloom of virtue, stain of sin,
    Rend thou the veil and pass alone within,
Stand naked there and feel thyself forlorn!
Nay! in what world, then Spirit, wast thou born?
    Or to what World-Soul art thou entered in?
    Feel the Self fade, feel the great life begin,
With Love re-rising in the cosmic morn.
    The inward ardour yearns to the inmost goal;
        The endless goal is one with the endless way;
    From every gulf the tides of Being roll,
        From every zenith burns the indwelling day;
    And life in Life has drowned thee soul in Soul;
        And these are God, and thou thyself art they.
                Frederick William Henry Myers

A LAST APPEAL

English 1843–1901

O somewhere, somewhere, God unknown,
    Exist and be!
I am dying; I am all alone;
    I must have Thee!

God! God! my sense, my soul, my all,
    Dies in the cry:—
Saw'st thou the faint star flame and fall?
    Ah! it was I.

Frederick William Henry Myers

LO, AS SOME BARD

English 1843–1901

Lo, as some bard on isles of the Ægean
    Lovely and eager when the earth was young,
Burning to hurl his heart into a pæan,
    Praise of the hero from whose loins he sprung;—

He, I suppose, with such a care to carry,
    Wandered disconsolate and waited long,
Smiting his breast, wherein the notes would tarry,
    Chiding the slumber of the seed of song:

Then in the sudden glory of a minute
    Airy and excellent the proem came,
Rending his bosom, for a god was in it,
    Waking the seed, for it had burst in flame.

So even I athirst for his inspiring,
    I who have talked with Him forget again,
Yes, many days with sobs and with desiring
    Offer to God a patience and a pain;

Then thro' the mid complaint of my confession,
    Then thro' the pang and passion of my prayer,

Leaps with a start the shock of his possession,
   Thrills me and touches, and the Lord is there.

Lo, if some pen should write upon your rafter
   Mene and mene in the folds of flame,
Think you could any memories thereafter
   Wholly retrace the couplet as it came?

Lo, if some strange intelligible thunder
   Sang to the earth the secret of a star,
Scarce could ye catch, for terror and for wonder,
   Shreds of the story that was pealed so far:—

Scarcely I catch the words of his revealing,
   Hardly I hear Him, dimly understand,
Only the Power that is within me pealing
   Lives on my lips and beckons to my hand.

Whoso has felt the Spirit of the Highest
   Cannot confound nor doubt Him nor deny:
Yea with one voice, O world, tho' thou deniest,
   Stand thou on that side, for on this am I.

Rather the earth shall doubt when her retrieving
   Pours in the rain and rushes from the sod,
Rather than he for whom the great conceiving
   Stirs in his soul to quicken into God.

Aye, tho' thou then shouldst strike him from his glory
   Blind and tormented, maddened and alone,

Even on the cross would he maintain his story,
Yes and in hell would whisper, I have known.

Frederick William Henry Myers

A NEW HYMN FOR SOLITUDE

Irish 1843–1913

I found Thee in my heart, O Lord,
  As in some secret shrine;
I knelt, I waited for Thy word,
  I joyed to name Thee mine.

I feared to give myself away
  To that or this; beside
Thy altar on my face I lay,
  And in strong need I cried.

Those hours are past. Thou art not mine,
  And therefore I rejoice,
I wait within no holy shrine,
  I faint not for the voice.

In Thee we live; and every wind
  Of heaven is Thine; blown free
To west, to east, the God unshrined
  Is still discovering me.

Edward Dowden

SEEKING GOD

Irish 1843–1913

I said, "I will find God," and forth I went
To seek him in the clearness of the sky,

But he over me, stood unendurably
Only a pitiless sapphire firmament
Ringing the world,—blank splendor; yet intent
Still to find God, "I will go seek," said I,
"His way upon the waters," and drew nigh
An ocean marge weed-strewn and foam-besprent;
And the waves dashed on idle sand and stone,
And very vacant was the long, blue sea;
But in the evening as I sat alone,
My window open to the vanishing day,
Dear God! I could not choose but kneel and pray,
And it sufficed that I was found of Thee.
Edward Dowden

HOLY LAND

American 1844–1909

This is the earth He walked on; not alone
    That Asian country keeps the sacred stain;
  Ah, not alone the far Judæan plain,
Mountain and river! Lo, the sun that shone
On Him, shines now on us; when day is gone
    The moon of Galilee comes forth again,
  And lights our path as His; an endless chain
Of years and sorrows makes the round world one.
The air we breathe, He breathed—the very air
    That took the mold and music of His high
And Godlike speech. Since then shall mortal dare
    With base thought front the ever sacred sky—
Soil with foul deed the ground whereon He laid,
In holy death, His pale immortal head!
Richard Watson Gilder

Lyra Mystica
UNDYING LIGHT

American 1844–1909

When in the golden western summer skies
   A flaming glory starts, and slowly fades
   Through crimson tone on tone to deeper shades,
   There falls a silence, while the daylight dies
Lingering—but not with human agonies
   That tear the soul, or terror that degrades;
   A holy peace the failing world pervades,
   Nor any fear of that which onward lies.
For well, ah well, the darkened vale recalls
   A thousand times ten thousand vanished suns;
   Ten thousand sunsets from whose blackened walls
Reflamed the white and living day that runs,
   In light which brings all beauty to the birth,
   Deathless forever round the ancient earth.

O Thou the Maker and Lord of Life and Light!
   Full heavy are the burdens that do weigh
   Our spirits earthward, as through twilight gray
   We journey to the end of rest and night;
Tho' well we know to the deep inward sight
   Darkness is but Thy shadow, and the day
   Where Thou art never dies, but sends its ray
   Through the wide universe with restless might.
O Lord of Light, steep Thou our souls in Thee!
   That when the daylight trembles into shade,
   And falls the silence of mortality,

Lyra Mystica

And all is done, we shall not be afraid
  But pass from light to light; from earth's dull gleam
  Into the very heart and heaven of our dream.
                  Richard Watson Gilder

THE INVISIBLE

American 1844–1909

Such pictures of the heavens were never seen.
We stood at the steep edge of the abyss
And looked out on the making of the suns.
The skies were powdered with the white of stars
And the pale ghosts of systems yet to be;
While here and there a nebulous spiral told,
Against the dark, the story of the orbs—
From the impalpable condensing slow
Through ages infinite.

                Each mighty shape
Seemed as the shape of speed—a whirling wheel
Stupendously revolving,
And yet no eye of man may see it stir.
(That moveless motion brings to the human brain
A hint of the large measurements of time—
Eternity made present.)

                Such new sense
Of magnitudes that make our world an atom
Might crush the soul, did not this saving thought
Leap to the mind and lift it to clear heights:—
" 'Tis but the unseen that grows not old nor dies,

Lyra Mystica

Suffers not change, nor waning, nor decay.
This that we see—this casual glimpse within
The seething pit of space; these million stars

And worlds in making, these are naught but matter;
These are all but the dust of our feet,
And we who gaze forth fearless on the sight
Find not one equal, facing from the vast
Our sentient selves. Not one, sole, lonely star
In all that infinite glitter and deep light
Can make one conscious movement; all are slaves
To law material, immutable—
That Power immense, mysterious, intense,
Unseen as our own souls, but which must be
Like them, the home of thought, with will and might
To stamp on endless matter the soul's will.
Yea, in these souls of ours triumphant dwells
Some segment of the large creative Power—
A thing beyond the things of sight and sense;
A strength to think, a force to conquer force.
One are we with the ever-living One."
Richard Watson Gilder

JOHANNES MILTON SENEX

English 1844–1930

Since I believe in God the Father Almighty,
Man's Maker and Judge, Overruler of Fortune,
'Twere strange should I praise anything and refuse
    Him praise,

Lyra Mystica

Should love the creature, forgetting the Creator,
Nor unto Him in sorrow and suffering turn me:
Nay, how could I withdraw me from His embracing?

But since that I have seen not, and cannot know Him,
Nor in my earthly temple apprehend rightly
His wisdom and the heav'nly purpose eternal;
Therefore will I be bound to no studied system
Nor argument, nor with delusion enslave me,
Nor seek to please Him in any foolish invention,
Which my spirit within me, that loveth beauty
And hateth evil, hath reproved as unworthy:

But I cherish my freedom in loving service,
Gratefully adoring for delight beyond asking
Or thinking, and in hours of anguish and darkness
Confiding always on His excellent greatness.
                              Robert Bridges

ALL IN ALL

American 1845–1909

We know Thee, each in part—
  A portion small;
But love Thee, as Thou art—
  The All in all:
For Reason and the rays thereof
Are starlight to the noon of Love.
                      John Bannister Tabb

Lyra Mystica

CHRIST AND THE PAGAN

American 1845–1909

I had no God but these,
The sacerdotal Trees,
And they uplifted me.
"I hung upon a Tree."

The sun and moon I saw,
And reverential awe
Subdued me day and night.
"I am the perfect Light."

Within a lifeless Stone—
All other gods unknown—
I sought Divinity.
"The Corner-Stone am I."

For sacrificial feast,
I slaughtered man and beast,
Red recompense to gain.
"So I, a Lamb, was slain.

"Yea; such My hungering Grace
That wheresoe'er My face
Is hidden, none may grope
Beyond eternal Hope."

John Bannister Tabb

AN INTERPRETER

American 1845–1909

What, O Eternity,
Is Time to thee?—

Lyra Mystica

What to the boundless All
My portion small?

Lift up thine eyes, my soul!
Against the tidal roll
  Stands many a stone,
  Whereon the breakers thrown
Are dashed to spray—
  Else were the Ocean dumb.

So, in the way
  Of tides eternal, thou
  Abidest now;
And God Himself doth come
  A suppliant to thee,
  Love's prisoned thought to free.
John Bannister Tabb

CRYING ABBA, FATHER

British 1845–1926

Abba, in Thine eternal years
  Bethink Thee of our fleeting day;
  We are but clay;
Bear with our foolish joys, our foolish tears,
  And all the wilfulness with which we pray!

I have a little maid who, when she leaves
Her father and her father's threshold, grieves,
But being gone, and life all holiday,
Forgets my love and me straightway;

Yet, when I write,
Kisses my letters, dancing with delight,
Cries "Dearest father!" and in all her glee
For one brief live-long hour remembers me.
Shall I in anger punish or reprove?
Nay, this is natural; she cannot guess
How one forgotten feels forgetfulness;
And I am glad thinking of her glad face,
And send her little tokens of my love.
And Thou—wouldst Thou be wroth in such a case?

> And crying Abba, I am fain
> To think no human father's heart
> Can be so tender as Thou art,
> So quick to feel our love, to feel our pain.

When she is froward, querulous or wild,
Thou knowest, Abba, how in each offense
I stint not patience lest I wrong the child,
Mistaking for revolt defect of sense,
For wilfulness mere spriteliness of mind;
Thou know'st how often, seeing, I am blind;
How when I turn her face against the wall
And leave her in disgrace,
And will not look at her or speak at all,
I long to speak and long to see her face;
And how, when twice, for something grievous done,
I could but smite, and though I lightly smote,
I felt my heart rise strangling in my throat;
And when she wept I kissed the poor red hands.
All these things, Father, a father understands;
And am not I Thy son?

Abba, in Thine eternal years
   Bethink Thee of our fleeting day;
From all the rapture of our eyes and ears
   How shall we tear ourselves away?
   At night my little one says nay,
With prayers implores, entreats with tears
For ten more flying minutes' play;
How shall we tear ourselves away?
Yet call, and I'll surrender
   The flower of soul and sense,
Life's passion and its splendor,
   In quick obedience.

If not without the blameless human tears
By eyes which slowly glaze and darken shed,
Yet without questionings or fears
For those I leave behind when I am dead.
Thou, Abba, knowst how dear
My little child's poor playthings are to her;
What love and joy
She has in every darling doll and precious toy;
Yet when she stands between my knees
To kiss good-night, she does not sob in sorrow,
"Oh father, do not break or injure these!"
She knows that I shall fondly lay them by
For happiness to-morrow;
She leaves them trustfully. And shall not I?

   Whatever darkness gather
     O'er coverlet or pall,
   Since Thou art Abba, Father,
     Why should I fear at all?

Lyra Mystica

Thou'st seen how closely, Abba, when at rest
My child's head nestles to my breast;
And how my arm her little form enfolds,
Lest in the darkness she should feel alone;
And how she holds
My hands, my hands, my two hands in her own?

   A little easeful sighing
      And restful turning round,
   And I too, on Thy love relying,
      Shall slumber sound.

William Canton

WHERE THE BLESSED FEET HAVE TROD

English 1846–1914, or 1862–1913

Not alone in Palestine those blessed Feet have trod,
For I catch their print,
I have seen their dint
On a plot of chalky ground,
    Little villas dotted round;
On a sea-worn waste,
Where a priest, in haste,
Passeth with the Blessed Sacrament to one dying, frail,
Through the yarrow, past the tamarisk, and the plaited snail:
Bright upon the grass I see
    Bleeding Feet of Calvary—
And I worship, and I clasp them round!
On this bit of chalky, English ground,

Lyra Mystica

Jesu, Thou art found: my God I hail,
    My Lord, my God!

Michael Field

PER ASPERA

American 1850–1927

Thank God, a man can grow!
He is not bound
With earthward gaze to creep along the ground;
Though his beginnings be but poor and low,
Thank God, a man can grow!
The fire upon his altars may burn dim,
    The torch he lighted may in darkness fail
    And nothing to rekindle it avail,—
Yet high beyond his dull horizon's rim,
Arcturus and the Pleiads beckon him.

Florence Earle Coates

MEN TOLD ME, LORD!

American 1851–1931

Men told me, Lord, it was a vale of tears
Where thou hadst placed me; wickedness and woe
My twain companions whereso I might go;
That I through ten and three-score weary years
Should stumble on, beset by pains and fears,
Fierce conflict round me, passions hot within,
Enjoyment brief and fatal, but in sin.
When all was ended then I should demand
Full compensation from thine austere hand:

For 'tis thy pleasure, all temptation past,
To be not just but generous at last.

Lord, here am I, my three score years and ten
Are counted to the full; I've fought thy fight,
Crossed thy dark valleys, scaled thy rocks' harsh height,
Borne all the burdens thou dost lay on men
With hand unsparing, three score years and ten.
Before thee now I make my claim, Oh, Lord!
What shall I pay thee as a meet reward?

David Starr Jordan

CHRISTMAS NIGHT

English 1853–1922

"If I cannot see Thee present I will mourn Thee absent, for this also is a proof of love."
—*Thomas à Kempis*

We do not find Him on the difficult earth,
    In surging human-kind,
In wayside death or accidental birth,
    Or in the "march of mind."

Nature, her nests, her prey, the fed, the caught,
    Hide Him so well, so well,
His steadfast secret there seems to our thought
    Life's saddest miracle.

He's but conjectured in man's happiness,
    Suspected in man's tears,

Or lurks beyond the long, discouraged guess,
  Grown fainter through the years.

. . . .

But absent, absent now? Ah, what is this,
  Near as in child-birth bed,
Laid on our sorrowful hearts, close to a kiss?
  A homeless childish head.

Alice Meynell

A GENERAL COMMUNION

English 1853–1922

I saw the throng, so deeply separate,
  Fed at one only board—
The devout people, moved, intent, elate,
  And the devoted Lord.

O struck apart! not side from human side,
  But soul from human soul,
As each asunder absorbed the multiplied,
  The ever unparted, whole.

I saw this people as a field of flowers,
  Each grown at such a price
The sum of unimaginable powers
  Did no more than suffice.

A thousand single central daisies they,
  A thousand of the one;
For each, the entire monopoly of day;
  For each, the whole of the devoted sun.

Alice Meynell

Lyra Mystica

I AM THE WAY

English 1853–1922

Thou art the Way
Hadst Thou been nothing but the goal,
    I cannot say
If Thou hadst ever met my soul.

I cannot see—
I, child of process—if there lies
    An end for me,
Full of repose, full of replies.

I'll not reproach
The road that winds, my feet that err,
    Access, Approach
Art Thou, Time, Way, and Wayfarer.

Alice Meynell

TO THE MOTHER OF CHRIST THE SON OF MAN

English 1853–1922

We too (one cried), we too,
We the unready, the perplexed, the cold,
Must shape the Eternal in our thoughts anew,
    Cherish, possess, enfold.

Thou sweetly, we in strife,
It is our passion to conceive Him thus
In mind, in sense, within our house of life;
    That seed is locked in us.

We must affirm our Son
From the ambiguous Nature's difficult speech,
 Gather in darkness that resplendent One,
  Close as our grasp can reach.

  Nor shall we ever rest
From this our task. An hour sufficed for thee,
 Thou innocent! He lingers in the breast
  Of our humanity.

Alice Meynell

THE TREASURE

English 1853–1922

 Three times have I beheld
Fear leap in a babe's face, and take his breath,
 Fear, like the fear of eld
That knows the price of life, the name of death.

 What is it justifies
This thing, this dread, this fright that has no tongue,
 The terror in those eyes
When only eyes can speak—they are so young?

 Not yet those eyes had wept.
What does fear cherish that it locks so well?
 What fortress is thus kept?
Of what is ignorant terror sentinel?

 And pain in the poor child,
Monstrously disproportionate, and dumb

In the poor beast, and wild
In the old decorous man, caught, overcome?

Of what the outposts these?
Of what the fighting guardians? What demands
That sense of menaces,
And then such flying feet, imploring hands?

Life: There's nought else to seek;
Life only, little prized; but by design
Of nature prized. How weak,
How sad, how brief! O how divine, divine!

Alice Meynell

THE UNKNOWN GOD

English 1853–1922

One of the crowd went up,
And knelt before the Paten and the Cup,
Received the Lord, returned in peace, and prayed
Close to my side. Then in my heart I said:

"O Christ, in this man's life—
This stranger who is Thine—in all his strife,
All his felicity, his good and ill,
In the assaulted stronghold of his will,

"I do confess Thee here,
Alive within this life; I know Thee near
Within this lonely conscience, closed away
Within this brother's solitary day.

"Christ in his unknown heart,
His intellect unknown—this love, this art,
This battle and this peace, this destiny
That I shall never know, look upon me!

"Christ in his numbered breath,
Christ in his beating heart and in his death,
Christ in his mystery! From that secret place
And from that separate dwelling, give me grace!"

Alice Meynell

TO A DAISY

English 1853–1922

Slight as thou art, thou art enough to hide
  Like all created things, secrets from me,
  And stand like a barrier to eternity,
And I, how can I praise thee well and wide

From where I dwell—upon the hither side?
  Thou little veil for so great mystery,
  When shall I penetrate all things and thee,
And then look back? For this I must abide

Till thou shalt grow and fold and be unfurled
Literally between me and the world.
  Then shall I drink from in beneath a spring,

And from a poet's side shall read his book.
O daisy mine, what will it be to look
  From God's side even of such a simple thing?

Alice Meynell

THE REPLY OF SOCRATES

American 1854–1925

This from that soul incorrupt whom Athens had doomed to the death,
When Crito brought promise of freedom: "Vainly thou spendest thy breath!
Dost remember the wild Corybantes? feel they the knife or the rod?
Heed they the fierce summer sun, the frost, or winterly flaws?—
If any entreat them they answer, "We hear but the flutes of the God!"

"So even am I, O my Crito! Thou pleadest a losing cause!
Thy words are but sound without import—I hear but the voice of the Laws;
And, know thou, the voice of the Laws is to me as the flutes of the God."
Thus spake that soul incorrupt, and wherever, since hemlock was quaffed,
A man has stood forth without fear—has chosen the dark, deep draught!—
Has taken the lone one way, nor the path of dishonour has trod—
Behold! He, too, hears but the voice of the Laws, the flutes of the God!

Edith M. Thomas

Lyra Mystica

PATMOS

American 1854–1925

All around him Patmos lies,
Who hath spirit-gifted eyes,
Who his happy sight can suit
To the great and the minute.
Doubt not but he holds in view
A new earth and heaven new;
Doubt not but his ear doth catch
Strain nor voice nor reed can match:
Many a silver, sphery note
Shall within his hearing float.

All around him Patmos lies,
Who unto God's priestess flies:
Thou, O Nature, bid him see,
Through all guises worn by thee,
A divine apocalypse.
Manifold his fellowships:
Now the rocks their archives ope;
Voiceless creatures tell their hope
In a language symbol-wrought;
Groves to him sigh out their thought;
Musings of the flower and grass
Through his quiet spirit pass.
'Twixt new earth and heaven new
He hath traced and holds the clue,
Number his delights ye may not;
Fleet the year but these decay not.
Now the freshets of the rain,

Bounding on from hill to plain,
Show him earthly streams have rise
In the bosom of the skies.
Now he feels the morning thrill,
As upmounts, unseen and still,
Dew the wing of evening drops.
Now the frost, that meets and stops
Summer's feet in tender sward,
Greets him, breathing heavenward.
Hieroglyphics writes the snow,
Through the silence falling slow;
Types of star and petaled bloom
A white missal-page illume.
By these floating symbols fine,
Heaven-truth shall be divine.

All around him Patmos lies,
Who hath spirit-gifted eyes;
He need not afar remove,
He need not the times reprove,
Who would hold perpetual lease
Of an isle in seas of peace.

Edith M. Thomas

INSPIRATIONS

Anglo-American 1854–1928

Sometimes, I know not why, nor how, nor whence,
   A change comes over me, and then the task
   Of common life slips from me. Would you ask
What power is this which bids the world go hence?
   Who knows? I only feel a faint perfume

Steal through the rooms of life; a saddened sense
Of something lost; a music as of brooks
That babble to the sea; pathetic looks
  Of closing eyes that in a darkened room
  Once dwelt on mine: I feel the general doom
Creep nearer, and with God I stand alone.
  O mystic sense of sudden quickening!
Hope's lark-song rings, or life's deep undertone
  Wails through my heart—and then I needs must sing.

William James Dawson

LET US BESIDE THE RIVER REST AWHILE

Anglo-American 1854–1928

Let us beside the river rest awhile,
For now the last light lingers like God's smile,
And you and I, like two tired travellers,
Have come all soiled to Life's last dusty mile.

To this strange House of Life through doors of light
We enter in, and scarce have moved aright
When a Shape summons us from pleasant talk,
And we pass out again thro' doors of night.

All kings and lovers go the self-same road,
And know not if it lead to sleep or God;
And after some few years a little dust
Alone is left, which the wind blows abroad.

Lo, I have seen great houses desolate,
And with loud moan the corpse borne out in state;

Then, after some brief months, the Bride pass in
With light and laughter thro' the self-same gate.

And lo, it is the same bell rings for both;
Laughter of bells for plighted wedding troth,
And moan of bells when slow incurious hands
Lay on the dead man's face the funeral cloth.

Let us a little time with talk run on
Of things which we have seen, or hoped, or done;
It is but little time we have, and still
A pleasant place is this great Babylon.

Warm hostelries it hath where we have slept,
Bright rooms where we our merry feasts have kept,
And we were loth to go, did we not think
Of O so many places where we wept!

The grass-blade springs, the bird is tossed along
Its skiey road of brightness and of song,
And neither knows from what warm Hand it sprang,
Or how the life was nourished and grew strong.

And since, like these, I know not whence I came,
It were in me small scorn or little shame
That I am loth to go: let Him decide
Who timed my coming and gave me my name.

. . . .

Let us be still. And yet at times this thought
Perplexes me—Why was I made and wrought
With so much skill of cunning workmanship,
Only to be cast down and brought to naught?

Lyra Mystica

It were as tho' the Maker made a star,
Lit it, and for an hour bade it afar
Flash splendours forth: then struck it out and cried,
"Go now, and lie where dark and dead things are!"

Or as a Schoolmaster, who takes a boy
And trains his mind in learning's eager joy;
Then, mocking, cries, "Perfect art thou in vain,
Be broken thou with Truth thy broken toy."

O verily, verily, this is not God's way,
Not thus the Maker toils upon his clay;
Be it He breaks us here, yet shall He not,
Think you, make us anew some other day?

O verily, verily, this is not God's plan,
To spend eternities in making man,
And then for all His skill to end in naught,
To end at that same point where it began.

The meanest artist, with the feeblest glance
Into his Art's concealed significance,
Attains a method surer with the years;
In God's Art only is there no advance?

The greatest artist likewise feels the sense
Of Progress as a thing unfixed, immense,
And all his Art, a single wave that flows
Out of the Soul's unbounded opulence.

Can God then be content to contemplate
His work as finished, be it soon or late,

Which one marred creature of His hand upbraids,
And craves fresh chances in a better state?

. . . .

It cannot be the brain that soared sublime
Into the height and mysteries of Time,
Now is a pulp wherein corruption thrives,
Or on the fields a little leaven of lime.

Something survives that scorns corruption's hands.
Something that worked thro' us its high commands;
There is a Spirit that moved behind the brain,
And somewhere there's a House not made with hands.

All that aspired, at last shall find its mark;
See, how each morn the little eager lark
Throbs up the sky all hungry for the dawn,
And finds the punctual light beyond the Dark.

O Soul, be sure that this must be God's plan
To warm the germ of God concealed in man,
Till it outsoar in scorn the ended flesh,
As seeds the husk in which their life began.

Thus by degrees, on secret promptings fed,
By sweet divine illusions charmed and led,
Man pushes on in search of earthly good,
Till, losing earth, he finds God's heaven instead.

Even as plants unveil a tiny eye,
Think the Sun near, and strive to touch the sky;
And straining upward, get their growth, to find
Always there is a Higher above the High.

Lyra Mystica

For hearts and brains that let Earth's prizes slip
Comes there at last no higher scholarship?
A power commensurate with the Soul's demand?
A loftier dialect to the poet's lip?

All, all leads up to that we do not see,
Powers that shall ripen, worlds that yet shall be—
Time like a twilight swallowed up at last
In the broad radiance of eternity.

All is not buried in the great abyss,
Brains that stored truth, and Love that found its bliss
In death of self: O, God Himself is not
So rich to bear such shameful waste as this.

. . . .

So, Friend, we part; long while in Babylon
My feet on many a foolish quest have gone,
Now Death cries, "For a longer journey rise,
Nor put thy worn-out pilgrim sandals on.

"Alone, barefooted, garmentless, and stark,
Lo, thou shalt pass within the doors of Dark,
But fear thou not: a voice attends thee there,
And lo, a Hand shall guide thee toward the mark!"

Plant thou the Rose to grow above my head,
Let lilies be the broidery of my bed;
Let me be laid face-forward to the sun,
And write not over me that I am dead.

I see and seek the Star of Bethlehem;
If any question, thou shalt answer them,

"This man, who toiled in Babylon so long,
Hath gone to find God's new Jerusalem."
William James Dawson

DESIRE

Scottish 1855–1905

The desire of love, joy:
The desire of life, peace:
The desire of the soul, heaven:
The desire of God . . . a flame-white secret for ever.
Fiona Macleod (William Sharp)

THE MYSTIC'S PRAYER

Scottish 1855–1905

Lay me to sleep in sheltering flame,
  O Master of the Hidden Fire!
Wash pure my heart, and cleanse for me
  My soul's desire.

In flame of sunrise bathe my mind,
  O Master of the Hidden Fire,
That, when I wake, clear-eyed may be
  My soul's desire.

Fiona Macleod (William Sharp)

THE RUNE OF AGE

Scottish 1855–1905

O Thou that on the hills and wastes of Night art Shepherd,

Lyra Mystica

Whose folds are flameless moons and icy planets,
Whose darkling way is gloomed with ancient sorrows:
Whose breath lies white as snow upon the olden,
Whose sigh it is that furrows breasts grown milkless,
Whose weariness is in the loins of man:
And is the barren stillness of the woman:
O Thou whom all would flee, and all must meet,
Thou that the Shadow art of Youth Eternal,
The gloom that is the hush'd air of the Grave,
The sigh that is between last parted love,
The light for aye withdrawing from weary eyes,
The tide from stricken hearts for ever ebbing!

O thou the Elder Brother whom none loveth,
Whom all men hail with reverence or mocking,
Who broodest on the brows of frozen summits
Yet dreamest in the eyes of babes and children:
Thou, Shadow of the Heart, the Mind, the Life,
Who art that dusk What-is that is already Has-been,
To Thee this rune of the fathers to the sons
And of the sons to the sons, and mothers to new
 mothers—
To Thee who art Aois,
To Thee who art Age!

Breathe Thy frosty breath upon my hair, for I am
 weary!
Lay Thy frozen hand upon my bones that they support
 not,
Put Thy chill upon the blood that it sustain not;
Place the crown of Thy fulfilling on my forehead;

Throw the silence of Thy spirit on my spirit;
Lay the balm and benediction of Thy mercy
On the brain-throb and the heart-pulse and the life-
    spring—
For Thy child that bows his head is weary,
For Thy child that bows his head is weary.
I the shadow am that seeks the Darkness.
Age, that hath the face of Night unstarr'd and moonless,
Age, that doth extinguish star and planet,
Moon and sun and all the fiery worlds,
Give me now Thy darkness and Thy silence.

Fiona Macleod (William Sharp)

THE VALLEY OF SILENCE

Scottish 1855–1905

In the secret Valley of Silence
    No breath doth fall;
No wind stirs in the branches;
    No bird doth call:
    As on a white wall
      A breathless lizard is still,
    So silence lies on the valley
      Breathlessly still.

In the dusk-grown heart of the valley
    An altar rises white:
No rapt priest bends in awe
    Before its silent light:
    But sometimes a flight
      Of breathless words of prayer

White-wing'd enclose the altar,
  Eddies of prayer.
        Fiona Macleod (William Sharp)

THE WHITE PEACE

Scottish 1855–1905

It lies not on the sunlit hill
  Nor on the sunlit plain:
Nor ever on any running stream
  Nor on the unclouded main—

But sometimes, through the Soul of Man,
  Slow moving o'er his pain,
The moonlight of a perfect peace
  Floods heart and brain.
        Fiona Macleod (William Sharp)

WHITE STAR OF TIME

Scottish 1855–1905

Each love-thought in thy mind doth rise
  As some white cloud at even,
Till in sweet dews it falls on me
  Athirst for thee, my Heaven!

My Heaven, my Heaven, thou art so far!
  Stoop, since I cannot climb:
I would this wandering fire were lost
  In thee, white Star of Time!
        Fiona Macleod (William Sharp)

Lyra Mystica

AT BEACH ST. MARY

American 1856–1921

The long brown arm thrusts out to sea
    A headland lost in sliding sands;
So Time indents Eternity;
    We live on Being's borderlands.

Man builds his lighthouse of Desire,
    Waits here to greet a coming sail;
Brings golden oil for Hope's faint fire,
    And will not let his beacon fail.

Here on the fronting height abide
    The prophets with their faith divine;
Here see they first the moon-drawn tide
    Tremble along Life's limit-line.

Afar beyond, from shores unseen,
    Thrusts out an arm enflowered and strong;
And they who watch there hear, I ween,
    The same deep-billowed ocean-song.

And deeper than the sea, below
    Unmeasured calm or thunder-shock,
'Neath darksome mystery and glow,
    Firm lies the floor of hidden rock.

Frank W. Gunsaulus

Lyra Mystica

THE HOUND OF HEAVEN
English 1859–1907

I fled Him, down the nights and down the days;
  I fled Him, down the arches of the years;
I fled Him, down the labyrinthine ways
  Of my own mind; and in the midst of tears
I hid from Him, and under running laughter.
      Up vistaed hopes I sped;
      And shot, precipitated,
Adown Titanic glooms of chasmèd fears,
  From those strong Feet that followed, followed after
      But with unhurrying chase,
      And unperturbèd pace,
  Deliberate speed, majestic instancy,
      They beat—and a Voice beat
      More instant than the Feet—
"All things betray thee, who betrayest Me."

      I pleaded, outlaw-wise,
By many a hearted casement, curtained red,
  Trellised with intertwining charities;
(For, though I knew His love Who followèd,
      Yet was I sore adread
Lest, having Him, I must have naught beside).
But, if one little casement parted wide,
  The gust of His approach would clash it to.
  Fear wist not to evade, as Love wist to pursue.
Across the margent of the world I fled,
  And troubled the gold gateways of the stars,
  Smiting for shelter on their clangèd bars;
      Fretted to dulcet jars

And silvern chatter the pale ports o' the moon.
I said to Dawn: Be sudden—to Eve: Be soon;
   With thy young skiey blossoms heap me over
      From this tremendous Lover—
Float thy vague veil about me, lest He see!
   I tempted all His servitors, but to find
My own betrayal in their constancy,
In faith to Him their fickleness to me,
   Their traitorous trueness, and their loyal deceit.
To all swift things for swiftness did I sue;
   Clung to the whistling mane of every wind.
      But whether they swept, smoothly fleet,
   The long savannahs of the blue;
      Or whether, Thunder-driven,
   They clanged his chariot 'thwart a heaven,
Plashy with flying lightnings round the spurn o' their feet:—
Fear wist not to evade as Love wist to pursue.
      Still with unhurrying chase,
      And unperturbèd pace,
Deliberate speed, majestic instancy,
      Came on the following Feet,
      And a Voice above their beat—
"Naught shelters thee, who wilt not shelter Me."

I sought no more that after which I strayed
   In face of man or maid;
But still within the little children's eyes
   Seems something, something that replies,
They at least are for me, surely for me!
I turned me to them very wistfully;

Lyra Mystica

But just as their young eyes grew sudden fair
  With dawning answers there,
Their angel plucked them from me by the hair.
"Come then, ye other children, Nature's—share
With me" (said I) "your delicate fellowship;
  Let me greet you lip to lip,
  Let me twine with you caresses,
      Wantoning
  With our Lady Mother's vagrant tresses,
      Banqueting
  With her in her wind-walled palace,
  Underneath her azured dais,
  Quaffing, as your taintless way is,
      From a chalice
Lucent-weeping out of the dayspring."
    So it was done:
I in their delicate fellowship was one—
Drew the bolt of Nature's secrecies.
  I knew all the swift importings
  On the wilful face of skies;
  I knew how the clouds arise
  Spumed of the wild sea-snortings;
      All that's born or dies
  Rose and drooped with; made them shapers
Of mine own moods, or wailful or divine;
  With them joyed and was bereaven.
  I was heavy with the even,
  When she lit her glimmering tapers
  Round the day's dead sanctities.
  I laughed in the morning's eyes.

I triumphed and I saddened with all weather,
  Heaven and I wept together,
And its sweet tears were salt with mortal mine;
Against the red throb of its sunset-heart
    I laid my own to beat,
    And share commingling heat;
But not by that, by that, was eased my human smart.
In vain my tears were wet on Heaven's grey cheek.
For ah! we know not what each other says,
  These things and I; in sound *I* speak—
Their sound is but their stir, they speak by silences.
Nature, poor stepdame, cannot slake my drouth;
  Let her, if she would own me,
Drop yon blue bosom-veil of sky, and show me
  The breasts o' her tenderness:
Never did any milk of hers once bless
    My thirsting mouth.
    Nigh and nigh draws the chase,
    With unperturbèd pace,
  Deliberate speed, majestic instancy;
    And past those noisèd Feet
    A voice comes yet more fleet—
"Lo! naught contents thee, who content'st not Me!"

Naked I wait Thy love's uplifted stroke!
My harness piece by piece Thou hast hewn from me,
    And smitten me to my knee;
  I am defenceless utterly.
  I slept, methinks, and woke,
And, slowly gazing, find me stripped in sleep.

Lyra Mystica

In the rash lustihead of my young powers,
  I shook the pillaring hours
And pulled my life upon me; grimed with smears,
I stand amid the dust o' the mounded years—
My mangled youth lies dead beneath the heap.
My days have crackled and gone up in smoke,
Have puffed and burst as sun-starts on a stream.
  Yea, faileth now even dream
The dreamer, and the lute the lutanist;
Even the linked fantasies, in whose blossomy twist
I swung the earth a trinket at my wrist,
Are yielding; cords of all too weak account
For earth with heavy griefs so overplussed.
  Ah, is Thy love indeed
A weed, albeit an amaranthine weed,
Suffering no flowers except its own to mount?
  Ah! must—
  Designer infinite!—
Ah! must Thou char the wood ere Thou canst limn with it?
My freshness spent its wavering shower i' the dust;
And now my heart is as a broken fount,
Wherein tear-drippings stagnate, spilt down ever
  From the dank thoughts that shiver
Upon the sighful branches of my mind.
  Such is; what is to be?
The pulp so bitter, how shall taste the rind?
I dimly guess what Time in mists confounds;
Yet ever and anon a trumpet sounds
From the hid battlements of Eternity;
Those shaken mists a space unsettle, then

Round the half-glimpsed turrets slowly wash again.
    But not ere him who summoneth
    I first have seen, enwound
With glooming robes purpureal, cypress-crowned;
His name I know, and what his trumpet saith.
Whether man's heart or life it be which yields
    Thee harvest, must Thy harvest-fields
    Be dunged with rotten death?

    Now of that long pursuit
    Comes on at hand the bruit;
That Voice is round me like a bursting sea:
    "And is thy earth so marred,
    Shattered in shard on shard,
Lo, all things fly thee, for thou fliest Me!
Strange, piteous, futile thing!
Wherefore should any set thee love apart?
Seeing none but I makes much of naught" (He said),
"And human love needs human meriting:
    How hast thou merited—
Of all man's clotted clay the dingiest clot?
    Alack, thou knowest not
How little worthy of any love thou art!
Whom wilt thou find to love ignoble thee,
    Save Me, save only Me?
All which I took from thee I did but take,
    Not for thy harms,
But just that thou might'st seek it in My arms.
    All which thy child's mistake
Fancies as lost, I have stored for thee at home:
    Rise, clasp My hand, and come!"

Halts by me that footfall:
Is my gloom, after all,
Shade of His hand, outstretched caressingly?
"Ah, fondest, blindest, weakest,
I am He Whom thou seekest!
Thou dravest love from thee, who dravest Me."

Francis Thompson

DESIDERIUM INDESIDERATUM

English 1859–1907

O gain that lurk'st ungained in all gain!
O love we just fall short of in all love!
O height that in all heights art still above!
O beauty that dost leave all beauty pain!
Thou unpossessed that mak'st possession vain,
See these strained arms which fright the simple air,
And say what ultimate fairness holds thee, Fair!
They girdle Heaven, and girdle Heaven in vain;
They shut, and lo! but shut in their unrest.
Thereat a voice in me that voiceless was:—
"Whom seekest thou through the unmarged arcane,
And not discern'st to thine own bosom prest?"
I looked. My clasped arms athwart my breast
Framed the august embraces of the Cross.

Francis Thompson

THE KINGDOM OF GOD

English 1859–1907

O world invisible, we view thee,
O world intangible, we touch thee,

O world unknowable, we know thee,
Inapprehensible, we clutch thee!

Does the fish soar to find the ocean,
The eagle plunge to find the air—
That we ask of the stars in motion
If they have rumour of thee there?

Not where the wheeling systems darken,
And our benumbed conceiving soars!—
The drift of pinions, would we hearken,
Beats at our own clay-shuttered doors.

The angels keep their ancient places;—
Turn but a stone, and start a wing!
'Tis ye, 'tis your estranged faces,
That miss the many-splendoured thing.

But (when so sad thou canst not sadder)
Cry;—and upon thy so sore loss
Shall shine the traffic of Jacob's ladder
Pitched betwixt Heaven and Charing Cross.

Yea, in the night, My Soul, my daughter,
Cry,—clinging Heaven by the hems;
And, lo, Christ walking on the water
Not of Gennesareth, but Thames!

Francis Thompson

Lyra Mystica

EACH IN HIS OWN TONGUE

American 1859–1924

A fire-mist and a planet,
  A crystal and a cell,
A jellyfish and a saurian,
  And caves where the cavemen dwell;
Then a sense of law and beauty,
  And a face turned from the clod—
Some call it Evolution,
  But others call it God.

A haze on the far horizon,
  The infinite, tender sky,
The ripe, rich tint of the cornfields,
  And the wild geese sailing high—
And all over upland and lowland
  The charm of the goldenrod—
Some of us call it Autumn,
  And others call it God.

Like tides on a crescent sea beach,
  When the moon is new and thin,
Into our hearts high yearnings
  Come welling and surging in—
Come from the mystic ocean,
  Whose rim no foot has trod—
Some of us call it Longing,
  And others call it God.

A picket frozen on duty—
  A mother starved for her brood—

Socrates drinking the hemlock,
  And Jesus on the rood;
And millions who, humble and nameless,
  The straight, hard pathway trod—
Some call it Consecration,
  And others call it God.

William H. Carruth

AFTER ST. AUGUSTINE

English 1861–1907

Sunshine let it be or frost,
  Storm or calm, as Thou shalt choose;
Though Thine every gift were lost,
  Thee Thyself we could not lose.

Mary Elizabeth Coleridge

BORDERLANDS

American 1861–1920

Through all the evening,
All the virginal long evening,
Down the blossomed aisle of April it is dread to walk alone;
For there the intangible is nigh, the lost is ever-during;
And who would suffer again beneath a too divine alluring,
Keen as the ancient drift of sleep on dying faces blown?

Yet in the valley,
At a turn of the orchard alley,

When a wild aroma touched me in the moist and
    moveless air,
Like breath indeed from out Thee, or as airy vesture
    round Thee,
Then was it I went faintly, for fear I had nearly
    found Thee,
O hidden, O Perfect, O Desired! O first and final
    Fair!

Louise Imogen Guiney

SUMMUM BONUM

American 1861–1920

Waiting on Him who knows us and our need,
Most need have we to dare not, nor desire,
But as He giveth, softly to suspire
Against His gift with no inglorious greed,
For this is joy, though still our joys recede;
And, as in octaves of a noble lyre,
To move our minds with His, and clearer, higher,
Sound forth our fate: for this is strength indeed.

Thanks to His love let earth and man dispense
In smoke of worship when the heart is stillest,
A praying more than prayer: "Great good have I,
Till it be greater good to lay it by;
Nor can I lose peace, power, permanence,
For these smile on me from the thing Thou willest!"

Louise Imogen Guiney

Lyra Mystica

VESTIGIA

Canadian-American 1861–1929

I took a day to search for God,
And found Him not. But, as I trod
   By rocky ledges, through woods untamed,
   Just where one scarlet lily flamed,
I saw His footprints in the sod.

Then suddenly, all unaware,
Far off in the deep shadows, where
   A solitary hermit thrush
   Sang through the holy twilight hush—
I heard His voice upon the air.

And even as I marvelled how
God gives us heaven here and now,
   In a stir of wind that hardly shook
   The poplar leaves beside the brook—
His hand was light upon my brow.

At last with evening as I turned
Homeward, and thought what I had learned
   And all that there was still to prove,
   I caught the glory of His love
Where the last fires of sunset burned.

Back to the world with quickening start
I looked and longed for any part
   In making saving beauty be . . .
   And from that kindly ecstasy
I knew God dwelt within my heart.

Bliss Carman

Lyra Mystica

VENI CREATOR

Canadian-American 1861–1929

I

Lord of the grass and hill,
Lord of the rain,
White Overlord of will,
Master of pain,

I who am dust and air
Blown through the halls of death,
Like a pale ghost of prayer,—
I am thy breath.

Lord of the blade and leaf,
Lord of the bloom,
Sheer Overlord of grief,
Master of doom,

Lonely as wind or snow,
Through the vague world and dim,
Vagrant and glad I go;
I am thy whim.

Lord of the storm and lull,
Lord of the sea,
I am thy broken gull,
Blown far alee.

Lord of the harvest dew,
Lord of the dawn,

Star of the paling blue
Darkling and gone,

Lord of the mountain height
Where the first winds are stirred,
Out of the wells of night
I am thy word.

Lord of the haunted hush,
Where raptures throng,
I am thy hermit thrush,
Ending no song.

Lord of the frost and cold,
Lord of the North,
When the red sun grows old
And day goes forth,

I shall put off this girth,—
Go glad and free,
Earth to my mother earth,
Spirit to thee.

2

Lord of my heart's elation,
Spirit of things unseen,
Be thou my aspiration
Consuming and serene!

Bear up, bear out, bear onward
This mortal soul alone,

To selfhood or oblivion,
Incredibly thine own,—

As the foamheads are loosened
And blown along the sea,
Or sink and merge forever
In that which bids them be,

I, too, must climb in wonder,
Uplift at thy command,—
Be one with my frail fellows
Beneath the wind's strong hand,

A fleet and shadowy column
Of dust or mountain rain,
To walk the earth a moment
And be dissolved again.

Be thou my exaltation
Or fortitude of mien,
Lord of the world's elation
Thou breath of things unseen!

Bliss Carman

SANCTUARIES

Irish 1861-1931

Thou givest me greenest sanctuaries,
As birds have the trees.
The birds have the trees and I
Deep shadow and blue sky,

A well of waters, a palm tree,
A bird and a bee.

As though I were Thine only one
Thou makest for me alone
A hearth-fire in the wintry cold,
A walled city, a sweet fold,
A winged sentinel to tell
To the night: All's well!

Thou spreadest over me and mine
The night a-shine
With strange and wonderful eyes of stars;
And weary of the day's wars
Into the nest of love we creep
And lie asleep.

Hearts are Thy sanctuaries: Thou hast set
Wide open a heart's gate
Where I come in and am at rest,
A bed for my heart, a nest,
Sure comfort, surplusage of love.
Thou givest enough!

Woods are Thy sanctuaries and all
Dear gardens musical,
And fields and groves where it may be
Thine angel walks with me.
Thine angel! Nay, but Thou dost walk
With me and talk.

Katharine Tynan

Lyra Mystica

THE IMAGE

Irish 1861–1931

When a wild grace I see,
  A turn o' the neck, a curl, sweet hands, clear eyes,
Gentleness, courtesy, dignity;
  In all these gifts Thee I surmise, surprise.

All beauty and delight:
  Skin like a rose, a beauteous shape, an air
Free and enchanting, give my weary sight
  Glimpses of Thee, Thou Beauty past compare.

Strength, courage also are Thine,
  And joy of youth and wings that cleave the blue,
Low singing and soft voices: I divine
  In these Thy beauty ancient yet ever new.

O, when my startled eye
  Perceives this beauty league-long, sea and isle
And eagle-crested mountains wild and high,
  I catch Thy Maker's thought—I see Thy smile.

Some mirror out of range
  Flashes reflex of Heaven on this sweet earth,
Brooding for ever, beautiful, without change,
  The bluebell sea, the thousand streams' soft mirth.

All beauty is of Thee:
  Kindness and quietness, moon and stars and sun,
Gardens and woods, the bird in the new-fledged tree,
  And sleep, O Kindest One!

Katharine Tynan

Lyra Mystica

OF AN ORCHARD

Irish 1861–1931

Good is an orchard, the saint saith,
To meditate on life and death,
With a cool well, a hive of bees,
A hermit's grot below the trees.

Good is an orchard: very good,
Though one should wear no monkish hood;
Right good when spring awakes her flute,
And good in yellowing time of fruit:

Very good in the grass to lie
And see the net-work 'gainst the sky,
A living lace of blue and green
And boughs that let the gold between.

The bees are types of souls that dwell
With honey in a quiet cell;
The ripe fruit figures goldenly
The soul's perfection in God's eye.

Prayer and praise in a country home
Honey and fruit: a man might come
Fed on such meats to walk abroad
And in his Orchard talk with God.

Katharine Tynan

SHEEP AND LAMBS

Irish 1861–1931

All in the April evening,
April airs were abroad;

The sheep with their little lambs
    Passed me by on the road.

The sheep with their little lambs
    Passed me by on the road;
All in the April evening
    I thought on the Lamb of God.

Up in the blue, blue mountains
    Dewy pastures are sweet;
Rest for the little bodies,
    Rest for the little feet.

But for the Lamb of God,
    Up on the hill-top green,
Only a Cross of shame
    Two stark crosses between.

All in the April evening,
    April airs were abroad;
I saw the sheep with their lambs,
    And thought on the Lamb of God.

Katharine Tynan

THE FLYING WHEEL

Irish 1861–1931

When I was young the days were long,
Oh, long the days when I was young:
So long from morn to evenfall
As they would never end at all.

Now I grow old Time flies, alas!
I watch the years and seasons pass.
Time turns him with his fingers thin
A wheel that whirls while it doth spin.

There is no time to take one's ease,
For to sit still and be at peace:
Oh, whirling wheel of Time, be still,
Let me be quiet if you will!

Yet still it turns so giddily,
So fast the years and seasons fly,
Dazed with the noise and speed I run
And stay me on the Changeless One.

I stay myself on Him who stays
Ever the same through nights and days:
The One Unchangeable for aye,
That was and will be: the one Stay,

O'er whom Eternity will pass
But as an image in a glass;
To whom a million years are nought,—
I stay myself on a great Thought.

I stay myself on the great Quiet
After the noises and the riot;
And in a garnished chamber sit
Far from the tumult of the street.

Oh, wheel of Time, turn round apace!
But I have found a resting place.

You will not trouble me again
In the great peace where I attain.
                     Katharine Tynan

THE PAVILIONS OF PEACE

Irish 1865-1930

Within the circle of His peace
The Lord of life abides and is.

Out of His peace I can not go,
Now that its still delight I know.

Clad in its beam I spend the day,
A poor weed dressed in a silver ray.

Earth's fields at evening mourn the light:
In His pavilions there is no night.

Peace holds the darkness, till it seems
His hand upon me in my dreams.

And when I wake, in light it falls,
A window in my chamber walls.

Dressed in His peace the hills arise,
And shine like towers of Paradise.

The green trees standing in the sun,
Are flames of His brightness every one.

Flowers, blown in a secret place,
In their day of beauty desire His face.

Lit by His thought, His children's eyes
Are lamps before His mysteries.

Within the peace of His great halls,
Where moon and star ingem the walls,

I have had gifts at His hand of light,
That make one treasure of day and night;

Chrism of the eyes, a seal on the mouth,
A harp at the ear set, a sun in the south.

Through His pavilions flows white peace,
The fountain of my felicities.

Out of His peace may I never go;
I should perish of thirst for that stream's white flow.

Grace Rhys

INTROIT

Irish 1865-1930

Oh Lord, my cup is small,
Since I must Thee contain;
I can hold no more than the shell on the sand
Can hold of the splendid main;
No more than the leaf on the forest branch
Can hold of the rain.

Lyra Mystica

Because the cup is small,
It should the cleaner be;
Clean of the choking cares of life
That hinder receiving Thee.
I will cast them all out of my heart until
The way is free.

Dark shadows stand within,
Dark and with hidden face;
The mournful faces of many a sin;
Can I drive them from their place?
Three angels are come to lead them forth
To the burying place.

What shall be done with my joys?
Alas, they must wake and go;
Like a flock of doves I drive them out,
And they wander to and fro;
Like a flock of doves on summer wing,
They pass and go.

Only my loves are left;
Those flowers of different stain;
They were gathered in gardens of Paradise,
I will not uproot them again;
They shall bend down their necks to the soles of Thy feet,
As the grass to the rain.

Ah, when Thou comest in!
The seven lights divide,
The crystal curtains are lifted up,

Low doors are opened wide.
The doors of my heart are open thrown
To greet the tide.

Joy sits upon the flood,
Thy music wakes the day,
The empty lamp that waited the flame
Is lit by a merciful ray.
In the heart of Thy servant Thy throne is set:
Oh, wilt Thou stay?

Grace Rhys

THE POET'S PRAYER

English 1868–1915

That I have felt the rushing wind of Thee:
That I have run before Thy blast to sea;
That my one moment of transcendent strife
Is more than many years of listless life;
Beautiful Power, I praise Thee: yet I send
A prayer that sudden strength be not the end.
Desert me not when from my flagging sails
Thy breathing dies away, and virtue fails:
When Thou hast spent the glory of that gust,
Remember still the body of this dust.
Not then when I am boundless, without bars,
When I am rapt in hurry to the stars;
When I anticipate an endless bliss,
And feel before my time the final kiss,
Not then I need Thee: for delight is wise,
I err not in the freedom of the skies;

Lyra Mystica

I fear not joy, so joy might ever be,
And rapture finish in felicity.
But when Thy joy is past, comes in the test,
To front the life that lingers after zest:
To live in mere negation of Thy light,
A more than blindness after more than sight.
'Tis not in flesh so swiftly to descend,
And sudden from the spheres with earth to blend;
And I, from splendour thrown, and dashed from dream,
Into the flare pursue the former gleam.
Sustain me in that hour with Thy left hand,
And aid me, when I cease to soar, to stand;
Make me Thy athlete even in my bed,
Thy girded runner though the course be sped;
Still to refrain that I may more bestow,
From sternness to a larger sweetness grow.
I ask not that false calm which many feign,
And call that peace which is a dearth of pain.
True calm doth quiver like the calmest star;
It is that white where all the colours are;
And for its very vestibule doth own
The tree of Jesus and the pyre of Joan.
Thither I press: but O do Thou meanwhile
Support me in privations of Thy smile.
Spaces Thou hast ordained the stars between,
And silences where melody hath been:
Teach me those absences of fire to face,
And Thee no less in silence to embrace,
Else shall Thy dreadful gift still people Hell,
And men not measure from what height I fell.

Stephen Phillips

Lyra Mystica

STARLIGHT

American 1869-1905

They think me daft, who nightly meet
My face turned starward, while my feet
Stumble along the unseen street;

But should man's thoughts have only room
For earth, his cradle and his tomb,
Not for his Temple's grander gloom?

And must the prisoner all his days
Learn but his dungeon's narrow ways
And never through its grating gaze?

Then let me linger in your sight,
My only amaranths! blossoming bright
As over Eden's cloudless night,

The same vast belt, and square, and crown,
That on the Deluge glittered down,
And lit the roofs of Bethlehem town!

Ye make me one with all my race,
A victor over time and space,
Till all the path of men I pace.

Far-speeding backward in my brain
We build the Pyramids again,
And Babel rises from the plain;

Lyra Mystica

And climbing upward on your beams
I peer within the Patriarch's dreams,
Till the deep sky with angels teems.

My comforters!—Yea, why not mine?
The power that kindled you doth shine,
In man a mastery divine;

That love which throbs in every star,
And quickens all the worlds afar,
Beats warmer where his children are.

The shadow of the wings of Death
Broods over us; we feel his breath:
"Resurgam" still the spirit saith.

These tired feet, this weary brain,
Blotted with many a mortal stain,
May crumble earthward—not in vain.

With swifter feet that shall not tire,
Eyes that shall fail not at your fire,
Nearer your splendors I aspire.

Edward Rowland Sill

I STOOD WITHIN THE HEART OF GOD

American 1869–1910

I stood within the heart of God;
    It seemed a place that I had known:
(I was blood-sister to the clod,
    Blood-brother to the stone).

I found my love and labor there,
  My house, my raiment, meat and wine,
My ancient rage, my old despair,—
  Yea, all things that were mine.

I saw the spring and summer pass,
  The trees grow bare, the winter come;
All was the same as once it was
  Upon my hills at home.

Then suddenly in my own heart
  I felt God walk and gaze about;
He spoke; His words seemed held apart
  With gladness and with doubt.

"Here is my meat and wine," He said,
  "My love, my toil, my ancient care;
Here is my cloak, my book, my bed,
  And here my old despair;

Here are my seasons: winter, spring,
  Summer the same, and autumn spills
The fruits I look for; everything
  As on my heavenly hills."

William Vaughn Moody

THE FINAL FAITH

American 1869-1926

Not often, when the carnal dance is mad—
  Not often, in our youth's audacity,
Shall one, aware, have final faith in thee,

Lyra Mystica

O soul, for he who knows thee shall be sad
Betimes, and youth would be forever glad.
   Then, craving freedom, never are we free;
   Through many-coloured mists we call or flee,
And in illusion's raiment are we clad.

But when the humiliation of the flesh
   Is ours, like truant children going home
   We turn to thee, the beautiful and best,
Whose dew-remembered flowers are ever fresh—
   Whose winds are from the snows and ocean-foam—
Who hast the starlight on thy marble breast.

George Sterling

THE SOURCE

American 1874–1922

  I know, whatever God may be,
  All Life it was that lighted me
  This little flame whereby I see.

  I know All Strength did stir this hand
  To serve somehow the poor command
  Of whatsoe'er I understand.

  And from All Love there throbs the stress
  Of pity and of wistfulness
  Both to be blessèd and to bless.

  O Light of Light, that still doth pour
  On star and glow-worm known before,
  I am alive . . . forevermore!

Josephine Preston Peabody

Lyra Mystica

IN THE SILENCE

American 1874–1922

Where didst Thou tarry, Lord, Lord,
  Who heeded not my prayer?
All the long day, all the long night,
  I stretched my hands to air.

"There was a bitterer want than thine
  Came from the frozen North;
Laid hands upon My garment's hem
  And led Me forth.

"It was a lonely Northern man:
  Where there was never tree
To shed its comfort on his heart,
  There he had need of Me.

"He kindled us a little flame
  To hope against the storm;
And unto him, and unto Me,
  The light was warm."

And yet I called Thee, Lord, Lord,—
  Who answered not, nor came:
All the long day, and yesterday,
  I called Thee by Thy name.

"There was a dumb, unhearing grief
  Spake louder than thy word.
There was a heart called not on Me;
  But yet I heard.

"The sorrow of a savage man
  Shaping him gods, alone,
Who found no love in the shapen clay
  To answer to his own.

"His heart knew what his eyes saw not;
  He bade Me stay, and eat;
And unto him, and unto Me,
  The cup was sweet.

"Too long we wait for thee and thine,
  In sodden ways and dim.
And where the man's need cries on Me,
  There have I need of him.

"Along the borders of despair
  Where sparrows seek no nest,
Nor ravens food, I sit at meat,
  —The unnamed Guest."

Josephine Preston Peabody

AN AIR OF COOLNESS PLAYS UPON HIS FACE

American 1876–1928

Out of the four and twenty hours,
To take one sheaf of moments
To open the house and air it
In the May morning of Eternity,
Will not, O my dear Self,
Leave all your cares and duties
Naked to the little foxes,

But guard them with a golden bayonet!
Efficient would we be with the farming,
The baking, the children,—
Swing wide the dormer windows of Now
To the sunlit breezes of Forever!

Sarah N. Cleghorn

THE ANODYNE

American 1876–1928

In the late evening, when the house is still,
For an intense instant,
I lift my clean soul out of the soiled garments of mortality.
No sooner is it free to rise than it bends back earthward
And touches mortal life with hands like the hands that troubled the waters of Bethesda.
So this incorruptible touches the corrupt;
This immortal cools with a touch
The beaded forehead of mortality.

Sarah N. Cleghorn

HEART OF GOD

American 1879–1932

O great heart of God,
Once vague and lost to me,
Why do I throb with your throb to-night,
In this land, eternity?

O little heart of God,
Sweet intruding stranger,

You are laughing in my human breast,
A Christ-child in a manger.

Heart, dear heart of God,
Beside you now I kneel,
Strong heart of faith. O heart not mine,
Where God has set His seal.
Wild thundering heart of God
Out of my doubt I come,
And my foolish feet with prophets' feet,
March with the prophets' drum.

Vachel Lindsay

A CHANT OUT OF DOORS

American 1883–1928

God of grave nights,
God of brave mornings,
God of silent noon,
Hear my salutation!
    For where the rapids rage white and scornful
    I have passed safely, filled with wonder;
    Where the sweet pools dream under willows
    I have been swimming, filled with joy.

God of round hills,
God of green valleys,
God of clear springs,
Hear my salutation!
    For where the moose feeds I have eaten berries,
    Where the moose drinks I have drunk deep;
    And under clear skies have I known love.

God of great trees,
God of wild grasses,
God of little flowers,
Hear my salutation!
    For where the deer crops and the beaver plunges
    Near the river I have pitched my tent;
    Where the pines cast aromatic needles
    On the still flowers I have known peace.

God of grave nights,
God of brave mornings,
God of silent noon,
Hear my salutation.

Marguerite Wilkinson

OUT OF THE DARK

American 1883–1928

Out of the troubled dark I came
Into bright silence where I heard a Name
Sounded without a voice.
Time narrowed, then,
Into an instant, and the world of men
Rolled into space, and left me to rejoice
In solitude that was not solitude.
And quietly my spirit was renewed,
While through and through and over and under all
The Name was sounded, call upon ringing call.

Time widened out into eternity;
Power was upon me so that I could see

Lyra Mystica

Light beyond light, rivers of silver flowing,
Sheer lakes of rosy and golden color, blowing
Torrents of tumbled glory, amber and green,
White rays impetuous, violet pools serene,
And a broad azure tide whose waves are curled
Around the margin of the farthest world.
Light followed darkness and time died. For me
Silence was crying out of mystery.
"Oh, bow and worship, bend you and adore,
God is forevermore . . .
All marvel of vision overwhelming sight
Is but one darkened threshold of His light
Where, by His mercy on your lowly star,
One small door of His Heaven stands ajar."

Marguerite Wilkinson

SONNETS OF THE NEW BIRTH

American 1883–1928

2

Alone I climb the hanging crags of prayer,
Steep beyond steep, cry beyond broken cry,
And never a sluggard is more slow than I,
And never a dullard falls more heavily where
The aim is rising, climbing to bright air,
To watch with God while Heaven and earth go by.
O bruised and fallible, into His far sky
I reach. I clutch at Him for Whom I care.

Steep beyond steep I climb above my pain
When the bright answer wavers and grows dim;
Cry beyond broken cry, again, again,
From the rough crags up to the heavens' high rim,
Until His light is shed in me like rain,
Until I lose the light and rest in Him.

4

Trials by fire, by water, and by air,
Unknowing darkness of the eternal cloud,
And the bright throes by which the soul is bowed
Down to the utter dust, inert and spare;
All the hard strife that Jesus bent to share,
Alone, forever lonely in the crowd,
All costly pain that yet shall make Him proud;—
Whoever holds Him shall have strength to bear.

O strong my Lord, down to Thy wounded feet
I bend my face; I keep the mighty tryst
With life and death, the future and the past,
Since every rhythm of Thy will is sweet.
By the strong Cross that I have taken and kissed,
Grant me the hidden manna, Lord, at last.

12

There is no light but love. This I have learned.
There is no other glory anywhere
But love has made it and has made it fair.
Love is the only sun that ever burned.

Lyra Mystica

Each far-reflecting moon and star discerned
Through and beyond our azure wheel of air
Has but one ancient wonder to declare—
How all that goes from love must be returned.

Bend your bright orbits when they lead away,
O blessed luminaries; so will I
Turn in my farthest darkness toward the Light
That colors mountains, fills the common day
With power, and quickens every mothering cry
In a blind race that would give birth to sight.

Marguerite Wilkinson

OF CHILDREN

Syrian 1883–1931

And a woman who held a babe against her bosom said,

Speak to us of Children.

And he said:

Your children are not your children.

They are the sons and daughters of Life's longing for itself.

They come through you but not from you,

And though they are with you yet they belong not to you.

You may give them your love but not your thoughts,

For they have their own thoughts.

You may house their bodies but not their souls,

For their souls dwell in the house of tomorrow, which you cannot visit, not even in your dreams.

You may strive to be like them, but seek not to make them like you.

For life goes not backward nor tarries with yesterday.

You are the bows from which your children as living arrows are sent forth.

The Archer sees the mark upon the path of the infinite, and He bends you with His might that His arrows may go swift and far.

Let your bending in the Archer's hand be for gladness;

For even as He loves the arrow that flies, so He loves also the bow that is stable.

Kahlil Gibran

OF REASON AND PASSION

Syrian 1883–1931

And the priestess spoke again and said:
Speak to us of Reason and Passion.
And he answered, saying:
Your soul is oftentimes a battlefield, upon which your reason and your judgment wage war against your passion and your appetite.

Would that I could be the peacemaker in your soul, that I might turn the discord and the rivalry of your elements into oneness and melody.

But how shall I, unless you yourselves be also the peacemakers, nay, the lovers of all your elements?

Your reason and your passion are the rudder and the sails of your seafaring soul.

If either your sails or your rudder be broken, you

can but toss and drift, or else be held at a standstill in mid-seas.

For reason, ruling alone, is a force confining; and passion, unattended, is a flame that burns to its own destruction.

Therefore let your soul exalt your reason to the height of passion, that it may sing;

And let it direct your passion with reason, that your passion may live through its own daily resurrection, and like the phoenix rise above its own ashes.

I would have you consider your judgment and your appetite even as you would two loved guests in your house.

Surely you would not honor one guest above the other; for he who is more mindful of one loses the love and the faith of both.

Among the hills, when you sit in the cool shade of the white poplars, sharing the peace and serenity of distant fields and meadows—then let your heart say in silence, "God rests in reason."

And when the storm comes, and the mighty wind shakes the forest, and thunder and lightning proclaim the majesty of the sky—then let your heart say in awe, "God moves in passion."

And since you are a breath in God's sphere, and a leaf in God's forest, you too should rest in reason and move in passion.

Kahlil Gibran

Lyra Mystica

THE SOLDIER IN FRANCE

American 1886-1918

My shoulders ache beneath my pack,
(Lie easier, Cross, upon His back).

I march with feet that burn and smart,
(Tread, holy Feet, upon my heart).

Men shout at me who may not speak,
(They scourged Thy back and smote Thy cheek).

I may not lift a hand to clear
My eyes of salty drops that sear,

(Then shall my fickle soul forget
Thy agony of Bloody Sweat?)

My rifle hand is stiff and numb,
(From Thy pierced palm red rivers come).

Lord, Thou didst suffer more for me
Than all the hosts of land and sea,

So let me render back again
This millionth of Thy gift. Amen.

Joyce Kilmer

I SEE HIS BLOOD UPON THE ROSE

Irish 1887–1916

I see His blood upon the rose
And in the stars the glory of His eyes,

His body gleams amid eternal snows,
His tears fall from the skies.

I see His face in every flower;
The thunder and the singing of the birds
Are but His voice—and carven by His power
Rocks are His written words.

All pathways by His feet are worn,
His strong heart stirs the ever-beating sea,
His crown of thorns is twined with every thorn,
His cross is every tree.

Joseph M. Plunkett

THIS CORRUPTIBLE

American 1887–1928

The Body, long oppressed,
And pierced, then prayed for rest,
(Being but apprenticed to the other Powers;)
And kneeling in that place
Implored the thrust of grace
Which makes the dust lie level with the flowers.

Then did that fellowship
Of three, the Body strip;
Beheld his wounds, and none among them mortal;
The Mind severe and cool;
The Heart still half a fool;
The fine-spun Soul, a beam of sun can startle.

These three, a thousand years
Had made adventurers
Amid all villainies the earth can offer;
Applied them to resolve
From the universal gulph
What pangs the poor material flesh may suffer.

"This is a pretty pass;
To hear the growing grass
Complain; the clay cry out to be translated;
Will not this grosser stuff
Receive reward enough
If stabled after labouring, and baited?"

Thus spoke the Mind in scorn:
The Heart, which had outworn
The Body, and was weary of its fashion,
Preferring to be dressed
In skin of bird or beast
Replied more softly, in a feigned compassion:

"Anatomy most strange
Crying to chop and change;
Inferior copy of a higher image;
While I, the noble guest,
Sick of your second-best
Sigh for embroidered archangelic plumage;

"For shame, thou fustian cloak!"
And then the Spirit spoke;
Within the void it swung securely tethered

By strings composed of cloud;
It spoke both low and loud
Above a storm no lesser star had weathered:

"O lodging for the night!
O house of my delight!
O lovely hovel builded for my pleasure!
Dear tenement of clay
Endure another day
As coffin sweetly fitted to my measure.

"Take Heart, and call to Mind
Although we are unkind;
Although we steal your shelter, strength, and clothing;
'Tis you who shall escape
In some enchanting shape
Or be dissolved to elemental nothing.

"You the unlucky slave,
Are the lily on the grave;
The wave that runs above the bones a-whitening;
You are the new-mown grass;
And the wheaten bread of the Mass;
And the fabric of the rain, and the lightning.

"If one of us elect
To leave the poor suspect
Imperfect bosom of the earth our parent;
And from the world avert
The spirit or the Heart
Upon a further and essential errand;

"His chain he cannot slough
Nor cast his substance off;
He bears himself upon his flying shoulder;
The Heart, infirm and dull;
The Mind, in any skull;
Are captive still, and wearier and colder.

" 'Tis you who are the ghost,
Disintegrated, lost;
The burden shed; the dead who need not bear it;
O grain of God in power,
Endure another hour!
It is but for an hour," said the Spirit.

Elinor Wylie

PRAYER

From the Persian

He prayed, but to his prayer no answer came,
And choked within him sank his ardour's flame,
No more he prayed, no more the knee he bent,
While round him darkened doubt and discontent;
Till in his room one eve there shone a light
And he beheld an angel-presence bright,
Who said, "O faint-heart, why has thou resigned
Praying, as though thy God were deaf and blind?"
"I prayed," he said, "but nothing won by prayer,
Long disappointment has induced despair."
"Fool!" cried the angel, "every prayer of thine
Of God's immense compassion was a sign;
Each cry of thine, 'O Lord!' itself contains

The answer, 'Here am I'; thy very pains,
Ardour and love and longing and each tear
Are His attraction, prove Him very near."

The cloud dispersed; once more the suppliant prayed,
Nor ever failed to find the promised aid.

C. F.

THE OARSMEN

East Indian Contemporary

Do you hear the tumult of death afar,
The call midst the fire-floods and poisonous clouds
—The Captain's call to the steersman to turn the ship to an unnamed shore,
For that time is over—the stagnant time in the port—
Where the same old merchandise is bought and sold in an endless round,
Where dead things drift in the exhaustion and emptiness of truth.

They wake up in sudden fear and ask, "Comrades, what hour has struck? When shall the dawn begin?"
The clouds have blotted away the stars—
Who is there then can see the beckoning finger of the day?
They run out with oars in hand, the beds are emptied, the mother prays, the wife watches by the door;
There is a wail of parting that rises to the sky,

And there is the Captain's voice in the dark:
"Come, sailors, for the time in the harbour is over!"

All the black evils in the world have overflowed their banks,
Yet, oarsmen, take your places with the blessing of sorrow in your souls!
Whom do you blame, brothers? Bow your heads down!
The sin has been yours and ours.

The heat growing in the heart of God for ages—
The cowardice of the weak, the arrogance of the strong, the greed of fat prosperity, the rancour of the wronged, pride of race, and insult to man—
Has burst God's peace, raging in storm.

Like a ripe pod, let the tempest break its heart into pieces, scattering thunders.
Stop your bluster of dispraise and of self-praise,
And with the calm of silent prayer on your foreheads sail to that unnamed shore.

We have known sins and evils every day and death we have known;
They pass over our world like clouds mocking us with their transient lightning laughter.
Suddenly they have stopped, become a prodigy,
And men must stand before them saying:
"We do not fear you, O Monster! for we have lived every day by conquering you,
"And we die with the faith that Peace is true, and Good is true, and true is the eternal One!"

Lyra Mystica

If the Deathless dwell not in the heart of death,
If glad wisdom bloom not bursting the sheath of sorrow,
If sin do not die of its own revealment,
If pride break not under its load of decorations,
Then whence comes the hope that drives these men
    from their homes like stars rushing to their death
    in the morning light?
Shall the value of the martyrs' blood and mothers' tears
    be utterly lost in the dust of the earth, not buying
    Heaven with their price?
And when Man bursts his mortal bounds, is not the
    Boundless revealed that moment?

Rabindranath Tagore

From FRUIT-GATHERING

East Indian Contemporary

"What is there but the sky, O Sun, that can hold thine image?"

"I dream of thee, but to serve thee I can never hope," the dewdrop wept and said, "I am too small to take thee unto me, great lord, and my life is all tears."

"I illumine the limitless sky, yet I can yield myself up to a tiny drop of dew," thus the Sun said, "I shall become but a sparkle of light and fill you, and your little life will be a laughing orb."

Rabindranath Tagore

Lyra Mystica

AUTUMN

East Indian Contemporary

Today the peace of autumn pervades the world.
In the radiant noon, silent and motionless, the wide stillness rests like a tired bird spreading over the deserted fields to all horizons its wings of golden green.
Today the thin thread of the river flows without song, leaving no mark on its sandy banks.
The many distant villages bask in the sun with eyes closed in idle and languid slumber.
In the stillness I hear in every blade of grass, in every speck of dust, in every part of my own body, in the visible and invisible worlds, in the planets, the sun, and the stars, the joyous dance of the atoms through endless time—the myriad murmuring waves of Rhythm surrounding Thy throne.

Rabindranath Tagore

IN SALUTATION TO THE ETERNAL PEACE

East Indian Contemporary

Men say the world is full of fear and hate,
And all life's ripening harvest-fields await
The restless sickle of relentless fate.

But I, sweet Soul, rejoice that I was born,
When from the climbing terraces of corn
I watch the golden orioles of Thy morn.

Lyra Mystica

What care I for the world's desire and pride,
Who know the silver wings that gleam and glide,
The homing pigeons of Thine eventide?

What care I for the world's loud weariness,
Who dream in twilight granaries Thou dost bless
With delicate sheaves of mellow silences?

Say, shall I heed dull presages of doom,
Or dread the rumoured loneliness and gloom,
The mute and mythic terror of the tomb?

For my glad heart is drunk and drenched with Thee,
O inmost wine of living ecstasy!
O intimate essence of eternity!

Sarojini Naidu

THE SOUL'S PRAYER

East Indian Contemporary

In childhood's pride I said to Thee:
"O Thou, who mad'st me of Thy breath,
Speak, Master, and reveal to me
Thine inmost laws of life and death.

"Give me to drink each joy and pain
Which Thine eternal hand can mete,
For my insatiate soul would drain
Earth's utmost bitter, utmost sweet.

"Spare me no bliss, no pang of strife,
Withhold no gift or grief I crave,

Lyra Mystica

The intricate lore of love and life
And mystic knowledge of the grave."

Lord, Thou didst answer stern and low:
"Child, I will hearken to thy prayer,
And thy unconquered soul shall know
All passionate rapture and despair.

"Thou shalt drink deep of joy and fame,
And love shall burn thee like a fire,
And pain shall cleanse thee like a flame,
To purge the dross from thy desire.

"So shall thy chastened spirit yearn
To seek from its blind prayer release,
And spent and pardoned, sue to learn
The simple secret of My peace.

"I, bending from my sevenfold height,
Will teach thee of My quickening grace,
Life is a prism of My light,
And Death the shadow of My face."

Sarojini Naidu

THE HOLY FACE

French Contemporary

You cannot efface from your heart a certain image,
And that image is the face imprinted on Veronica's handkerchief;
It is a sensitive, drawn face, and the chin is covered with a tufted beard.

The expression is so austere that it terrifies us; and the
   old sinner planted deep within us
Trembles down to his original root; and the misery of
   that face is so profound
That, all abashed, we stand like children who behold
   their father weeping and do not know the reason.
It is vain to spread before those eyes the power and
   glory of the world.—
Those eyes, which, with a mere lift of the lashes,
   created the Universe,
Now are lowered, and cruel tears are streaming from
   them.
The forehead sweats blood.
But consider now, the mouth of God—the mouth, my
   son, of the Word.
What bitterness it savors, what ineffable sorrow it tastes!
The corner of the lips are opened in an agonized smile
As He weeps with all His being, drenching us with His
   pity.
There can be no more food or rest for us until we have
   consoled that sorrow.
It is the sorrow of the Son of Man who has voluntarily
   tasted and redressed our sins.
It is the sorrow of the Son of God
At being unable to render up to His Father the hearts
   of all men through the sacrifice of His crucifixion.

Paul Claudel

Lyra Mystica
RAPTURE
German Contemporary

1

I feel a breath from other planets blowing
And pallid through the darkness wax the faces
That even now so kind and near were glowing.

Gray and more gray are tree and path and meadow
So that I scarcely know familiar places,
And thou, dear summoner of my pain, bright shadow,

Too far in deeper glow dissolved hast floated
To deem me, after this wild tumult's mazes,
To any earthly love or awe devoted.

Melted I am in music, circling, driven,
In boundless gratitude and nameless praises,
Will and desireless to the eternal given.

2

A tempest wafts me and I am elated,
In passionate madness of the women grieving
Who deep in dust their prayers have consecrated.

Then I behold the milky mists dislimning
A noble clearness filled with sunshine leaving
Wherein the farthest mountain peaks are swimming.

The ground beneath me, white and soft, is shaken...
By monstrous chasms I mount high and higher
Above the last cloud's silver edge to waken.

In seas of crystal radiance to dip under—
I am a spark of the eternal fire,
And of the eternal voice I am the thunder!

Stefan George

UXBRIDGE ROAD

English Contemporary

The Western Road goes streaming out to seek the cleanly wild,
It pours the city's dim desires towards the undefiled,
It sweeps betwixt the huddled homes about its eddies grown
To smear the little space between the city and the sown:
The torments of that seething tide who is there that can see?
There's one who walked with starry feet the western road by me!

He is the Drover of the soul; he leads the flock of men
All wistful on that weary track, and brings them back again.
The dreaming few, the slaving crew, the motley caste of life—
The wastrel and artificer, the harlot and the wife—
They may not rest, for ever pressed by one they cannot see:

The one who walked with starry feet the western road
    by me.

He drives them east, he drives them west, between the
    dark and light;
He pastures them in city pens, he leads them home at
    night.
The towery trams, the threaded trains, like shuttles to
    and fro
To weave the web of working days in ceaseless travel
    go.
How harsh the woof, how long the weft! Who shall
    the fabric see?
The one who walked with starry feet the western road
    by me!

Throughout the living joyful year at lifeless tasks to
    strive,
And scarcely at the end to save gentility alive;
The villa plot to sow and reap, to act the villa lie,
Beset by villa fears to live, midst villa dreams to die;
Ah, who can know the dreary woe? and who the
    spendour see?
The one who walked with starry feet the western road
    by me.

Behold! he lent me as we went the vision of the seer;
Behold! I saw the life of men, the life of God shine
    clear.
I saw the hidden Spirit's thrust; I saw the race fulfil
The spiral of its steep ascent, predestined of the Will.

Yet not unled, but shepherded by one they may not see—
The one who walked with starry feet the western road by me!

Evelyn Underhill

SUPERSENSUAL

English Contemporary

When first the busy, clumsy tongue is stilled,
Save that some childish, stammering words of love
The coming birth of man's true language prove:
    When, one and all,
The wistful, seeking senses are fulfillèd
With strange, austere delight:
    When eye and ear
Are inward turned to meet the flooding light,
The cadence of thy coming quick to hear:
    When on thy mystic flight,
Thou Swift yet Changeless, herald breezes bring
To scent the heart's swept cell
With incense from the thurible of spring,
The fragrance which the lily seeks in vain:
    When touch no more may tell
The verities of contact unexpressed,
And, deeply pressed,
To that surrender which is holiest pain,
We taste thy very rest—
    Ah, then we find
Folded about by kindly-nurturing night,

Instinct with silence sweetly musical,
The rapt communion of the mind with Mind.
  Then may the senses fall
  Vanquished indeed, nor dread
That this their dear defeat be counted sin:
  For every door of flesh shall lift its head,
Because the King of Life is entered in.

Evelyn Underhill

IMMANENCE

English Contemporary

I come in the little things,
Saith the Lord:
Not borne on morning wings
Of majesty, but I have set My Feet
Amidst the delicate and bladed wheat
That springs triumphant in the furrowed sod.
There do I dwell in weakness and in power;
Not broken or divided, saith our God!
In your strait garden plot I come to flower:
About your porch My Vine,
Meek, fruitful, doth entwine;
Waits at the threshold, Love's appointed hour.

I come in the little things,
Saith the Lord:
Yea, on the glancing wings
Of eager birds, the softly pattering feet
Of furred and gentle beasts, I come to meet
Your hard and wayward heart. In brown bright eyes

That peep from out the brake, I stand confest.
On every nest
Where feathery patience is content to brood
And leaves her pleasure for the high emprize
Of motherhood—
There doth my Godhead rest.

I come in the little things,
Saith the Lord:
My starry wings
I do forsake,
Love's highway of humility to take:
Meekly I fit my stature to your need.
In beggar's part
About your gates I shall not cease to plead—
As man to speak with man—
Till by such art
I shall achieve My Immemorial plan,
Pass the low lintel of the human heart.

Evelyn Underhill

CHRIST IN FLANDERS

English Contemporary

We had forgotten You, or very nearly—
You did not seem to touch us very nearly—
Of course we thought about You now and then;
Especially in any time of trouble—
We knew that You were good in time of trouble—
But we are very ordinary men.

And there were always other things to think of—
There's lots of things a man has got to think of—
His work, his home, his pleasure, and his wife;
And so we only thought of You on Sunday—
Sometimes, perhaps, not even on a Sunday—
Because there's always lots to fill one's life.

And, all the while, in street, or lane, or byway—
In country lane, in city street, or byway—
You walked among us, and we did not see.
Your feet were bleeding as You walked our pavements—
How did we miss Your footprints on our pavements?—
Can there be other folk as blind as we?

Now we remember; over here in Flanders—
(It isn't strange to think of You in Flanders)—
This hideous warfare seems to make things clear.
We never thought about You much in England;
But now that we are far away from England
We have no doubts, we know that You are here.

You helped us pass the jest along the trenches—
Where, in cold blood, we waited in the trenches—
You touched its ribaldry and made it fine.
You stood beside us in our path and weakness—
We're glad to think You understand our weakness—
Somehow it seems to help us not to whine.

We think about You kneeling in the Garden—
Ah! God! the agony of that dread Garden—

We know You prayed for us upon the Cross.
If anything could make us glad to bear it,
'Twould be the knowledge that You willed to bear it—
Pain—death—the uttermost of human loss.

Though we forgot You, You will not forget us—
We feel so sure that You will not forget us—
But stay with us until this dream is past.
And so we ask for courage, strength and pardon—
Especially, I think, we ask for pardon—
And that You'll stand beside us to the last.

L. W.

THE EVERY DAY OF LIFE

English Contemporary

Oh, sweet life's daily round;
Life's sacramental breaking of its bread,
Outpouring of its wine;
The wonted, the perpetual usual,
The oft-repeated joys—recurrences
Of dear, familiar duties; glad
Observances; intimacies; retreats,
Sudden and momentary, into unseen haunts
Come of the spirit's need; rewards
Unlooked for in a strange, sweet hour;
And, betwixt duty and duty, vision,
Quick, clear—a shaft of radiant light
Making all plain that erst was half-perceived.
'Twixt dawn and dark to venture gratefully
The shining, laden hours,

Peace hidden in each, and in the spirit peace—
How blessed! A life's praise indeed is praise;
Heaven's arches ring with men's melodious days.
                              Annie Sophia Waples

REDEMPTION

English Contemporary

All living creatures' pain,
The sufferings of the lowliest thing that creeps
Or flies a moment ere it sinks and sleeps,
Are too Redemption's tears and not in vain—
For nothing idly weeps.
Earth is through these fulfilling that it must
As in Christ's own eternal Passion chain,
And flowering from the dust.

The driven and the drudging ass
Crushed by the bondage of its bitter round,
Repeats the Gospel in that narrow bound;
God is reflected in the blade of grass,
And *there* is Calvary's ground.
O not an insect or on leaf or sod
But in its measure is a looking-glass,
And shows Salvation's God.

All thus are carrying on,
And do work out, the one Redemption's tale;
Each is a little Christ on hill or dale,
The hell where Mercy's light has never shone
Is with that Mercy pale,

And though flesh turns from agony they dread,
Even as they groan and travail it is gone—
Love riseth from the dead.

Frederick William Orde Ward

INVENTION

English Contemporary

I envy not the Lark his song divine,
Nor thee, O Maid, thy beauty's faultless mould.
Perhaps the chief felicity is mine,
Who hearken and behold.

The joy of the Artificer Unknown
Whose genius could devise the Lark and thee—
This, or a kindred rapture, let me own,
I covet ceaselessly!

Sir William Watson

IMMORTALITY

English Contemporary

I that had life ere I was born
Into this world of dark and light,
Waking as one who wakes at morn
From dreams of night,

I am as old as Heaven and Earth—
But sleep is death without decay,
And since each morn renews my birth,
I am no older than the day.

Old though my outward form appears,
Though it at last outworn shall lie,
This, that is servile to the years,
This is not I—

I, who outwear the form I take,
When I put off this garb of flesh,
Still in immortal youth shall wake
And somewhere clothe my life afresh.

A. St. John Adcock

THE FRINGE OF HEAVEN

English Contemporary

Now have I left the world and all its tears,
And high above the sunny cloud-banks fly,
Alone in all this vast and lonely sky—
This limpid space in which the myriad spheres
Go thundering on, whose song God only hears
High in his heavens. Ah! how small seem I,
And yet I know he hears my little cry
Down there among Man's cruel jests and sneers.

And I forget the grief which I have known,
And I forgive the mockers and their jest,
And in this mighty solitude alone,
I taste the joys of everlasting rest,
Which I shall know when I have passed away
To live in Heaven's never-fading day.

Paul R. Bewsher

Lyra Mystica

A COLLOQUY

English Contemporary

Why hurt so hard by little pricks,
By chasing cares so clouded over,
Heart of mine?
Holding what no storm can unfix,
Nor time corrupt, O tender lover,
Why repine?

In you so deep a fountain springs
Of faith and joy beyond all speech,
O happy heart!
How should these meanly thwarting things
Men do, the petty creeds they preach,
In you have part?

It is because, my heart replies,
There lives such Beauty to adore
Within, for ever—
Because I dwell in Paradise,
That the world's chafing is a sore,
A fret, a fever.

Were there no fountain welling strong
Within, no vision heavenly-rare
Before my eyes,
There'd be for me no world of wrong
Without, lamenting to compare
With Paradise.

Laurence Binyon

Lyra Mystica
OVER THE CITY
English Contemporary

    Over the great city
Where the wind rushes through the parks and gardens,
In the air, the high clouds brooding,
In the lines of street perspective, the lamps, the traffic,
The pavements and the innumerable feet upon them,
I *am:* make no mistake—do not be deluded,

Think not because I do not appear at first glance—because the centuries have gone by and there is no assured tidings of me that therefore I am not there.
Think not because all goes to its own way that therefore I do not go my own way through all.

The fixed bent of hurrying faces in the street—each turned towards its own light, seeing no other—yet I am the light towards which they all look.
The toil of so many hands towards so many multifarious ends, yet my hands know the touch and twining of them all.

All come to Me at last.
There is no love like Mine;
For all other love takes one and not another;
And other love is pain, but This is joy eternal.
                                Edward Carpenter

SO THIN A VEIL

English Contemporary

So thin a veil divides
Us from such joy, past words,
Walking in daily life—the business of the hour, each
    detail seen to;
Yet carried, rapt away, on what sweet floods of other
    Being:
Swift streams of music flowing, light far back through
    all Creation shining,
Loved faces looking—
Ah! from the true, the mortal self
So thin a veil divides!

Edward Carpenter

TURRIS EBURNEA

A Song of God's Fool the Mystic

English Contemporary

My soul is like a fencèd tower,
And holds a secret room:
I hide me in it many an hour
Amid its dim perfume:
I have my holy bloom,
The Rose of Heaven in flower:
I hold my inner bower
In strait and dreaming gloom,
My soul my fencèd tower.

The Rose of soil angelical,
That shines not over earth,
I have its buds and petals all,
Inestimable of worth,
Its blood-red calyces
Dyed with the wine of God,
Roots earthy from that sod,
Which dews in Syon bless,
And leaves of loveliness.

Its radiant heart unfolds to me,
Its starry soul is plain
In glimmering felicity,
Dyed deep with love and pain:
Any while my glad eyes gaze
Upon its petalled crown,
I hear a song come down
With thanksgiving and praise
Of the celestial town.

The moon, that torch Dianian,
Dreams ever paganly:
But I am only a simple man
In a white tower by the sea:
There comes a liturgy,
Even for a little span,
Great voices Christian,
Songs of my Lord to me,
To me, a simple man.

A tower of ivory it is
Beside a shoreless sea:

Lyra Mystica

I look out of my lattices
And the saints appear to me,
A singing company
From heaven's high palaces,
Chaunting their litanies:
White luting Cecily
Their first choir-maiden is.

The sea-wave crashes in my ears;
Again their viols cease:
I have been here for endless years,
And the room is full of peace.
Dim-sliding harmonies
And dreaming voice of seers
Come past all barriers:
With God I have no fears,
And round me roll His seas.

Wilfred Rowland Childe

UNDER A WILTSHIRE APPLE TREE

English Contemporary

Some folks as can afford,
So I've heard say,
Set up a sort of cross
Right in the garden way
To mind 'em of the Lord.

But I, when I do see
Thik apple tree
An' stoopin' limb

Lyra Mystica

All spread wi' moss,
I think of Him
And how He talks wi' me.
I think of God.

And how He trod
That garden long ago;
He walked, I reckon, to and fro
And then sat down
Upon the groun'
Or some low limb
What suited Him,
Such as you see
On many a tree,
And on thik very one
Where I at set o' sun
Do sit and talk wi' He.

And, mornings, too, I rise and come
An' sit down where the branch be low;
A bird do sing, a bee do hum,
The flowers in the border blow,
And all my heart's so glad and clear
As pools be when the sun do peer,
As pools a-laughing in the light
When mornin' air is swep' an' bright,
As pools what got all Heaven in sight,
So's my heart's cheer
When He be near.

He never pushed the garden door,
He left no foot mark on the floor;

I never heard 'Un stir nor tread
And yet His hand do bless my head,
And when 'tis time for work to start
I takes Him with me in my heart.
And when I die, pray God I see
At very last thik apple tree
An' stoopin' limb,
And think of Him
And all He been to me.

Anna de Bary

A PRAYER

English Contemporary

Lord, not for light in darkness do we pray,
Not that the veil be lifted from our eyes,
Nor that the slow ascension of our day
      Be otherwise.

Not for a clearer vision of the things
Whereof the fashioning shall make us great,
Not for remission of the peril and stings
      Of time and fate.

Not for a fuller knowledge of the end
Whereto we travel, bruised yet unafraid,
Nor that the little healing that we lend
      Shall be repaid.

Not these, O Lord. We would not break the bars
Thy wisdom sets about us; we shall climb

Lyra Mystica

Unfetter'd to the secrets of the stars
    In Thy good time.

We do not crave the high perception swift
When to refrain were well, and when fulfill,
Nor yet the understanding strong to sift
    The good from ill.

Not these, O Lord, for these Thou hast revealed.
We know the golden season when to reap
The heavy-fruited treasure of the field,
    The hour to sleep.

Not these. We know the hemlock from the rose,
The pure from stained, the noble from the base,
The tranquil light of holy truth that glows
    On Pity's face.

We know the paths wherein our feet should press,
Across our hearts are written Thy decrees:
Yet now, O Lord, be merciful to bless
    With more than these.

Grant us the will to fashion as we feel,
Grant us the strength to labor as we know,
Grant us the purpose, ribb'd and edg'd with steel,
    To strike the blow.

Knowledge we ask not,—knowledge Thou hast lent,
But, Lord, the will,—there lies our bitter need,
Give us to build above the deep intent
    The deed, the deed.

John Drinkwater

Lyra Mystica
ENOUGH

English Contemporary

"You toil in your attic the whole day long
For pitiful fire and bread,
But the joy in your heart slips out in a song"—
"I can see the sky," she said.

"Pain is your comrade and Want your guest,
They sit by your board and bed,
But you laugh at your work with a child's gay zest"—
"There are birds on the roof," she said.

Never a lover is yours to kiss,
Never a child to tend,
But your eyes are alight with a secret bliss"—
"God", she said, "is my Friend."

Rose Fyleman

I KNOW NOT

English Contemporary

I know not where
The glories of the heavenly city are,—
In dazzling sun, in moon, in quivering star,—
Yet faith can pierce the clouds and find thee there.

I know not how
To each one of thy children thou canst come,
And make within so many hearts thy home;
Yet, Lord, I feel thee dwelling with me now.

I know not when
Thy voice shall reach a soul—hereafter, now—
Yet unto thee shall every kingdom bow,
Whose voice shall quicken all the sons of men.

How souls shall hear
Thy call—in joy, in effort, failure, loss,
In pain, in patient bearing of a cross—
Thou shalt appoint, and unto each be dear.

The wonder strange
Who shall explain, how dreary waste of snow
Into a garden of fair hopes can grow,
Save thou, O Lord, who work'st the wondrous change?

What need to know?
When all my questioning is laid to rest—
A seeker spent, upon a tender breast—
Soothed by sweet voice like murmuring waters' flow.

Elizabeth Gibson

PLOUGHMAN AT THE PLOUGH

English Contemporary

He, behind the straight plough, stands
Stalwart; firm shafts in firm hands.

Naught he cares for wars and naught
For the fierce disease of thought.

Only for the winds, the sheer
Naked impulse of the year,

Only for the soil which stares
Clean into God's face, he cares.

In the stark might of his deed
There is more than art or creed;

In his wrist more strength is hid
Than the monstrous Pyramid;

Stauncher than stern Everest
Be the muscles of his breast;

Not the Atlantic sweeps a flood
Potent as the ploughman's blood.

He, his horse, his ploughshare, these
Are the only verities.

Dawn to dusk, with God he stands,
The earth poised on his broad hands.

Louis Golding

THE SECOND CRUCIFIXION

English Contemporary

Loud mockers in the roaring street
  Say Christ is crucified again:
Twice pierced His gospel-bearing feet,
  Twice broken His great heart in vain.

I hear and to myself I smile,
For Christ talks with me all the while.

Lyra Mystica

No angel now to roll the stone
  From off His unawaking sleep,
In vain shall Mary watch alone,
  In vain the soldiers vigil keep.

Yet while they deem my Lord is dead
My eyes are on His shining head.

Ah! never more shall Mary hear
  That voice exceeding sweet and low
Within the garden calling clear:
  Her Lord is gone, and she must go.

Yet all the while my Lord I meet
In every London lane and street.

Poor Lazarus shall wait in vain,
  And Bartimeus still go blind;
The healing hem shall ne'er again
  Be touched by suffering humankind.

Yet all the while I see them rest,
The poor and outcast, on His breast.

No more unto the stubborn heart
  With gentle knocking shall He plead,
No more the mystic pity start,
  For Christ twice dead is dead indeed.

So in the street I hear men say,
Yet Christ is with me all the day.

Richard Le Gallienne

Lyra Mystica

THOU CANST CHOOSE THE EASTERN CIRCLE

English Contemporary

Thou canst choose the Eastern Circle for thy part,
  And within its sacred precincts thou shalt rest;
  Thou shalt fold pale, slender hands upon thy breast,
Thou shalt fasten silent eyes upon thy heart.
If there steal within the languor of thine ark
  The thunder of the waters of the earth,
  The human, simple cries of pain and mirth,
The wails of little children in the dark,
Thou shalt contemplate thy Circle's radiant gleam,
  Thou shalt gather self and God more closely still:
  Let the piteous and the foolish moan at will,
So thou shelter in the sweetness of thy dream.

Thou canst bear a blood-stained Cross upon thy breast,
  Thou shalt stand upon the common, human sod,
  Thou shalt lift unswerving eyes unto thy God,
Thou shalt stretch torn, rugged hands to east and west.
Thou shalt call to every throne and every cell—
  Thou shalt gather all the answers of the earth,
  Thou shalt wring repose from weariness and dearth,
Thou shalt fathom the profundity of hell—
But thy height shall touch the height of God above,
  And thy breadth shall span the breadth of pole to pole,
  And thy depth shall sound the depth of every soul,
And thy heart the deep Gethsemane of Love.

Ruth Temple Lindsay

Lyra Mystica

From THE EVERLASTING MERCY

English Contemporary

O glory of the lighted mind.
How dead I'd been, how dumb, how blind.
The station brook, to my new eyes,
Was babbling out of Paradise,
The waters rushing from the rain
Were singing Christ has risen again.
I thought all earthly creatures knelt
From rapture of the joy I felt.
The narrow station-wall's brick ledge,
The wild hop withering in the hedge,
The lights in huntsman's upper storey
Were parts of an eternal glory,
Were God's eternal garden flowers.
I stood in bliss at this for hours.

O glory of the lighted soul.
The dawn came up on Bradlow Knoll,
The dawn with glittering on the grasses,
The dawn which pass and never passes.

"It's dawn," I said, "And chimney's smoking,
And all the blessed fields are soaking.
It's dawn, and there's an engine shunting;
And hounds, for huntsman's going hunting.
It's dawn, and I must wander north
Along the road Christ led me forth."

So up the road I wander slow
Past where the snowdrops used to grow

With celandines in early springs,
When rainbows were triumphant things
And dew so bright and flowers so glad,
Eternal joy to lass and lad.
And past the lovely brook I paced,
The brook whose source I never traced,
The brook, the one of two which rise
In my green dream in Paradise,
In wells where heavenly buckets clink
To give God's wandering thirsty drink,
By whose clean cots of carven stone
Where the clear water sings alone.
Then down, past that white-blossomed pond,
And past the chestnut trees beyond,
And past the bridge the fishers knew,
Where yellow flag flowers once grew,
Where we'd go gathering cops of clover,
In sunny June times long since over.
O clover-cops half white, half red,
O beauty from beyond the dead.
O blossom, key to earth and heaven,
O souls that Christ has new forgiven.

John Masefield

SONNETS

English Contemporary

In the full summer of that unearthly gleam
Which lights the spirit when the brain gives birth,
Of a perfected I, in happy hours,
Treading above the sea that trembles there,
A path through thickets of immortal flowers

That only grow where sorrows never were.
And, at a turn, of coming face to face
With Beauty's self, that Beauty I have sought
In women's hearts, in friends, in many a place,
In barren hours passed at grips with thought,
Beauty of woman, comrade, earth and sea,
Incarnate thought come face to face with me.

If I could come again to that dear place
Where once I came, where Beauty lived and moved,
Where, by the sea, I saw her face to face,
That soul alive by which the world has loved;
If, as I stood at gaze among the leaves,
She would appear again, as once before,
While the red herdsman gathered up his sheaves
And brimming waters trembled up the shore;
If, as I gazed, her Beauty that was dumb,
In that old time, before I learned to speak,
Would lean to me and revelation come,
Words to the lips and color to the cheek,
Joy with its searing-iron would burn me wise,
I should know all; all powers, all mysteries.

Men are made human by the mighty fall
The mighty passion led to, these remain.
The despot, at the last assaulted wall,
By long disaster is made man again.
The faithful fool who follows the torn flag,
The woman marching by the beaten man,
Make with their truth atonement for the brag,
And earn the pity for the too proud plan.

For in disaster, in the ruined will,
In the soiled shreds of what the brain conceived,
Something above the wreck is steady still,
Bright above all that cannot be retrieved,
Grandeur of soul, a touching of the star
That good days cover but by which we are.

John Masefield

THE SECRET GARDEN

English Contemporary

There is somewhere a Secret Garden, which none hath seen
In a place apart
But amid the bramble-bound world, the thicket, the screen
To the ununderstanding of heart.

There is somewhere a Secret Garden, where none hath been,
Where Night and Day
Commingle; where the sun and the starlight's sheen
Shines ever; where ever the moony fountains play
Lifting their lily-like throats, tossing their spray;
Where ever the rainbow meets red-hued serene;
Where the flame-dripping branches are brighter green;
Where the Gardener walks in His Garden unheard, unseen.

There is somewhere a Secret Garden: a door in a wall,
Opened: how shine within

Flower and fruit and torrent of blossoms which cannot fall!
Whence a jubilant din
Floats abroad of birds of scintillant feather
Swelling ecstatic throats in chorus together;
Or the cry of one, crying alone a sad and a silver call
Rings from the Secret Garden where none hath been.

There everlastingly the Gardener walks
Unseen, unmarked, unheard
Save as He goes
Humbled and hushed and happy falls each bird,
Each fountain throws
Gentlier upward, changing from blue to rose,
And there is seen
Glimpse of a radiant robe, a darkling mien
'Twixt the sheeted light and the sparkling drift where it blows.

There the flowers wait,
Abasing each noble head,
Till He draw nigh,
Then exalt their lovely faces to Him, rose little, rose great,
Flowers of pale and flowers of passionate dye,
Under His eye
Till softly He lift a hand and the hand is spread
Blessing their beauty, their peace with a word like a sigh.

There is somewhere a Secret Garden, where none hath been,

Or, glimpsed, lost to his grief,
There would I bide, though I ever abode unseen:
A snail or a stone under the lowliest leaf.

Robert Nichols

THE ORIGIN OF LIFE

English Contemporary

In the beginning slowly grope we back
Along the narrowing track,
Back to the deserts of the world's pale prime—
The mire, the clay, the slime.
And then, what then? Surely to something less:
Back—back to nothingness!

You dare not halt upon that dwindling way,
There is no gulf to stay
Your footsteps to the last. Go back you must
Far, far below the dust.
Descend, descend grade by dissolving grade;
We follow unafraid.

Dissolve, dissolve this moving world of men
Into thin air, and then,
O pioneers, O warriors of the light,
In that abysmal night
Will you have courage then to rise and tell
Earth of this miracle?

Will you have courage then to bow the head
And say, when all is said:

"Out of nothingness arose our thought,
This blank abysmal nought
Woke and brought forth that lighted city street,
Those towers, that armored fleet"?

When you have seen those vacant primal skies
Beyond the centuries:
Watched the pale mists across their darkness flow,
As in a lantern show,
Weaving by merest "chance" out of thin air
Pageants of praise and prayer;

Watched the great hills like clouds arise and set
And one named Olivet;
When you have seen as a shadow passing away
One child clasp hands and pray;
When you have seen emerge from that dark mire
One martyr, ringed with fire;

Or from that nothingness, by special grace,
One woman's love-lit face,
Will you have courage then to front that law,
From which our sophists draw
Their only right to flout one human creed,
That nothing can proceed—
Not even thought, not even love, from less
Than its own nothingness?

The law is yours, but dare you waive your pride
And kneel where you denied?
The law is yours; dare you rekindle, then,

One faith for faithless men
And say you found, on that dark road you trod,
In the beginning—God?

Alfred Noyes

THE PARADOX

"I Am That I Am"

English Contemporary

I

All that is broken shall be mended;
All that is lost shall be found;
  I will bind up every wound
When that which is begun shall be ended.
Not peace I brought among you but a sword
  To divide the night from the day,
When I sent my worlds forth in their battle-array
  To die and to live,
  To give and to receive,
    Saith the Lord.

. . . .

9

I am that I am; the Container of all things; kneel, lift
    up your hands
To the high Consummation of good and of evil which
    none understands;
The divine Paradox, the ineffable Word, in whose
    light the poor souls that ye trod

Underfoot as too vile for their fellows are at terrible
    union with God!
    Am I not over both evil and good,
  The righteous man and the shedder of blood?
    Shall I save or slay?
  I am neither the night nor the day,
    Saith the Lord.
Judge not, oh ye that are round my footstool, judge
    not, ere the hour be born
  That shall laugh you also to scorn.

10

  Ah, yet I say unto all that have sinned,
    East and West and South and North
    The wings of my measureless love go forth
To cover you all: they are free as the wings of the
    wind.

11

But one thing is needful; and ye shall be true
    To yourselves and the goal and the God that ye
        seek;
Yea, the day and the night shall requite it to you
    If ye love one another, if your love be not weak.

12

Since I sent out my worlds in their battle-array
    To die and to live,
    To give and to receive,

Lyra Mystica

Not peace, not peace, I have brought among you but
    a sword,
  To divide the night from the day,
    Saith the Lord;
Yet all that is broken shall be mended,
  And all that is lost shall be found,
  I will bind up every wound,
When that which is begun shall be ended.

Alfred Noyes

THE PILGRIM

English Contemporary

When I am recompensed and lean secure
Against the white cairn of the far hill-top,
Let me not then—I pray thee, King of Heaven—
Hinder that other pilgrim who ascends
By the same harsh, forbidding ways I climbed;
Maybe a worthier than I, and armed
With brighter buckler, more celestial blade,
Yet railing with parched tongue because he bleeds.

Remind me well when I shall say "Desist!"
When I cry out "Judgment belongs to Heaven!
Look to your feet in quiet, rouse not the Fiend;
You show a foraying spirit else, not God's,"
Blasting him from my fastness when he rails.

Remind me, King of Heaven, bestow thy power,
That I may lean to him with flickering brain,
Smite so upon the silence, lend him my mind,

Be to his arm a shadowy minister.
For thus, unseen, throughout Heaven's Universe,
Thought marches swift to action, glows to power,
And lives are nourished down dim distances.

Remind me, King of Heaven, that when I climbed,
Troubled and bleeding, up the mountain flanks
I still could see the sun, while ministers
Of tenderest kindness drifted to my side,
And Thy white manna fell ere flash of Day.
Remind my soul how each must climb his way.
Herbert E. Palmer

HE IS THE LONELY GREATNESS OF THE WORLD

English Contemporary

He is the lonely Greatness of the World—
        (His eyes are dim),
His power it is holds up the Cross
        That holds up Him.

He takes the sorrow of the threefold hour—
        (His eyelids close),
Round Him and round, the wind—His Spirit—where
        It listeth blows.

And so the wounded Greatness of the World
        In silence lies—
And death is shattered by the light from out
        Those darkened eyes.
Madeleine Caron Rock

BY THOSE HEIGHTS WE DARE TO DARE

English Contemporary

By those heights we dare to dare,
By the greatness of our prayer,
Ever growing, loftier reaching
To a royaller beseeching,
By the olden woes washed painless, white and stainless
 in the tears of bitter price,
By the strength of our assurance to endurance of the
 need of sacrifice,
Not by dreaming but by using,
Not by claiming but refusing,
Then shall dawn on eyes unsealing the revealing of a
 self that knows and grows,
And the stream of thy devotion find the ocean when
 its meaning overflows.
So take the thread that seemed so frail,
Have faith to hope and never quail,
For all the weary woes of earth
And all the hollowness of mirth,
Accept but this divine in man
Believe "I ought to" means "I can,"
And comprehend the perfect plan.

Lift thee o'er thy "here" and "now,"
Look beyond thine "I" and "thou,"
Every effort points the next,
And the way grows unperplexed
To wider ranges, larger scope,
All things possible to hope!

Till thou feel the breath of morning shadow scorning
    and on spirit wings unfurled
  Win the way to realms of wonder,
  Rolling starward with the thunder,
Flashing earthwards with the lightning to the brightening the dark edges of the world,
  Till the vastness shall absorb thee,
  And the light of lights enorb thee,
  And the wings on which thou soarest
  Thou wilt need to shade thine eyes,
  For the radiance thou adorest,
  For the nearness of sunrise;
  Then thy strongest strength shall be
  In thine own humility,
  Wrapt into the holiest holy
  In thy worship vastly aisled,
  Bend the knee and whisper lowly
  "Our Father" with the child!

Sir James Rennell Rodd

BY SEVERN'S BANKS

English Contemporary

One voice is from the homeland and the hills,
One voice is from the grey unrestful sea.
Here where at dusk the tingling silence thrills
I linger companied with memory;
  Hearing at times the boom
Of the far fog-ship sounding through the gloom;
At times the cry of nightbirds, and the sigh
Of slumberous waters nigh.

Lyra Mystica

O crying from the bygone and the known—
O murmur from the hidden and mystic deep
To which we pass alone
Through paths of sleep—
I cannot hear you clear;
Earth's dust is in mine ear,
The distant voice is muffled by the near.
I stand
As on a frontierland
Of things that with a step shall be revealed,
The hitherside of regions mist-concealed;
Yet still it seems
There must be instant waking from my dreams,
When it shall be
That the unheard is heard, the unseen appear—
The message that I almost hear,
The vision that I almost see.

Arthur L. Salmon

I LIVED MY DAYS APART

English Contemporary

I lived my days apart,
Dreaming fair songs for God,
By the glory of my heart
Covered and crowned and shod.

Now God is in the strife,
And I must seek Him there,
Where death outnumbers life,
And fury smites the air.

Lyra Mystica

I walk the secret way
With anger in my brain.
O music through my clay,
When will you sound again?

Siegfried Sassoon

IT WERE NOT HARD, WE THINK, TO SERVE HIM

English Contemporary

It were not hard, we think, to serve Him,
  If we could only see;
If He would stand with that gaze intense,
Burning into our bodily sense;
If we might look on that face most tender,
The brow where the scars are burned to splendour,
Might catch the light of His smile so sweet,
And find the marks in His hands and feet,
  How loyal we should be!
It were not hard, we think, to serve Him,
  If we could only see!

It were not hard, he says, to see Him,
  If we would only serve,
He that doeth the Will of Heaven,
To him shall knowledge and sight be given!
While for His presence we sit repining,
Never to see His countenance shining.
They who toil where His reapers be,
The glory of His smile may always see,
  And their faith will never swerve,

Lyra Mystica

It were not hard, he says, to see Him,
   If we would only serve.

Margaret Seebach

ON CHRISTMAS EVE

English Contemporary

Earth a transition underwent
   Into an awed astonishment,
Pools, hills, and fields their deep communion made;
   Hesperus flying high and bright
   Sang through the dusk, Hail, holy Night!
And trees with all their boughs reached up and prayed.

Through the torn veil of time and space
   I walked in Wychwood face to face
With starlit Bethlehem, and turning thence,
   By Charlbury to a barn I came
   Shot through its chinks with rosy flame,
While in my heart burned myrrh and frankincense.

W. Force Stead

THE VOICE OF GOD

English Contemporary

I bent unto the ground
And I heard the quiet sound
Which the grasses make when they
Come up laughing from the clay.

"We are the voice of God," they said:
Thereupon I bent my head

Down again that I might see
If they truly spoke to me.

But around me everywhere
Grass and tree and mountain were
Thundering in a mighty glee,
"We are the voice of deity."

And I leapt from where I lay,
I danced upon the laughing clay,
And to the rock that sang beside,
"We are the voice of God," I cried.

James Stephens

O THOU, IN WHOM WE LIVE AND BREATHE

British Contemporary

O thou, in whom we live and breathe,
Who enlightenest our souls with the radiance of thy glory
Who art in thyself the perfect reward of all toil, all sacrifice, all agony,
Holy and almighty, yet infinitely close and dear,
Heart of our hearts, soul of our souls
Self of our true selves.

Thou, who by the inward and secret workings of thy spirit
Urgest us for ever upward that we may find ourselves in thee:
Thou, who leavest us not desolate,

But in loneliness and in grief art very nigh unto us;
Thou, who redeemest our feeble and froward wills,
Bending them by thy holy inward influence
That they may of their own accord desire what thou desirest
Work for thy ends, and love with thy love:

O thou, our God, lover of our souls,
Ineffable reward of all labour,
Unspeakable joy shining through tears,—
Be with us and save us this day,
That we may bear company with thee,
Put on thee, wear thee in our mortal bodies,
Gain to-day the substance of eternal life in thee.

J. S. Hoyland

FATHER, WE THANK THEE

British Contemporary

Father,
We thank thee—even whilst we suffer—for the tragedy of thy world,
For the conflict of lower good with higher.

We thank thee for the setting of the battle,
For the toil and weariness and pain
Whereon is built up the only true good—
The character which is both human and divine,
Wherein love and faithfulness, cheerful self-sacrifice, and steady devotion to a noble cause
Combine perfectly to show forth thy nature to men.

We thank thee for the relics of the beast within us,
And for all that deludes us with a false semblance of satisfaction,
Because these things are foes to be fought and conquered,
And only upon victory over them can be built purity and self-mastery.

We thank thee for sorrow and loneliness,
For all that rends from us sweet and gracious human companionship,
Because without victory over these foes there cannot be eternal love,
Nor a full experience of thy divine compassion.

We thank thee for pain and poverty and loss,
For all that robs us of what we hold so dear,
Because without these we cannot gain thyself.
Nor find forgetfulness of ourselves in service of thy little ones.

We thank thee, our God, for all the tragedy of thy world,
For the conflict of lower good with higher,
For the foes which are but the raw material of our victory,
Nay, of thy victory in us.

J. S. Hoyland

Lyra Mystica

O THOU WHO LOVEST WITH DIVINE PASSION

British Contemporary

O thou who lovest, with divine passion,
These thy poor creatures, whom thou hast made,
With whom, in whom, thou for ever yearnest
To endure, to triumph, and to die,
Teach us to-day how we should love thee.

Show us how adorable thou art,
Show us thy beauty, thy sufficiency, thy glory;
Reveal unto us, who are so lightly led away by things of
    time and sense,
Thine own eternal loveliness: that loveliness which now
    and through eternity
Shall satisfy our souls with divine contentment that can
    never fade nor fail.

Teach us to love thee, O our God—our Friend who art
    closer than child or wife,—
Teach us to love thee, our Lover, who art nearer and
    sweeter than any earthly love,—
Teach us to love thee, in whom all earthly love is con-
    summated and perfected:
Receive us into thy divine communion, which is the
    life of the Universe
And the exceeding sweet solace of our poor human
    hearts.

J. S. Hoyland

Lyra Mystica

IN THIS, O NATURE, YIELD

British Contemporary

In this, O nature, yield, I pray, to me.
  I pace and pace, and think and think, and take
The fevered hands, and note down all I see
  That some dim distant light may haply break.

The painful faces ask, can we not cure?
  We answer, No, not yet; we seek the laws.
O God reveal through all this thing obscure,
  The unseen, unknown, million-murdering cause.

Sir Ronald Ross

REPLY

British Contemporary

I

This day relenting God
  Hath placed within my hand
A wondrous thing; and God
  Be praised. At his command,

Seeking His secret deeds
  With tears and toiling breath,
I find thy cunning seeds,
  O million-murdering Death.

I know this little thing
  A myriad men will save.

O Death, where is thy sting?
  Thy victory, O Grave?

2

Before Thy feet I fall,
  Lord, who made high my fate;
For in the mighty small
  Thou showedst the mighty great.

Henceforth I will resound
  But praises unto Thee;
Tho' I was beat and bound,
  Thou gavest me victory.

Tho' in these depths of night
  Deep-dungeon'd I was hurl'd,
Thou sentest me a light
  Wherewith to mend the world.

O Exile, while thine eyes
  Were weary with the night
Thou weepst; now arise
  And bless the Lord of Light.

Hereafter let the lyre
  Be bondsman to His name;
His thunder and His fire
  Will fill thy lips with flame.

He is the Lord of Light;
  He is the Thing That Is;

He sends the seeing sight;
  And the right mind is His.

Sir Ronald Ross

THE IMMORTAL HOUR

Scottish Contemporary

Still as the great waters lying in the West,
  So is my spirit still.
I lay my folded hands within Thy breast,
  My will within Thy will.
O Fortune, idle pedlar, pass me by.
O Death, keep far from me who cannot die.
The passion-flowers are lacing o'er the sill
Of my low door.—As dews their sweetness fill,
  So do I rest in Thee.
It is mine hour. Let none set foot therein.
It is mine hour unflawed of pain or sin.
'Tis laid and steeped in silence, till it be
A solemn dazzling crystal, to outlast
And storm the eyes of poets when long-past
Is all the changing dream of Thee and Me.

Rachel Annand Taylor

IN SUMMER FIELDS

Scottish Contemporary

Sometimes, as in the summer fields
I walk abroad, there comes to me
So strange a sense of mystery,

Lyra Mystica

My heart stands still, my feet must stay,
I am in such strange company.

I look on high—the vasty deep
Of blue outreaches all my mind;
And yet I think beyond to find
Something more vast—and at my feet
The little bryony is twined.

Clouds sailing as to God go by,
Earth, sun, and stars rushing on;
And faster than swift time, more strong
Than rushing of the worlds, I feel
A something Is, of name unknown.

And turning suddenly away,
Grown sick and dizzy with the sense
Of power, and mine own impotence,
I see the gentle cattle feed
In dumb unthinking innocence.

The great Unknown above; below,
The cawing rooks, the milking-shed;
God's awful silence overhead;
Below, the muddy pool, the path
The thirsty herds of cattle tread.

Sometimes, as in the summer fields
I walk abroad, there comes to me
So wild a sense of mystery,
My senses reel, my reason fails,
I am in such strange company.

Lyra Mystica

Yet somewhere, dimly, I can feel
The wild confusion dwells in me,
And I, in no strange company,
Am the lost link 'twixt Him and these,
And touch Him through the mystery.

Christina Catherine Fraser-Tytler

PERFECTION

Irish Contemporary

Who seeks perfection in the art
Of driving well an ass and cart,
Or painting mountains in a mist,
Seeks God although an Atheist.

Francis Carlin

THE ROSE OF THE WORLD

Irish Contemporary

Who dreamed that beauty passes like a dream?
  For these red lips, with all their mournful pride,
  Mournful that no new wonder may betide,
Troy passed away in one high funeral gleam,
  And Usna's children died.

We and the labouring world are passing by:
  Amid men's souls, that waver and give place,
  Like the pale waters in their wintry race,
Under the passing stars, frame of the sky,
  Lives on this lonely face.

Lyra Mystica

Bow down, archangels, in your dim abode:
    Before you were, or any hearts to beat,
    Weary and kind, one lingered by His seat;
He made the world to be a grassy road
    Before her wandering feet.

William Butler Yeats

THE QUEST

Irish Contemporary

For years I sought the Many in the One,
I thought to find lost waves and broken rays,
The rainbow's faded colours in the sun—
The dawns and twilights of forgotten days.

But now I seek the One in every form,
Scorning no vision that a dewdrop holds,
The gentle Light that shines behind the storm,
The Dream that many a twilight hour enfolds.

Eva Gore-Booth

BY THE MARGIN OF THE GREAT DEEP

Irish Contemporary

When the breath of twilight blows to flame the misty skies,
All its vaporous sapphire, violet glow and silver gleam
With their magic flood me through the gateway of the eyes;
    I am one with the twilight's dream.

When the trees and skies and fields are one in dusky
  mood,
Every heart of man is rapt within the mother's breast:
Full of peace and sleep and dreams in the vasty
  quietude,
   I am one with their hearts at rest.

From our immemorial joys of hearth and home and
  love
Strayed away along the margin of the unknown tide,
All its reach of soundless calm can thrill me far above
   Word or touch from the lips beside.

Aye, and deep and deep and deeper let me drink and
  draw
From the olden fountain more than light or peace or
  dream,
Such primeval being as o'erfills the heart with awe,
   Growing one with its silent stream.
George William Russell (A. E.)

THE DIVINE VISION

Irish Contemporary

This mood hath known all beauty, for it sees
O'erwhelmèd majesties
In these pale forms, and kingly crowns of gold
On brows no longer bold,
And through the shadowy terrors of their hell
The love for which they fell,
And how desire which cast them in the deep

Called God too from His sleep.
Oh, Pity, only seer, who looking through
A heart melted like dew,
Seest the long perished in the present thus,
For ever dwell in us.
Whatever time thy golden eyelids ope
They travel to a hope;
Not only backward from these low degrees
To starry dynasties,
But, looking far where now the silence owns
And rules from empty thrones,
Thou seest the enchanted hills of heaven burn
For joy at our return.
Thy tender kiss hath memory we are kings
For all our wanderings.
Thy shining eyes already see the after
In hidden light and laughter.

George William Russell (A. E.)

A VISION OF BEAUTY

Irish Contemporary

Where we sat at dawn together, while the star-rich heavens shifted,
We were weaving dreams in silence, suddenly the veil was lifted.
By a hand of fire awakened, in a moment caught and led
Upward to the heaven of heavens—through the star-mists overhead

Flare and flaunt the monstrous highlands; on the sapphire coast of night
Fall the ghostly froth and fringes of the ocean of the light.
Many coloured shine the vapors: to the moon-eye far away
'Tis the fairy ring of twilight, mid the spheres of night and day,
Girdling with a rainbow cincture round the planet where we go,
We and it together fleeting, poised upon the pearly glow;
We and it and all together flashing through the starry spaces
In a tempest dream of beauty lighting up the face of faces.
Half our eyes behold the glory; half within the spirit's glow
Echoes of the noiseless revels and the will of Beauty go.
By a hand of fire uplifted—to her star-strewn palace brought,
To the mystic heart of beauty and the secret of her thought:
Here of yore the ancient Mother in the fire mists sank to rest,
And she built her dreams about her, rayed from out her burning breast:
Here the wild will woke within her lighting up her flying dreams,
Round and round the planets whirling break in woods and flowers and streams,

And the winds are shaken from them as the leaves
    from off the rose,
And the feet of earth go dancing in the way that
    beauty goes,
And the souls of earth are kindled by the incense of
    her breath
As her light alternate lures them through the gates of
    birth and death.
O'er the fields of space together following her flying
    traces,
In a radiant tumult thronging, suns and stars and
    myriad races
Mount the spirit spires of beauty, reaching onward to
    the day
When the Shepherd of the Ages draws his misty hordes
    away
Through the glimmering deep to silence, and within
    the awful fold
Life and joy and love forever vanish as a tale is told,
Lost within the Mother's being. So the vision flamed
    and fled,
And before the glory fallen every other dream lay
    dead.

George William Russell (A. E.)

THE TWILIGHT OF EARTH

Irish Contemporary

The wonder of the world is o'er:
    The magic from the sea is gone:

There is no unimagined shore,
   No islet yet to venture on.
The Sacred Hazel's blooms are shed,
The Nuts of Knowledge harvested.

Oh, what is worth this lore of age
   If time shall never bring us back
Our battle with the gods to wage
   Reeling along the starry track.
The battle rapture here goes by
In warring upon things that die.

Let the tale of him whose love
   Was sighed between white Deirdre's breasts,
It will not lift the heart above
   The sodden clay on which it rests.
Love once had power the gods to bring
All rapt on its wild wandering.

We shiver in the falling dew,
   And seek a shelter from the storm:
When man these elder brothers knew
   He found the mother nature warm,
A hearth fire blazing through it all,
A home without a circling wall.

We dwindle down beneath the skies,
   And from ourselves we pass away:
The paradise of memories
   Grows ever fainter day by day.
The shepherd stars have shrunk within,
The world's great night will soon begin.

Lyra Mystica

Will no one, ere it is too late,
   Ere fades the last memorial gleam,
Recall for us our earlier state?
   For nothing but so vast a dream
That it would scale the steeps of air
Could rouse us from so vast despair.

The power is ours to make or mar
   Our fate as on the earliest morn,
The Darkness and the Radiance are
   Creatures within the spirit born.
Yet, bathed in gloom too long, we might
Forget how we imagined light.

Not yet are fixed the prison bars;
   The hidden light and spirit owns
If blown to flame would dim the stars
   And they who rule them from their thrones:
And the round sceptred spirits thence
Would bow to pay us reverence.

Oh, while the glory sinks within
   Let us not wait on earth behind,
But follow where it flies, and win
   The glow again, and we may find
Beyond the Gateways of the Day
Dominion and ancestral sway.

George William Russell (A. E.)

Lyra Mystica
THE CITY
Irish Contemporary

*"Full of Zeus the cities: full of Zeus the harbours:
full of Zeus are all the ways of men."*

What domination of what darkness dies this hour,
And through what new, rejoicing, winged, ethereal power
O'erthrown, the cells opened, the heart released from fear?
Gay twilight and grave twilight pass. The stars appear
O'er the prodigious, smouldering, dusky, city flare.
The hanging gardens of Babylon were not more fair
Than these blue flickering glades, where childhood in its glee
Re-echoes with fresh voice the heaven-lit ecstasy.
Yon girl whirls like an eastern dervish. Her dance is
No less a god-intoxicated dance than his,
Though all unknowing the arcane fire that lights her feet,
What motions of what starry tribes her limbs repeat.
I, too, firesmitten, cannot linger: I know there lies
Open somewhere this hour a gate to Paradise,
Its blazing battlements with watchers thronged, O where?
I know not, but my flame-winged feet shall lead me there.
O, hurry, hurry, unknown shepherd of desires,
And with thy flock of bright imperishable fires
Pen me within the starry fold, ere the night falls

Lyra Mystica

And I am left alone below immutable walls.
Or am I there already, and is it Paradise
To look on mortal things with an immortal's eyes?
Above the misty brilliance the streets assume
A night-dilated blue magnificence of gloom
Like many-templed Ninevah, tower beyond tower,
Am I hurried on in this immortal hour.
Mine eyes beget new majesties: my spirit greets
The trams, the high-built glittering galleons of the streets
That float through twilight rivers from galaxies of light.
Nay, in the Fount of Days they rise, they take their flight,
And wend to the great deep, the Holy Sepulchre.
Those dark misshapen folk to be made lovely there
Hurry with me, not all ignoble as we seem,
Lured by some inexpressible and gorgeous dream.
The earth melts in my blood. The air that I inhale
Is like enchanted wine poured from the Holy Grail.
What was that glimmer then? Was it the flash of wings
As through the blinded mart rode on the King of Kings?
O stay, departing glory, stay with us but a day,
And burning seraphim shall leap from out our clay,
And plumed and crested hosts shall shine where men have been,
Heaven hold no lordlier court than earth at College Green.
Ah, no, the wizardy is over; the magic flame
That might have melted all in beauty fades as it came.

The stars are far and faint and strange. The night
    draws down.
Exiled from light, forlorn, I walk in Dublin Town.
Yet had I might to lift the veil, the will to dare,
The fiery rushing chariots of the Lord are there,
The whirlwind path, the blazing gates, the trumpets
    blown,
The halls of heaven, the majesty of throne by throne,
Enraptured faces, hands uplifted, welcome sung
By the thronged gods, tall, golden-coloured, joyful,
    young.

George William Russell (A. E.)

O LORD, WHERE SHALL I FIND THEE?

Jewish-American Contemporary

O Lord, where shall I find Thee?
   Hid is Thy lofty place;
And where shall I not find Thee,
   Whose glory fills all Space?

Who formed the world, abideth
   Within man's soul alway;
Refuge to them that seek Him,
   Ransom for them that stray.

Oh, how shall mortals praise Thee,
   When angels strive in vain—
Or build for Thee a dwelling,
   Whom worlds cannot contain?

Lyra Mystica

Yet when they bow in worship
  Before Thy throne, most high,
Closer than flesh or spirit,
  They feel Thy presence nigh.

Then they, with lips exulting,
  Bear witness Thou art One—
That Thou art their Creator,
  Ruler and God alone.

Who shall not yield Thee reverence,
  That holdest the world in thrall?
Who shall not seek Thy mercy,
  That feeds and succors all?

Longing to draw anear Thee,
  With all my heart I pray;
Then going forth to seek Thee,
  Thou meetst me on the way!

I find Thee in the marvels
  Of Thy creative might,
In visions in Thy temple,
  In dreams that bless the night.

Who saith he hath not seen Thee,
  Thy heavens refute his word;
Their hosts declare Thy glory,
  Though never voice be heard.

Dare mortal think such wonder?
  And yet, believe I must,

That God, the Uncreated,
   Dwells in this frame of dust.

That Thou, transcendent, holy,
   Joyest in Thy creatures' praise,
And comest where men are gathered
   To glorify Thy ways.

And where celestial beings
   Adore Thee, as they stand
Upon the heights eternal—
   And Thou, above their band,

Hast set Thy throne of Glory—
   Thou hearest when they call;
They sing Thine infinite wonders,
   And Thou upholdest all.

Solomon Solis-Cohen

FOR I KNOW THAT MY REDEEMER LIVETH

Jewish-American Contemporary

Shall the mole, in his night underground, call the beasts from the day-glare to flee?
Shall the owl charge the birds: "I am wise. Come, dwell in the shadows with me"?
Shall a man bind his eyes and proclaim: "It is vain that men weary to see"?

Let him walk in the gloom, whoso will; peace be with him. But whence is his right
To declare that the world is in darkness, because he has turned from the light,

Or to seek to o'ershadow my day with the pall of his self-chosen night?

I have listened, like David's great son, to the voice of the beast and the bird;
To the voice of the trees and the grass; yea, a voice from the stones I have heard;
And the sun and the moon and the stars in their courses, re-echo the word.

And one word speak the bird and the beast, and the hyssop that springs in the wall,
And the cedar that lifts its proud head upon Lebanon, stately and tall,
And the rocks, and the sea and the stars; and "Know" is the message of all.

For the answer hath ever been nigh unto him who would question and learn—
How to bring the stars near to his gaze; in what orbits the planets must turn;
Why the apple must fall from the bough; what the fuel that sunfires burn.

Whence came life? In the rocks is it writ, and no Finger hath graven it there?
Whence came light? Did its motions arise without impulse? Will Science declare,
That the Law ruling all hath upsprung from NoMind, that abideth NoWhere?

"Yea, I know!" cried the true man of old; and whoso'er wills it, may know.

Lyra Mystica

"My Redeemer—He liveth!" I seek for a sign of His
    presence, and lo,
As He spake to the light, and it was, so He speaks to
    my soul—and I know!

Solomon Solis-Cohen

SONNET

Spanish-American Contemporary

O world, thou choosest not the better part!
It is not wisdom to be only wise,
And on the inward vision close the eyes,
But it is wisdom to believe the heart.
Columbus found a world, and had no chart,
Save one that faith deciphered in the skies;
To trust the soul's invincible surmise
Was all his science and his only art.
Our knowledge is a torch of smoky pine
That lights the pathway but one step ahead
Across a void of mystery and dread.
Bid, then, the tender light of faith to shine
By which alone the mortal heart is led
Unto the thinking of the thought divine.

George Santayana

THE GUEST

American Contemporary

I

In Jewry had I dwelt of old,
    The Master would have supped with me,

Lyra Mystica

And I His handmaid would have been,
Like Martha—she of Bethany;
For Him the table had been set,
For Him the upper room prepared,
And all my costliest oil and nard
With Him had willingly been shared.

2

Then, when He left my cottage door
And to the Temple made His way,
I with the children would have strewn
Palm-branches in His path that day;
My voice with theirs had been upraised
To lift the anthem clear and sweet,
To David's Son and David's Lord,
Along the crowded city street.

3

And when, throughout the starry night,
Amidst the olive trees He wept,
Not far away would I have prayed,
And with Him would have vigil kept.
And when the dolorous path He trod
Up the steep road to Calvary,
Like Simon, at His side, would I
Have borne for Him the heavy tree.

4

Shamefast, heart-broken, I had stood
Beneath the Cross whereon He died,

The while the sun looked down aghast
To see its Maker crucified;
And hope within my heart had sprung
To see, like Aaron's rod of old,
Beside the rood on which He hung,
The flower of penitence unfold.

5

Perhaps the honor had been mine
To give that precious body room
For sepulture, and to have been
Among the earliest at the tomb,
When, bearing spices rare, they came,
Ere yet the shadowy night had fled,
And found, amazed, the broken seal,
And saw, where they had laid Him dead,

6

Angelic guards, in glistening white,
And heard with joy their message sweet;
Then, in the glowing Easter light,
I would have fallen at His feet
With Mary, whom He called by name,
Or journeyed with the two when He
They loved and mourned as lost drew near,
And made it plain that Calvary—
The bloody sweat—the cruel scourge—
The bitter cross on which He died—
Were but the lot the prophet saw
For Him who must be glorified.

. . . .

7

This to my heart I oft had said,
And once again thus ran my thoughts:
Had I been there in Jesus' day,
How willingly I would have wrought
For Him, as did the faithful few,
How glad to seize the chance to prove
Myself a follower of the Lord,
With all my goods and all my love.

. . . .

8

'Twas Easter eve; the first brave flowers
Of spring were budding 'neath the snow;
There lingered yet the wintry chill
That northern climes in April know.
I sat beside my cozy fire,
The flames cast shadows on the wall,
When suddenly—I know not how—
I seemed to hear my Master call:—

9

He called my name; I thrilled to think
The risen Christ had come to be
My Guest. In accents low He said,
"And wouldst thou minister to me?"
"Yea, Lord, Thou knowest that I would,
If Thou wilt only show me how."
Tender, and low, and lover-like,
He answered me: "I need thee now;

10

"Lift up thine eyes—the world is sad—
Its cup of sorrow overflows;
Today is my Gethsemane,
The nations' sorrows are my woes.
I weep alone where widowhood
And orphanage lift up their cry;
I grope in darkness, being blind;
That lonely prisoner is—I;

11

"I toss in speechless agony,
Or moan upon my narrow bed;
I weep beside my ruined home;
I perish for a crust of bread.
Think not what once thou wouldst have done
Hadst thou been there in Galilee,—
Where any child of earth has need,
There thou canst minister to Me."

12

While thus He spoke, my little room
Grew strangely large and strangely bright,
And when He vanished, a perfume,
Like Easter lilies, filled the night.
The Light has vanished; the perfume
Is mingled with the breath of spring;
But life can never be the same,

And service is a nobler thing.
I see the world with open eyes—
The world of need, the world of sin,—
And when the voice of duty calls,
 I bid the Lord Christ enter in.

Augusta Albertson

PRONOUNS

American Contemporary

The Lord said,
"Say, 'We'";
But I shook my head,
Hid my hands tight behind my back and said,
Stubbornly,
"I."

The Lord said,
"Say, 'We'";
But I looked upon them, grimy and all awry.
Myself in all those twisted shapes? Ah no!
Distastefully I turned my head away,
Persisting,
"They."

The Lord said,
"Say, 'We'";
And I,
At last,
Richer by a hoard
Of years,

And tears,
Looked in their eyes and found the heavy word
That bent my neck and bowed my head:
Like a shamed school-boy then I mumbled low,
"We,
Lord."

Karle Wilson Baker

THE FROZEN GRAIL

American Contemporary

Why sing the legends of the Holy Grail,
The dead Crusaders of the Sepulchre,
While these men live? Are the great bards all dumb?
Here is a vision to shake the blood of Song,
And make Fame's watchman tremble at his post.
What shall prevail against the spirit of man,
When cold, the lean and snarling wolf of hunger,
The threatening spear of ice-mailed Solitude,
Silence, and Space, and ghostly footed Fear
Prevail not? Dante, in his frozen hell,
Shivering, endured no bleakness like the void
These men have warmed with their own flaming will,
And peopled with their dreams. The wind from fierce
Arcturus in their faces, at their backs
The whip of the world's doubt, and in their souls
Courage to die—if death shall be the price
Of that cold cup that shall assuage their thirst,
They climb, and fall, and stagger toward the goal.
They lay themselves the road whereby they travel,

Lyra Mystica

And sue God for a franchise. Does He watch
Behind the lattice of the boreal lights?
In that Grail-chapel of their stern-vowed quest,
Ninety of God's long paces toward the North,
Will they behold the splendor of His face?
To conquer the world must man renounce the world?
These have renounced it. Had ye only faith
Ye might move mountains, said the Nazarene.
Why, these have faith to move the zones of man
Out to the point where All and Nothing meet.
They catch the bit of Death between their teeth
In one wild dash to trample the unknown
And leap the gates of knowledge. They have dared.

Elsa Barker

THE FALCONER OF GOD

American Contemporary

I flung my soul to the air like a falcon flying.
I said, "Wait on, wait on, while I ride below!
   I shall start a heron soon
   In the marsh beneath the moon—
A strange white heron rising with silver on its wings,
    Rising and crying
   Wordless, wondrous things;
   The secret of the stars, of the world's heart-strings
    The answer to their woe.
Then stoop thou upon him, and grip, and hold him so!"

My wild soul waited on as falcons hover.
I beat the reedy fens as I trampled past.

I heard the mournful loon
In the marsh beneath the moon.
And then, with feathery thunder, the bird of my desire
    Broke from the cover
  Flashing silver fire.
  High up among the stars I saw his pinions spire.
    The pale clouds gazed aghast
As my falcon stooped upon him, and gript and held
    him fast.

My soul dropped through the air—with heavenly
    plunder?—
Gripping the dazzling bird my dreaming knew?
  Nay! but a piteous freight,
  A dark and heavy weight
Despoiled of silver plumage, its voice forever stilled,—
    All of the wonder
  Gone that ever filled
  Its guise with glory. O bird that I have killed,
    How brilliantly you flew
Across my rapturous vision when first I dreamed of you!

Yet I fling my soul on high with new endeavor,
And I ride the world below with a joyful mind.
  I shall start a heron soon
  In the marsh beneath the moon—
A wondrous silver heron its inner darkness fledges!
    I beat forever
  The fens and the sedges.

The pledge is still the same—for all disastrous pledges,
　All hopes resigned!
My soul still flies above me for the quarry it shall find!

William Rose Benét

GOD

American Contemporary

Day and night I wander widely through the wilderness of thought,
Catching dainty things of fancy most reluctant to be caught,
Shining tangles leading nowhere presently unravel,
Tread strange paths of meditation very intricate to travel.

Gleaming bits of quaint desire tempt my steps beyond the decent,
I confound old solid glory with publicity too recent.
But my one unchanged obsession, wheresoe'er my feet have trod,
Is a keen, enormous, haunting, never-sated thirst for God.

Gamaliel Bradford

BEFORE THE DAWN

American Contemporary

Thou, for whom words have exhausted their sweetness—
Thou, the All-End of all human desire—

Thou, in whose Presence the ages are hourless,
        Gather me nigher!

Husht in the chambers where Reason lies sleeping,
Ere the Day claim us, to which we are told,—
Wrapped in the veil of Thy slumbering Beauty,
        Fold me, oh fold!

Fill me afresh with the wonder of wakening—
Draw me again with Thy splendour and might—
Open my lids but a moment, and grant me
        Sight of Thy sight!

Out of the furthest high Throne of Thy Dwelling,
A motionless Flame on the Bosom of Thought,
Deign to uncover Thyself, O Eternal
        Seeker and Sought!

Pure in the Body that offers Thee homage,
Blest in the Thought that embraces Thee far,
Next to Thy secret and innermost Breathing
        Thy worshippers are!

Forth to the Day that I know not awaiting,
Out to the highway Thy glory hath trod,
Glad as a child, and as passionless, fearless,
        Lead me, O God!

Alice Mary Buckton

Lyra Mystica

A PAGAN'S PRAYER

American Contemporary

You that uphold the world,
Uphold me.
You that light the sun,
Make me see,
Bear with me my sorrow:
Help me meet the morrow,
Patiently.

O'er the road we may know not
To end we must fear not,
Guide us, O mighty One!
March with us, heroes!

Alice Brown

THE HILL-BORN

American Contemporary

You who are born of the hills,
Hill-bred, lover of hills,
Though the world may not treat you aright,
Though your soul be aweary with ills:
This will you know above other men,
In the hills you will find your peace again.

You who were nursed on the heights,
Hill-bred, lover of skies,
Though your love and your hope and your heart,
Though your trust be hurt till it dies:

This will you know above other men,
In the hills you will find your faith again.

You who are brave from the winds,
Hill-bred, lover of winds,
Though the God whom you know seems dim,
Seems lost in a mist that blinds:
This will you know above other men,
In the hills you will find your God again.

Maxwell Struthers Burt

GOD'S GARDEN

American Contemporary

The years are flowers and bloom within
    Eternity's wide garden;
The rose for joy, the thorn for sin,
    The gardener, God, to pardon
All wilding growths, to prune, reclaim,
    And make them rose-like in His name.

Richard Eugene Burton

A LITTLE HILL AMONG NEW HAMPSHIRE HILLS

American Contemporary

A little hill among New Hampshire hills
Touches more stars than any height I know.
For there the whole earth—like a single being—fills
And expands with heaven.
It is the hill where Celia used to go

To watch Monadnock and the miles that met
In slow-ascending slopes of peace.

  She said: "When I am here, I find release
From every petty debt I owe,
The goods I bring with me increase,
The ills are riven
And blown away. And there remains a single debt
Toward all the world for me,
A single duty and one destiny."

  "There shall be many births of God
In this humanity,"
She said, "and many crucifixions on the hills,
Before we learn that where Christ trod
We all shall tread; and as he died to give
Himself to us, we too shall die—and live."

  "Though slowly knowledge comes, yet in the birth
Is joy," said Celia, "joy
As well as pain:
The clear and clouded beauty of the earth.
. . . This I forget in cities. For cities are a great
Impassable gate
Of tumult. But by mountains and by seas I gain
Path after path of peace."

Witter Bynner

RENUNCIATION

Wakeful all night I lay and thought of God,
Of heaven, and of crowns pale martyrs gain,
Of souls in high and purgatorial pain,
And the red path which murdered seers have trod:

I heard the trumpets which the angels blow
I saw the cleaving sword, the measuring rod,
I watched the stream of sound continuous flow
Past the gold towers where seraphs make abode.

But now I let that aching splendor go,
I dare not call the crownèd angels peers
Henceforth. I am content to dwell below
Mid common joys, with humble smiles and tears,
Delighted in the sun and breeze to grow,
A child of human hopes and fears.

Mark W. Call

I HAVE LIFTED MY EYES

American Contemporary

I have lifted my eyes to the strength of the hills
    At the dawn of the day;
Felt the quickening stir of power that thrills,
    Seen the night drift away;
Caught the first flush of dawn. Who is this, then, that fills
    With His spirit my clay?

He that slumbereth not while I slumber, nor sleeps
    While, protected, I sleep;
Who creates, shall sustain—who gave life shall renew—
    Who hath promised, shall keep:

My shade from the sun and my shelter from storm,
    In the dark a clear flame,

It is He—ever Friend and Preserver, O Soul!
  The Lord is His name!
                              Charles Poole Cleaves

QUO VADIS?

American Contemporary

Fare not abroad, O Soul, to win
  Man's friendly smile or favoring nod;
Be still, be strong, and seek within
  The comradeship of God.

Beyond lies not the journey's end,
  The fool goes wayfaring apart,
And even as he goes, his Friend
  Is knocking at his heart.
                              Myles E. Conolly

THE OPEN DOOR

American Contemporary

You, my son, have shown me God.
Your kiss upon my cheek has made me feel
The gentle touch of Him who leads us on.
The memory of your smile when young reveals
His face,
As mellowing years come on apace;
And when you went before, you left the gates
Of Heaven ajar—ajar,
That I might glimpse approaching from afar
The glories of His grace.

Lyra Mystica

Hold, son, my hand, guide me along the path
That coming, I may stumble not, nor roam,
Nor fail to show the way which leads us
Home.

Grace Coolidge

FAITH

American Contemporary

I know Thee, O God!
   Thy vastness I see;
The stars and the sod,
   All life, tell of Thee.

I know Thee, O God!
   My Father, my Friend;
Thou liftest the rod
   A gift to extend.

I know Thee, O God!
   Almighty, all kind;
In gloom tho' I trod,
   My way was defined.

I know Thee, O God!
   I know all is well
Tho' fate may be shod
   In sandals of hell!

I know Thee, O God!
   And Thou knowest me;

Lyra Mystica

    I move at Thy nod
      For what is to be.

    For good and not ill
      The long road I plod,
    To work Thy great will—
      I know Thee, O God!
                 Richard Lew Dawson

DEAF

American Contemporary

Oh, Lord, I cannot hear; didst speak, oh, Lord?
My soul is deaf; oh, speak so I may hear!

—Dawn trumpets on the hills, and draws her sword,
All glittering from its scabbard of the dews,
And, hearing, with a shout Day's hosts arise!
Quick, at Spring's footstep on the April snows
The daffodils pour fragrance to the skies.
The eager seas arise to clasp the land,
Then turn, with joyous patience, to retreat
Back to the deep, at some low-voiced command.
Men answer to the whirlwind and the fire,
And to melodious silences of peace;
To summonings of beauty, fear, desire—
The changing Word of that unchanging Voice
Which gives to Time, Eternity's demand.
All these, Thy children,—seas, and stars, and men—
Listen: and answer as they understand:

I do not answer, for no word is clear;
And yet I listen, Lord, I listen, too—
But nothing reaches me! I cannot hear.
My soul is deaf; Lord, speak that I may hear.

Margaret Deland

THE PASSER-BY

American Contemporary

This was the dream I saw before I woke;
  Silver and rose across the paling sky
The earliest glory of the morning broke;
  This was the voice I heard, when He went by.

One walked at midnight in a storm-swept land,
  His breast against the blast, his feet astray;
Out of the darkness came an unseen hand,
  That stayed his steps, and led him on his way,
  Safe-guided to the border-lands of day.

One sank outwearied in a swollen flood;
  The black cold water hurled him toward the sea;—
Close at his side a succoring strength withstood
  The gulfing waves, and bore him mightily
  Unto the haven where he sought to be.

One faltered stricken on a hard-fought field,
  The good sword shattered in his nerveless hand;
Even as he fell, an arm stretched out to shield
  His wounded breast; a sudden-flashing brand
  Flamed o'er his head, and victory swept the land.

Lyra Mystica

One wept alone beside a crumbling tomb,
    Desolate as the unforgotten dead;
Slow footsteps paused beside him in the gloom,
    And a hand waited resting on his head;—
    Words cannot utter what the Stranger said.

So passing by He went across the lands
    Through field and desert, mart and shrine and street;
The hungry and the weary kissed His hands,
    The guilty and forsaken clasped His feet,
    And at His touch earth's bitterness grew sweet.

This was the dream that lingered on my sight,
    While the last shadows lifted from the sea;
O Son of Man, O living Light of Light,
    Make real the vision of that love in me!

Mabel Earle

ON A SUBWAY EXPRESS

American Contemporary

I, who have lost the stars, the sod,
    For chilling pave and cheerless light,
Have made my meeting-place with God
    A new and nether Night—

Have found a fane where thunder fills
    Loud caverns, tremulous;—and these
Atone me for my reverend hills
    And moonlit silences.

Lyra Mystica

A figment in the crowded dark,
 Where men sit muted by the roar,
I ride upon the whirring Spark
 Beneath the city's floor.

In this dim firmament, the stars
 Whirl by in blazing files and tiers;
Kin meteors graze our flying bars,
 Amid the spinning spheres.

Speed! speed! until the quivering rails
 Flash silver where the head-light gleams,
As when on lakes the Moon impales
 The waves upon its beams.

Life throbs about me, yet I stand
 Outgazing on majestic Power;
Death rides with me, on either hand,
 In my communion hour.

You that 'neath country skies can pray,
 Scoff not at me—the city clod;—
My only respite of the Day
 Is this wild ride—with God.

Chester Firkins

THE GLORY OF THE GRASS

*"And she brought forth her first-born son, and wrapped
him in swaddling clothes, and laid him in a
manger. . . ." Luke 2:7*

In what far, green Judean field
Did those upgrowing grasses yield

Their promises of gentle strength
When they should cradle Him at length?

What secret grace did earth produce,
That made those grasses for His use?
What glory from the sun they drew,
And what of pity from the dew?

What lad with sudden singing heart,
From all the other lads apart,
Cut them and bound them in the sun
And went his way—his work all done?

What tender girl, dark-haired and brown,
Carried the sheaves into the town;
Nor felt the weight of all that load
Along the narrow, hilly road?

And then the night, when Mary's face
Grew pallid in that lowly place,
Who filled the manger, made the bed,
Where only dumb beasts long had fed?

The humblest thing that grows on earth,
You gave Him comfort at His birth,
And kept Him warm, and made a nest,
Wherein His tiny limbs might rest!

Still with strange blindness have we trod
Amongst the common fields of God,
Seeing but dimly as we pass
The ancient glory of the grass!

Claire Wallace Flynn

Lyra Mystica

LIFE'S EVENING

American Contemporary

Three score and ten! The tumult of the world
   Grows dull upon my inattentive ear:
The bugle calls are faint, the flags are furled,
   Gone is the rapture, vanished too the fear;
The evening's blessed stillness covers all,
   As o'er the fields she folds her cloak of grey;
Hushed are the winds, the brown leaves slowly fall,
   The russet clouds hang on the fringe of day.
What fairer hour than this? No stir of morn
   With cries of waking life, nor shafts of noon—
Hot tresses from the flaming sun-god born—
   Nor midnight's shivering stars and marble moon;
But softly twilight falls and toil doth cease,
While o'er my soul God spreads his mantle—peace.
                      William Dudley Foulke

THE SECRET WAY

American Contemporary

Stark on the window's early gray
   Lined out in squares by casement bars,
She saw her lily lift to take
   The sinking stars.

Within the room's delaying dark
   Intimate things lay dim and still
With all their daytime friendliness
   Gone false and chill.

Lyra Mystica

Her hand upon the coverlet,
  Her face low in the linen's cleft,
They were as wan as water-flowers
  By light bereft.

And never was bloom brought to her couch
  But shed the odor of a sigh
Because she was as white as they,
  And they must die.

"O Pale, lit deep within the dark
  Of your young eyes, a stifled light
Leaps thin and keen as melody
  And leavens night.

"It is a light that did not burn
  When you were gay at mart and fair;
O Pale, what is that starry fire,
  Fed unaware?"

Then softly she: "I may not tell
  What other eyes behold in mine;
But I have melted night and day
  In some wild wine.

"I may not read the graven cup
  Exhaustless as a brimming bell
Distilling silver; but I drank
  And all is well.

"One morn like this, bitter still,
  I waited for the early stir

Of those who slept the while I watched
  What muffled wonders were.

"I saw my lily on the sill;
  I saw my mirror on the wall
Take light that was not; and I saw
  My spectral taper tall.

"Why, I had known these quiet things
  Since I could speak. Yet suddenly
They all touched hands and in one breath
  They spoke to me.

"I may not tell you what they said.
  The strange part is that I must lie
And never tell you what we say—
  These things and I.

"I only know that common things
  Bear sudden little spirits set
Free by the rose of dawn and by
  Night's violet.

"I only know that when I hear
  Clear tone, the haunted echoes bear
Legions of little winged feet
  On printless air.

"And when warm color weds my look
  A word is uttered tremblingly,
With meaning full—but I know not
  What it may be.

"I only know that now I find
  Abiding beauty everywhere;
Or if it bide not, that it fades
  Is still more fair.

"I long to question those I love
  And yet I know not what to say;
I am alone as one upon
  Some secret way.

"My words are barren of my bliss;
  The strange part is that I must lie
And never tell you what we say—
  These things and I.

"So will it be when I am not.
  A little more perhaps to tell;
Yet then as now I may not say
  What I know well."

She died when all the east was red.
  And we are they who know her fate
Because we love the way of life
  That she had found too late.

Zona Gale

CONTOURS

American Contemporary

I am glad of the straight lines of the rain;
Of the free blowing curves of the grain;

Of the perilous swirling and curling of fire;
The sharp upthrust of a spire;
Of the ripples on the river
Where the patterns curl and quiver
And sun thrills;
Of the innumerable undulations of the hills.
But the true line is drawn from my spirit to some outward place . . .
That line I cannot trace.

Zona Gale

GIVE WAY!

American Contemporary

Shall we not open the human heart
Swing the doors till the hinges start;
  Stop our worrying, doubt, and din,
  Hunting heaven and dodging sin?
There is no need to search so wide,
Open the door and stand aside—
    Let God in!

Shall we not open the human heart
To loving labor in field and mart;
  Working together for all about
  The good, large labor that knows not doubt—
Can He be held in our narrow rim?
Do the work that is work for Him.
    Let God out!

Shall we not open the human heart,
Never to close and stand apart?

Lyra Mystica

God is a force to give way to!
God is a thing you have to do!
God can never be caught by prayer,
Hid in your heart and fastened there—
  Let God through!

                    Charlotte Perkins Gilman

BIRTH

American Contemporary

Lord, I am born!
I have built me a body
Whose ways are all open,
Whose currents run free,
From the life that is thine
Flowing ever within me,
To the life that is mine
Flowing outward through me.

I am clothed, and my raiment
Fits smooth the spirit,
The soul moves unhindered,
The body is free;
And the thought that my body
Falls short of expressing,
In texture and color
Unfoldeth on me.

I am housed, O my Father,
My body is sheltered,
My spirit has room

'Twixt the whole world and me,
I am guarded with beauty and strength,
And within it
Is room for still union,
And birth floweth free.

And the union and birth
Of the house, ever growing,
Have built me a city,—
Have borne me a state—
Where I live manifold,
Many-voiced, many hearted,
Never dead, never weary,
And oh! never parted!
The life of the Human,
So subtle—so great!

Lord, I am born!
From inmost to outmost
The ways are all open,
The current run free,
From thy voice in my soul
To my joy in the people—
I thank thee, O God,
For this body thou gavest,
Which enfoldeth the earth—
Is enfolded by thee!

Charlotte Perkins Gilman

SPRING'S SACRAMENT

American Contemporary

"Lift up your hearts!" The holy dews
   Asperge the woodland throng;
Dawn after dawn the lark renews
   His miracle of song;
While taper-like the crocus pricks
   Athwart the yearning sod;
The primrose lifts his golden pyx,
   And God looks forth to God.

The symbols blind, the visions fail,
   Our souls strain out to Thee;
Within the leaf, the light, the veil,
   Is Thy Felicity.
O Heart of all the world's desire,
   Breathe from around, above,
The mystic kiss of Fire to fire
   That Love will yield to love!

Harold E. Goad

LOVE HOLDS ME

American Contemporary

Love holds me in the hollow of His hand,
   And bids me try
To pierce the dark that He alone hath spanned,
   And reach the sky.

Love holds me in the hollow of His hand,
   And bids me sing,

While chanting stars and rushing worlds withstand
    My murmuring.

Love holds me in the hollow of His hand
    At peace to be;
Content that what I fail to understand
    Is best for me.

I sing my song, I struggle, hope or rest,
    He bends above;
My frail wings own for their unshaken nest
    Almighty Love.

Grace Duffield Goodwin

IN THE HOSPITAL

American Contemporary

Because on the branch that is tapping my pane
    A sun-wakened leaf-bud, uncurled,
Is bursting its rusty brown sheathing in twain,
    I know there is spring in the world.

Because through the sky-patch whose azure and white
    My window frames all the day long,
A yellow bird dips for an instant of flight,
    I know there is song.

Because even here, in this Mansion of Woe,
    Where creep the dull hours, leaden-shod,
Compassion and tenderness aid me, I know
    There is God.

Arthur Guiterman

Lyra Mystica

MIRACLES

American Contemporary

Thy miracles in Galilee
When all the world went after Thee
To bless their sick, to touch their blind,
O Gracious Healer of Mankind,
But fan my faith to brighter glow!
Have I not seen, do I not know
One greater miracle than these?
That Thou, the Lord of Life, shouldst please
To walk beside me all the way,
My Comrade of the Everyday!

Was I not blind to beauty too
Until Thy love came shining through
The dark of self and made me see
I share a glorious world with Thee?
Did I not falter till Thy hand
Reached out to mine? Did I not stand
Perplexed and mute and deaf until
I heard Thy gentle, "Peace, be still,"
And all the turmoil of my heart
Was silenced and I found my part?

Those other miracles I know
Were far away, were long ago,
But this, that I may see Thy face
Transforming all the commonplace,
May work with Thee, and watch Thee bless
My little loaves in tenderness;

This sends me singing on my way,
O Comrade of the Everyday!
                    Molly Anderson Haley

A CRAFTSMAN'S CREED

American Contemporary

I hold with none who think not work a boon,
Vouchsafed to man that he may aid his kind
With offerings from his chisel, wheel or loom
Fashioned with loving hand and loving mind.
All of the fine traditions and the skill,
Come from my elders through the long line down,
Are mine to use, to raise our craft's renown,
And mine to teach again with reverent will.
Thus do I live to serve, tho' least for pay,
With fingers which are masters of the tool,
And eyes which light to see the patterns play,
As it unfolds, obedient to each rule
Of our dear Art. So all my craft is praise
To God—at once part homage and part song.
My work's my prayer, I sing the whole day long,
As Faith and Beauty shape the forms I raise.
                    James P. Haney

BEFORE ACTION

By all the glories of the day,
And the cool evening's benison;
By the last sunset touch that lay
Upon the hills when the day was done:

By beauty lavishly outpoured,
And blessing carelessly received,
By all the days that I have lived,
Make me a soldier, Lord.

By all of all men's hopes and fears,
And all the wonders poets sing,
The laughter of unclouded years,
And every sad and lovely thing:
By the romantic ages stored
With high endeavor that was his,
By all his mad catastrophes,
Make me a man, O Lord.

I, that on my familiar hill,
Saw with uncomprehending eyes
A hundred of thy sunsets spill
Their fresh and sanguine sacrifice,
Ere the sun swings his noon-day sword
Must say goodbye to all of this:—
By all delights that I shall miss,
Help me to die, O Lord!

William Noel Hodgson

SAINT JOHN OF THE CROSS

American Contemporary

Night of the soul! Dark of divinest Fire!
  Memory, mind, and will alike are doomed;
  He dies to self, and as the God entombed,
By many deaths he ever mounts the higher.

Titanic passion! still he can aspire
　　Up the bleak mountain with one hope consumed,
　　Through the long watches by one Light illumed,
The Face of Him Who is the soul's Desire.

Sublime surrender, perfect gift of gifts:
　　All that he has he yields, nor seeks to see
　　　　Black vales below or blinding peaks above;
Upon his back the heavy Cross he lifts,
　　With stern eyes fixed upon Infinity—
　　　　Godhead! that holds the height and depth of Love.
　　　　　　　　　　　　　　Thomas S. Jones, Jr.

SAINT FRANCIS

American Contemporary

The mossy paths that bore the patient herd
　　Had led him far beyond the burning town
　　By quiet pools where leaping sunbeams drown,
And as he passed the lambs knew him and stirred;
From out the tangled boughs each shy wild bird
　　Like loosened leaves came fluttering slowly down
　　Upon his ragged robe of dusty brown
To hear the gentle music of his word.

But when the night sighed through the cloudy pine
　　The green wood trembled with a seraph's wings,—
　　　　A moment flamed the Vision, then was gone!
Long, long he lay beneath the matted vine,
　　So still amid the song of waking things,
　　　　And on his body Christ's Wounds red as dawn.
　　　　　　　　　　　　　　Thomas S. Jones, Jr.

Lyra Mystica

REFUGE

American Contemporary

Frail petals fold about the weary bee
  That lured by winds has wandered far astray
  To seek the haunting perfumes that the May
Scatters upon the earth so lavishly;
And murmuring a wistful melody,
  The little waves that danced all through the day
  On the stream's breast, at last have found the way
That winds along the meadows to the sea.

Though often blinded with the beauty here,
  Yet seeks the soul beyond the realms of space
    The Love that lies behind earth's fairest things,
And struggles through thick mists of doubt and fear
  To find in God a final resting place,—
    Refuge beneath the Shadow of His Wings.

                    Thomas S. Jones, Jr.

PRAYER

American Contemporary

There is a Garden birds seek without knowing,
  All of earth's loveliness lies drifted there,
  Where pain and adoration blent in prayer
Are as tall rows of deathless flowers growing;
And in the twilight mist their colors showing,
  As through a filmy veil, gleam pale and fair,
  While tender odors linger on the air,
Ethereal breath from unknown spaces blowing.

In shadows deeper than engulfing night
   These radiant blossoms of the soul were bred,—
      They spring from victories steadfast faith has won;
The winds that woo them are great Wings of Light,
   Their dew the tears of pity Angels shed,
      And in God's Smile they find their only sun.
                      Thomas S. Jones, Jr.

THE PARTING

American Contemporary

That He might better of Love's mystery tell
   Into a lonely mountain they withdrew,
   Day's golden fire cooled in deep wells of dew
About His Head with softened splendour fell;
And in each heart that heard the last farewell
   A quickening joy and deepening sorrow grew,
   And all were hushed—even the doubtful knew
His was the power of Heaven and of Hell.

When He had ceased, a mighty wind rushed by
   From far beyond the sunset's cloudless rim,
      And over them a glory seemed to bend;
Then like a star He rose into the sky,
   Sadly they watched the glowing light grow dim
      And heard the echoes ring, "Until the End."
                      Thomas S. Jones, Jr.

Lyra Mystica

THE ORDEAL

Henry Suso

American Contemporary

"Toward the last outpost of the world I ride;
  My blazon trails dishonored in the dust,
  My bright cuirass is stained with wind and rust,
No trophy to my saddle-horn is tied;
By God forsaken and by men denied,
  At phantom foemen—hatred, fear, and lust—
  Still do I lift my shield of faith and thrust,
Yet feel the spear-head enter my own side."

"Press forward, knight, thy foes are put to rout,
  These Hands will staunch, will heal each bleeding scar
  And lift on high thy trampled blazonry.
Here angels stand within the last redoubt,
  Here lie the frontiers of the Morning Star;
  I pierced thy breasts that ye might ride to Me."
Thomas S. Jones, Jr.

IN THE GARDEN OF THE LORD

American Contemporary

The word of God came unto me,
Sitting alone among the multitudes;
And my blind eyes were touched with light.
And there was laid upon my lips a flame of fire.

I laugh and shout for life is good,
Though my feet are set in silent ways.
In merry mood I leave the crowd
To walk in my garden. Ever as I walk
I gather fruits and flowers in my hands.
And with joyful heart I bless the sun
That kindles all the place with radiant life.
I run with playful winds that blow the scent
Of rose and jessamine in playful whirls.
At last I come where tall lilies grow,
Lifting their faces like white saints to God.
While the lilies pray, I kneel upon the ground;
I have strayed into the holy temple of the Lord.

Helen Keller

THE VOICES OF CHRISTMAS

American Contemporary

I cannot put the Presence by, of Him, the Crucified,
Who moves men's spirits with His love, as doth the moon the tide;
Again I see the Life He lived, the godlike Death He died.

Again I see upon the cross that great Soul-battle fought,
Into the texture of the world the tale of which is wrought
Until it hath become the woof of human deed and thought,—
And, joining with the cadenced bells that all the morning fill,

His cry of agony doth yet my inmost being thrill,
Like some fresh grief from yesterday that tears the heart-strings still.

I cannot put His presence by, I meet Him everywhere;
I meet Him in the country town, the busy market-square;
The Mansion and the Tenement attest His presence there.

Upon the funneled ships at sea He sets His shining feet;
The Distant Ends of Empire not in vain His Name repeat,—
And, like the presence of a rose, He makes the whole world sweet.

He comes to break the barriers down raised up by barren creeds;
About the globe from zone to zone, like sunlight He proceeds;
He comes to give the World's starved heart the perfect love it needs,—

The Christ, Whose friends have played Him false, Whom Dogmas have belied,
Still speaking to the hearts of men—tho' shamed and crucified,
The Master of the centuries Who will not be denied!

Harry Kemp

Lyra Mystica

THE GIFT

American Contemporary

He has taken away the things that I loved best:
  Love and youth and the harp that knew my hand.
Laughter alone is left of all the rest.
     Does He mean that I may fill my days with laughter,
  Or will it, too, slip through my fingers like spilt sand?

Why should I beat my wings like a bird in a net,
  When I can be still and laugh at my own desire?
The wise may shake their heads at me, but yet
     I should be sad without my little laughter.
  The crackling of thorns is not so bad a fire.

Will He take away even the thorns from under the pot,
  And send me cold and supperless to bed?
He has been good to me. I know He will not.
     He gave me to keep a little foolish laughter.
  I shall not lose it even when I am dead.

Aline Kilmer

HE IS THE LIGHT

American Contemporary

  He is the Light that fades not, never dies,
  But shines forever in His endless skies,
  Opes the babe's eye-lids in the quiet room,
  Illumines those dark ways beyond the tomb.

Tempered, His rays to weeping eyes are kind,
Shining with two-fold glory on the blind,
Giving alike to palace, prison, slave,
Dwelling with wistful glow on Pilate's grave,
Piercing the clouds of vast, fanatic years,
Till Ignorance disperses, disappears,
And we, who groped in darkness, find the Way,
Reading His mighty music in the Ray.
He is the Light that fades not, never dies,
But shines forever in His endless skies.

Henry Herbert Knibbs

TO THE VICTOR

American Contemporary

Man's mind is larger than his brow of tears;
This hour is not my all of time; this place
My all of earth; nor this obscene disgrace
My all of life; and thy complacent sneers
Shall not pronounce my doom to my compeers
While the Hereafter lights me in the face,
And from the Past, as from the mountain's base
Rise, as I rise, the long tumultuous cheers.

And who slays me must overcome a world,—
Heroes at arms, and virgins who became
Mothers of children, prophecy and song;
Walls of old cities with their flags unfurled;
Peaks, headlands, ocean and its isles of fame—
And sun and moon and all that made me strong!

William Ellery Leonard

Lyra Mystica

SONNET

American Contemporary

I dreamed last night I stood with God on high,
And saw the centuries glide, like falling rain,
Into the still pool of eternity,
Whose calm deeps scarcely rippled with their gain;
And everywhere, in flower and bud and tree,
In savage beast or stirring of the clod,
In the on-marching of humanity,
I seemed to see life reaching up to God;
And little joys that I had counted great,
And loss of love with all its wealth and gain,
Seemed less than that my soul drag not its weight,
Nor stay the age-long welding of life's chain.
O God, when self would seek its own delight,
Renew to me Thy vision of the night.

Snow Longley

REVELATION

American Contemporary

I made a pilgrimage to find the God:
I listened for His voice at holy tombs,
Searched for the print of His immortal feet
In dust of broken altars: yet turned back
With empty heart. But on the homeward road,
A great light came upon me, and I heard
The God's voice singing in a nestling lark;
Felt His sweet wonder in a swaying rose;
Received His blessing from a wayside well;

Looked on His beauty in a lover's face;
Saw His bright hand send signals from the suns.

Edwin Markham

PRAYER

American Contemporary

O my soul, I would have you rest upon the bosom of the Infinite
Which once enfolded you.
O my heart, I would have you beat to the measure of that greater heart
Of which you are a fragment.

I have heard the voice of the Infinite when men caressed my ears with loving words;
But I would hear it loudest when men assail me with envenomed tongues.
I have caught Life's song while silently I stood upon the lonely mountain peak;
But I would have her music in my ears amidst the din of cities.
I have seen the Cosmic Spirit sweep along the boundless plain;
But fain would I behold Life moving with majestic step
Through crowded streets and lowly places.
The breath of the Eternal One came sweetly to my nostrils
While I stood in clover-scented fields.
But I would be perfumed with everlasting fragrance,

Yea, I would watch man's sacred incense
Rising with man's most foul miasmas.

O my soul, I would have you rest upon the bosom of
    the Infinite
Which once enfolded you.
O my heart, I would have you beat to the measure of
    that greater heart
Of which you are a fragment.
                                Madeline Mason-Manheim

GOD'S WORLD

American Contemporary

O World, I cannot hold thee close enough!
    Thy winds, thy wide gray skies!
    Thy mists that roll and rise!
Thy woods this autumn day, that ache and sag
And all but cry with color! That gaunt crag
To crush! To lift the lean of that black bluff!
World, world, I cannot get thee close enough!

Long have I known a glory in it all,
    But never knew I this.
    Here such a passion is
As stretcheth me apart. Lord, I do fear
Thou'st made the world too beautiful this year.
My soul is all but out of me—let fall
No burning leaf; prithee, let no bird call.
                                Edna St. Vincent Millay

Lyra Mystica

From A CENTURY OF INDIAN EPIGRAMS

American Contemporary

Seated within this body's car
The silent Self is driven afar;
And the five senses at the pole
Like steeds are tugging restive of control.

And if the driver lose his way,
Or if the reins sunder, who can say
In what blind paths, what pits of fear
Will plunge the chargers in their mad career?

Drive well, O Mind, use all thy art,
Thou charioteer!—O feeling Heart,
Be thou a bridle firm and strong!
For the Lord rideth and the way is long.

Paul Elmer More

KINSHIP

American Contemporary

I am aware,
As I go commonly sweeping the stair,
Doing my part of the every-day care—
Human and simple my lot and share—
I am aware of a marvellous thing:
Voices that murmur and ethers that ring
In the far stellar spaces where cherubim sing;
I am aware of the passion that pours
Down the channels of fire through Infinity's doors;

    Forces terrific, with melody shod,
        Music that mates with the pulses of God.
I am aware of the glory that runs
From the core of myself to the core of the suns,
    Bound to the stars by invisible chains,
    Blaze of eternity now in my veins,
    Seeing the rush of ethereal rains,
Here in the midst of the every-day air—
        I am aware.

        I am aware,
As I sit quietly here in my chair,
Sewing or reading or braiding my hair—
Human and simple my lot and my share—
    I am aware of the systems that swing
    Through the aisles of creation on heavenly wing,
    I am aware of a marvellous thing,
Trail of the comets in furious flight,
Thunders of beauty that shatter the night,
    Terrible triumph of pageants that march
    To the trumpets of time through Eternity's arch.
I am aware of the splendour that ties
All the things of the earth with the things of the skies,
    Here in my body the heavenly heat,
    Here in my flesh the melodious beat
    Of the planets that circle Divinity's feet.
As I silently sit here in my chair,
        I am aware.

Angela Morgan

Lyra Mystica

A SONG OF THANKSGIVING

American Contemporary

Thank God I can rejoice
In human things—the multitude's glad voice,
The street's warm surge beneath the city light,
The rush of hurrying faces on my sight,
The million-celled emotion in the press
That would their human fellowship confess.
Thank Thee because I may my brother feed,
That Thou hast opened me unto his need,
Kept me from being callous, cold and blind,
Taught me the melody of being kind.
Thus, for my own and for my brother's sake—
    Thank Thee I am awake!

Thank Thee that I can trust!
That though a thousand times I feel the thrust
Of faith betrayed, I still have faith in man,
Believe him pure and good since time began—
Thy child forever, though he may forget
The perfect mould in which his soul was set.
Thank Thee that when love dies, fresh love springs up,
New wonders pour from Heaven's cup,
Young to my soul the ancient need returns,
Immortal in my heart the ardor burns;
My altar fires replenished from above—
    Thank Thee that I can love!

Thank Thee that I can hear,
Finely and keenly with the inner ear,

Below the rush and clamor of a throng
The mighty music of the under-song.
And when the day has journeyed to its rest,
Lo, as I listen, from the amber west,
Where the great organ lifts its glowing spires,
There sounds the chanting of the unseen choirs.
Thank Thee for sight that shows the hidden flame
Beneath all breathing, throbbing things the same,
Thy Pulse the pattern of the thing to be ...
    Thank Thee that I can see!

Thank Thee that I can feel!
That though Life's blade be terrible as steel,
My soul is stript and naked to the fang,
I crave the stab of beauty and the pang.
To be alive,
To think, to yearn, to strive,
To suffer torture when the goal is wrong,
To be sent back and fashioned strong
Rejoicing in the lesson that was taught
By all the good the grim experience wrought;
At last, exulting to *arrive* ...
    Thank God I am alive!

Angela Morgan

DUSK

It is impossible to be alone here, even in this little cabin room,
After beholding the Glory of God through the somber splendor of twilight loom,

And the violet dusk of the mountains quiver, and the
    Holy of Holies glow through the gloom.

Dusk as a brooding spirit whispered over the face of the
    harrowed field;
Dusk as a dim-winged dragon darkened over the bay
    where the flame-points reeled;
As an angel, veiled and flaming-sworded; watched at
    the gates of the unrevealed.

Over the bay the lights of the city, a thousand blossoms
    of yellow flame,
Gleamed and twinkled out of the blue and ash-gray
    darkness; and there came
A slow wind thence: a murmurous rumor: human
    passion, sadness, shame.

And I beheld God in the mountains; God in the iris
    glow of the sky;
And I beheld in the throbbing lights of the city, God
    in His agony—
A heart-beat; a lamentation; an impassioned, low,
    insatiate cry.

Kenneth Morris

WHO WALKS WITH BEAUTY

American Contemporary

Who walks with Beauty has no need of fear;
    The sun and moon and stars keep pace with him;
Invisible hands restore the ruined year,
    And time, itself, grows beautifully dim.

Lyra Mystica

One hill will keep the footprints of the moon,
  That came and went a hushed and secret hour;
One star at dusk will yield the lasting boon;
  Remembered Beauty's white, immortal flower.

Who takes of Beauty wine and daily bread,
  Will know no lack when bitter years are lean;
The brimming cup is by, the feast is spread—
  The sun and moon and stars his eyes have seen,
Are for his hunger and the thirst he slakes:
  The wine of Beauty and the bread he breaks.

David Morton

SYMBOL

American Contemporary

My faith is all a doubtful thing,
  Wove on a doubtful loom,
Until there comes, each showery spring,
  A cherry tree in bloom;

And Christ, who died upon a tree
  That death had stricken bare,
Comes beautifully back to me,
  In blossoms everywhere.

David Morton

QUIET

There is a flame within me that has stood
Unmoved, untroubled through a mist of years,
  Knowing nor love nor laughter, hope nor fears,

Nor foolish throb of ill, nor wine of good.
I feel no shadow of the winds that brood,
   I hear no whisper of a tide that veers,
   I weave no thought of passion, nor of tears,
Unfettered I of time, of habitude.
I know no birth, I know no death that chills;
   I fear no fate nor fashion, cause nor creed,
I shall outdream the slumber of the hills,
   I am the bud, the flower, I the seed:
     For I do know that in whate'er I see
     I am the part and it the soul of me.

John Spencer Muirhead

L'ENVOI

American Contemporary

Oh seek me not within a tomb;
Thou shalt not find me in the clay!
I pierce a little wall of gloom
To mingle with the Day!

I brothered with the things that pass,
Poor giddy Joy and puckered Grief;
I go to brother with the Grass
And with the sunning Leaf.

Not Death can sheathe me in a shroud;
A joy-sword whetted keen with pain,
I join the armies of the Cloud
The Lightning and the Rain.

Oh subtle in the sap athrill,
Athletic in the glad uplift,
A portion of the Cosmic Will,
I pierce the planet-drift.

My God and I shall interknit
As rain and Ocean, breath and Air;
And oh, the luring thought of it
Is prayer!

John G. Neihardt

PRAYER FOR PAIN

American Contemporary

I do not pray for peace nor ease,
Nor truce from sorrow:
No suppliant on servile knees
Begs here against to-morrow!

Lean flame against lean flame we flash,
O Fates that meet me fair;
Blue steel against blue steel we clash—
Lay on, and I shall dare!

But Thou of deeps the awful Deep,
Thou Breather in the clay,
Grant this my only prayer—Oh keep
My soul from turning gray!

For until now, whatever wrought
Against my sweet desires,

Lyra Mystica

My days were smitten harps strung taut,
My nights were slumbrous lyres.

And howsoe'er the hard blow rang
Upon my battered shield,
Some lark-like soaring spirit sang
Above my battlefield.

And through my soul of stormy night
The zigzag blue flame ran.
I asked no odds—I fought my fight—
Events against a man.

But now—at last—the gray mist chokes
And numbs me. *Leaves me pain!*
Oh let me feel the biting strokes
That I may fight again!

John G. Neihardt

THE QUEST

American Contemporary

I went seeking an unutterable Word
    To lift me out of my gloom,
And heard a mocking-bird singing
    On an apple tree in bloom.

I sat longing for ineffable things
    To satisfy my deep hunger,
And saw a mother bird hide her brood
    From lightning and thunder.

Lyra Mystica

I bowed, asking a Divine revelation
    To illumine my way to God;
And at my feet a shy little violet
    Lifted a face from the sod.

I sought too high for truth nearby,
    Standing aloof and apart:
For God is found in love and beauty—
    The Word is in thy heart.

                  Joseph Fort Newton

THE CRY OF MAN

American Contemporary

What roar as of breaking of Oceans, what cry as of seas on the iron-clanging coasts?
Lo, I peer through an acre of factory-sheds, I see in the blackness thin ghosts
With white faces a-flutter; a thousand machines throb, thunder and worry and whirl—
Only one Soul may I see: a great sunbeam splashes the face of a girl.
Not she a mere scarecrow that wags on a cornfield, rag-wrapped, bone-fingered, loose-shod,
For I see by the agonized whites of her eyes a terrible thirsting for God,
I see by her lips a cry for the Life—O God, I could gather her in,
Warm her with love, bear her off to the hills, and purge her of Pain and of Sin!

Lyra Mystica

Could I bear this, were you mine, O you child? Lo,
    as mine, are you sacred, as mine, you are Soul!
O, through you I reach out to God again, I see far-
    flashing the Goal
Of the rolling ages, the wild flight of Souls, the ages'
    vast Millions downtrod
With dust in their mouths crying for the Lord, in
    the search eternal for God!

O, Vision of the Ages, pouring forth Millions, O
    Vision of the Ages' Soul Flight,
Dropped from God's hand, winging over Earth, till
    caught by the tides of the Night,
Homing to the Lord by quick millions in Death—
    still, still through the great flight rolls
Revelation from God—the pouring of fire—the rush
    to new heights by all Souls!

For Souls that taste dust thirst for the Lord: in the
    sand-grain the pent Soul bursts,
Is a life-cell; breaks on, it is sponge; works out higher,
    is reptile; sees sunlight, and thirsts
More after God up through tiger, through ape; till the
    Soul through its simian ban
Strains for a flight to the stars, the roll'd Heavens, and
    bursts into glory of Man!

But, lo, we are half-Souls, dust-tasters—our cry is the
    cry eternal for God,
So strong that a Christ breaks through, and a Lincoln;
    and we of the dust, one with sod,

Born in an age of dust, lo, through such souls as even you, world-broken Girl,
See the Light, thirst anew; the last Visions of Ages on our eyes like new fight-flags unfurl!

Plato foretold it, Dante has sung it, Lincoln has lived it—our Souls
Know if they struggled but through a thin film they would burst twenty worlds toward our Goals—
A film! Yet a change as from Cæsar to Christ! The new great upper air
Blows all about us—we have but to rise one inch of the Soul to be there! . . .

Yea, brain-fragments alone glimmer and vanish—but we, we are human, our hands
Must build Temples even from the straw, from the stubble, pile-spiked in the sea's rushing sands!
Then how word our Vision? That Christ lived the Real: that we live the Unreal, and must
By our thirst, seek Realities: blowing from the world, from our planet, an Age of the Dust!

For we know, O you Child, that your Want is our Sin; that the Wild Excess that but gluts
Our Souls beyond God, is a Sin; either way the Door of Eternity shuts,
We are closed in with dust; Excess, yea, Excess is the lie we must meet with world-shock—
We must build life anew on the Rock of the Real—the Rock of the Real—the Christ-Rock!

Lyra Mystica

O Child, we must train you in godhood, and build a
    great Home and a Love for your Life—
We must give you a Faith; you must labor with joy;
    real woman, real mother, real wife!—
For Earth's but our cradle—there are stars for our feet
    —world to world cries the flying Ideal—
That which prepares us for Death, that alone, O that
    alone is the Real!

Which having, then shall our tears be dried? No, they
    shall lay the road's dust on to death!
Still lives the ancient strange struggle of the Soul, still
    walk with us Cain and Macbeth,
Still Judas and Nero!—O God, shall forever drag the
    great Soul on the Earth
Building, with blows of Pain, gods, his young gods,
    till Death flare, the last Fire-Birth!

Neither shall glory sit at our tables and circle us gliding
    in cars,
Neither shall Pleasure be tasted unpaid for—but Earth
    shall roll among stars
As of old with the terrible Cry of Man—God's infant
    cradle-swung
From the Sun and crying he knows not why till Death's
    sleep-chant has been sung.

O vast troubled heart of the human, forever, forever
    shall hunger be yours,
David shall brood there, Hamlet shall darken, and Joan,
    with the Faith that endures

The blaze of the fagots, shall lead you on Visions—
    Visions which found shall half-break,
Glass in your grasp, and fingers shall bleed, and the
    heart eternally ache!
One step alone in a thousand years toward God is all
    we can climb,
But oh, at the next step, lo, we shall find an Earth
    among new skies sublime,
Where all men are toiling, where all men are sunned
    by the Chance of touching the Peak,
Of struggling out a Soul, of lifting into God—O, the
    Chance, the Chance but to Seek!

To Seek! Not be bound and doomed in the dust! And
    the Seekers, the Millions, far-lifting
In the dim new ages, we know they shall fail—some
    crushed, some self-lost, some drifting
Back down the slopes—but the Chance shall be theirs,
    and ten thousand touching the Sun
Shall pull the race upwards to the City of Brothers,
    till on Earth God's will be done!

Till our streets shall be sunned with the joy of
    children, and our shops be busy with men
Toiling together great ends of the Earth, and our
    homes be hallowed again
With the Mother, the Child! Till our Schools shape
    Souls for an Earth-life ending in skies—
Till we know that a Soul is a Soul, and as such is holy
    before our eyes!

Then put off the coward—live with the Vision! Let me go to my work in the morning
With fire of God, let me strike in the open, let me cry, cry aloud the Age dawning—
Let *my* life be Real—faith in my heart! My Eternity hangs on this day—
God in me dies or leaps godward as I thunder my yea or my nay!

James Oppenheim

OVERTONES

I heard a bird at break of day
    Sing from the autumn trees;
A song so mystical and calm,
    So full of certainties,
No man, I think, could listen long
    Except upon his knees.
Yet this was but a simple bird
    Alone, among dead trees.

William Alexander Percy

IN PRAISE OF COMMON THINGS

American Contemporary

For stock and stone;
For grass, and pool; for quince tree blown
A virginal white in spring;
And for the wall beside,
Gray, gentle, wide;
For roof, loaf, everything,

I praise Thee, Lord;
For toil, and ache, and strife,
And all the commonness of life.

Hearty, yet dim,
Like country voices in a hymn,
The things a house can hold;
The memories in the air;
And down the stair
Fond footsteps known of old;
The chair, the book or two;
The little bowl of white and blue.

What would it be,
If loveliness were far from me?
A staff I could not take,
To hurry up and down,
From field to town;
Needs would my wild heart break;
Or, I would vacant go,
And, being naught, to nothing grow.

This is the best:
My little road from east to west,
The breadth of a man's hand,
Not from the sky too far,
Nor any star,
Runs through the unwalled land;
From common things that be,
Is but a step to run to Thee.

Lizette Woodworth Reese

GROWTH

American Contemporary

I climb that was a clod;
  I run whose steps were slow;
I reap the very wheat of God
  That once had none to sow.

Is Joy a lamp outblown?
  Truth out of grasping set?
But nay, for Laughter is mine own;
  I knock and answer get.

Nor is the last word said;
  Nor is the battle done;
Somewhat of glory and of dread
  Remains for set of sun.

For I have scattered seed
  Shall ripen at the end;
Old Age holds more than I shall need,
  Death more than I can spend.
            Lizette Woodworth Reese

TRUST

American Contemporary

I am Thy grass, O Lord!
  I grow up sweet and tall
But for a day; beneath Thy sword
  To lie at evenfall.

Yet have I not enough
  In that brief day of mine?
The wind, the bees, the wholesome stuff
  The sun pours out like wine.

Behold, this is my crown;
  Love will not let me be;
Love holds me here; Love cuts me down;
  And it is well with me.

Lord, Love, keep it but so;
  Thy purpose is full plain;
I die that after I may grow
  As tall, as sweet again.

Lizette Woodworth Reese

A RHAPSODIST'S SONG

American Contemporary

All the birds shall sing to me,
When I reach heaven.
All the leaves shall dance for me,
Seven times seven.
All the hills of bliss shall run,
Cloud-free from out its sun;
All the flowers, of all bowers,
Pour me fragrance, hours and hours;
All the air I breathe shall be
Joy's sweet leaven.

Mystic apples shall I pluck
For my soul's feeding.

Lyra Mystica

On a green palm-bed I'll lie,
Man and God reading.
I will fan me with the wings
Of my own imaginings;
And, to dally down each alley
Of its dream enverdured valley,
I will follow every breeze
Languorously leading.

When I wish to I will scale
Tops of mountain beauty.
I will learn how dawns are made,
How stars do their duty.
I will hold the high moon's sphere
Oft to my attentive ear.
And each comet, trailing from it
Leagues of light, shall be a plummet
For my soul through deeps of space
Strewn with death's booty.

Yes, I'll do this every day,
In the vales of Heaven.
For my need of it will be
Seven times seven:
Need of birds and mystic rills,
Need of apples for soul-ills;
Need of vision, where, elysian
Dews shall stir my heart's decision
To delight in love—and in
Life's Immortal leaven.

Cale Young Rice

Lyra Mystica
A LITANY FOR LATTER-DAY MYSTICS

American Contemporary

Out of the vastness that is God
   I summon the power to heal me.
It comes with peace ineffable
   And patience, to anneal me.
Ajar I set my soul-doors
   Toward unbounded Life
And let the infinitudes of it
   Flow through me, vigour-rife.

Out of the vastness that is God
   I summon the power to still me.
It comes from inner deeps divine
   With destinies that thrill me;
It follows the hush of every wrong;
   And every vain unrest
It banishes; and leaves a bliss
   Before all unpossessed.

Out of the vastness that is God
   I summon the strength to keep me,
And from all fleshly fears and fret
   With spirit-winds to sweep me.
I summon the faith that puts to flight
   All impotence and ills,
And that, through the wide universe,
   Well-being's breath distills.

Cale Young Rice

Lyra Mystica

I HAD A DREAM LAST NIGHT

American Contemporary

                     I had a dream last night:
A dream not like to any other dream
That I remember. I was all alone,
Sitting as I do now beneath a tree,
But looking not, as I am looking now,
Against the sunlight. There was neither sun
Nor moon, nor do I think of any stars;
Yet there was light, and there were cedar trees,
And there were sycamores. I lay at rest,
Or should have seemed at rest, within a trough
Between two giant roots. A weariness
Was on me, and I would have gone to sleep,
But I had not the courage. If I slept,
I feared that I should never wake again;
And if I did not sleep I should go mad,
And with my own dull tools, which I had used
With wretched skill so long, hack out my life.
And while I lay there, tortured out of death,
Faint waves of cold, as if the dead were breathing,
Came over me and through me; and I felt
Quick fearful tears of anguish on my face
And in my throat. But soon, and in the distance,
Concealed, importunate, there was a sound
Of coming steps,—and I was not afraid;
No, I was not afraid then, I was glad;
For I could feel, with every thought, the Man,
The Mystery, the Child, a footfall nearer.
Then, when he stood before me, there was no

Surprise, there was no questioning, I knew him,
As I had known him always; and he smiled.
"Why are you here?" he asked; and reaching down,
He took up my dull blades and rubbed his thumb
Across the edges of them and then smiled
Once more.—"I was a carpenter," I said,
"But there was nothing in the world to do."—
"Nothing?" said he.—"No, nothing," I replied.—
"But are you sure," he asked, "that you have skill?
And are you sure that you have learned your trade?
No, you are not."—He looked at me and laughed
As he said that; but I did not laugh then,
Although I might have laughed.—"They are dull," said he;
"They were not very sharp if they were ground;
But they are what you have, and they will earn
What you have not. So take them as they are,
Grind them and clean them, put new handles to them,
And then go learn your trade in Nazareth.
Only be sure that you find Nazareth."—
"But if I starve—when then?" said I.—He smiled.

Edwin Arlington Robinson

PSALM

American Contemporary

They have burned to Thee many tapers in many temples:
I burn to Thee the taper of my heart.

They have sought Thee at many altars, they have carried lights to find Thee:
I find Thee in the white fire of my heart.

They have gone forth restlessly, forging many shapes, images where they seek Thee, idols of deed and thought:
Thou art the fire of my deeds; Thou art the white flame of my dreams.

O vanity! They know things and codes and customs,
They believe what they see to be true; but they know not Thee,
Thou art within the light of their eyes that see, and the core of fire.

The white fire of my heart forges the shapes of my brain;
The white fire of my heart is a sun, and my deeds and thoughts are its dark planets;
It is a far flame of Thee, a star in Thy firmament.

With pleasant warmth flicker the red fires of the hearth,
And the blue, mad flames of the marsh flare and consume themselves:
I too am an ember of Thee, a little star; my warmth and my light travel a long way.

So little, so wholly given to its human quest,
And yet of Thee, wholly of Thee, Thou Unspeakable,
All the colors of life in a burning white mist
Pure and intense as Thou, O Heart of life!

Lyra Mystica

Frail is my taper, it flickers in the storm,
It is blown out in the great wind of the world;
Yet when the world is dead and the seas are a crust
  of salt,
When the sun is dark in heaven and the stars have
  changed their courses,
Forever somewhere with Thee, on the altar of life
Shall still burn the white fire of my heart.

Jessie E. Sampter

THE GREAT VOICE

American Contemporary

I who have heard solemnities of sound—
The throbbing pulse of cities, the loud roar
Of ocean on sheer ledges of gaunt rock,
The chanting of innumerable winds
Around white peaks, the plunge of cataracts,
The whelm of avalanches, and, by night,
The thunder's panic breath—have come to know
What is earth's mightiest voice—the desert's voice—
Silence, that speaks with deafening tones of God.

Clinton Scollard

FIRST FLIGHT

American Contemporary

Whither, when freed from fetters of the clay,
  Will be the first soul flight—
Into what realms of unimagined day,
  Across what depths of night?

Lyra Mystica

After stark hours of travail and of pain
    What blessing to be free—
To feel no bondage of the flesh—to gain
    The large serenity

Of peace beyond the bounds of mortal breath,
    Whatever be the goal!—
Fleeter than wings, man's mind conjectureth
    The first flight of the soul.

Clinton Scollard

SANCTUARY

American Contemporary

Let us put by some hour of every day
For holy things!—whether it be when dawn
Peers through the window pane, or when the noon
Flames, like a burnished topaz, in the vault,
Or when the thrush pours in the ear of eve
Its plaintive monody; some little hour
Wherein to hold rapt converse with the soul,
From sordidness and self a sanctuary,
Swept by the winnowing of unseen wings,
And touched by the White Light Ineffable.

Clinton Scollard

THE WHITE COMRADE

American Contemporary

    Under our curtain of fire,
    Over the clotted clods,

We charged, to be withered, to reel
And despairingly wheel
When the bugles bade us retire
From the terrible odds.

As we ebbed with the battle-tide,
Fingers of red-hot steel
Suddenly closed on my side.
I fell, and began to pray.
I crawled on my hands and lay
Where a shallow shell-crater yawned wide;
Then I swooned. . . .

When I woke, it was yet day.
Fierce was the pain of my wound,
Yet I saw it was death to stir,
For fifty paces away
Their trenches were.
In torture I prayed for the dark
And the stealthy step of my friend
Who, stanch to the very end,
Would creep to the danger zone
And offer his life as a mark
To save my own.

Night fell. I heard his tread,
Not stealthy, but firm and serene,
As if my comrade's head
Were lifted far from that scene
Of passion and pain and dread;
As if my comrade's heart

In carnage took no part;
As if my comrade's feet
Were set on some radiant street
Such as no darkness might haunt;
As if my comrade's eyes
No deluge of flame might surprise,
No death and destruction daunt,
No red-beaked bird dismay,
Nor sight of decay.

Then in the bursting shells' dim light
I saw he was clad in white.
For a moment I thought that I saw the smock
Of a shepherd in search of his flock,
Or some woman crazed by fright,
Clad in her wedding frock.
Alert were the enemy, too,
And their bullets flew
Straight at a mark no bullet could fail;
For the seeker was tall and his robe was bright;
But he did not flee nor quail.
Instead, with unhurrying stride
He came,
And gathering my tall frame,
Like a child, in his arms. . . .

I swooned, and awoke
From a blissful dream
In a cave by a stream.
My silent comrade had bound my side.
No pain now was mine, but a wish that I spoke,—

A mastering wish to serve this man
Who had ventured through hell my doom to revoke,
As only the truest of comrades can.
I begged him to tell me how best I might aid him,
And urgently prayed him
Never to leave me, whatever betide;—
When I saw he was hurt—
Shot through the hands that were clasped in prayer!
Then, as the dark drops gathered there
And fell in the dirt,
The wounds of my friend
Seemed to me such as no man might bear.
Those bullet-holes in the patient hands
Seemed to transcend
All horrors that ever these war-drenched lands
Had known or would know till the mad world's end.
Then suddenly I was aware
That his feet had been wounded too;
And, dimming the white of his side,
A dull stain grew.
"You are hurt, White Comrade!" I cried.
His words I already foreknew:
"These are old wounds," said he,
"But of late they have troubled me."

Robert Haven Schauffler

THE ELDER SACRAMENT

American Contemporary

Past this meadow on the shore
Glinting seagulls dip and soar.

Lyra Mystica

Boats festoon the purple bay;
And out beyond its rim of gray,
Languid in the August sheen
Mountain ridges, dusky green
As some faded tapestry,
Drowse at full length opposite me.
Soft across the sky of noon
Folds of thinnest clouds are strewn,
Blurring the hardness of its hue
Till blue is white and white is blue.
Then as the veils above me shift
So my senses drift and drift,
Lost beyond the will to think.
Motionless I eat and drink.

Lord of love and truth and power,
Thou art with me in this hour,
For Thy spirit is not lent
To a church-walled sacrament
More than to the simpler food
Of an open solitude;
And Thy rich outpouring grace
Fills this beauty-hallowed place,
Showing here Thy flesh indeed
And Thy blood to slake man's need
Freely given for all to share,
Bread of earth and wine of air.

Charles Wharton Stork

Lyra Mystica

FALTERINGS TOWARD THE UNKNOWN GOD

A Sonnet Sequence

American Contemporary

1

THE BIRTH OF WONDER

Cowering in fear, man felt himself alone
    In nature, till he sensed a hungry need
    Of comradeship no fellowman could feed.
He rose and stared up skyward. Had he gone
Astray from where the blue-gold splendor shone?
    He felt his hands and feet and body bleed
    From thorns, but in his heart a shining seed
Fell like a favor from a monarch's throne.

Struggling within him as in untilled earth,
    The seed struck root. Its hidden spark began
To spear up sun-ward into golden birth
As flame-flower, till he dreamed himself a part
    Of the high glow his arms were stretched to span;
But wonder-worship could not feed his heart.

2

SKY GODS

Millenniums passed. Man peopled earth and sky
    With his own image clad in strength or grace,
    Till of his thought was born a shining race,

Like mortals but too fair, it seemed, to die.
For them he feigned celestial kingdoms high
    Above the clouds, Valhallas throned in space
    Where he could never find their feasting place
Or startle their indifference with a cry.

And yet Olympian beings were at best
    But clay turned marble, for they sinned as much
    As man himself, no otherwise than he.
What wonder that they grew a bitter jest
    As man thought deeplier! Sky gods could not touch
    His spirit with the glow of sympathy.

3

HERCULES

Gods had come down to earth, had even died,
    Like summer flowers or the declining sun
    And been reborn. But now a mortal won
The crest that had flung back the titan's pride.
The strength of Hercules was deified
    But through obedience and the task well done.
    No favored course the hero had to run,
His locks were crowned not till his limbs were tried.

And when, his simple heart confused with blent
    Delight and awe, 'mid all the shining host
    In Jove's wide banquet hall the hero trod;
To Juno first, his former foe, he bent:
    'Twas she, who taxing to the uttermost
    His body and soul, had made of him a god.

4

JEHOVAH

Man felt himself as one, and ever had sought
    One changeless Lord Omnipotent though his
        mind—
    The window of the outer world—was blind
With ignorance first, then dazzled by vain thought.
He missed the ocean, by the waves distraught.
    In Nature's myriad forms he strove to find
    His archetype, till his praying soul divined
Beyond all form the unseen hand that wrought.

The Hebrews, grimly welded into one
    By scourges of affliction, in their need
    Laid hold on Jahveh, and he heard and blest.
But he might bless them in the tribe alone,
    Because their love was but for Israel's seed;
    Their hate recoiled in hatred from the rest.

5

THE DÆMON OF SOCRATES

Man longed to feel the tremor of God's will
    Not in far thunders from the judgment seat
    On Sinai, but persuasive as the sweet
Delight of wood-birds when the winds are still;
A voice to guide him in the whispered thrill
    Of his best thought, more near than hands or feet,
    But more imperative than his own heart's beat;
A fountain pulse where soul could drink its fill.

Socrates, dæmon-drunken, quaffed his death
    As a mere stirrup cup. Man's mind, he knew,
    Muddied with law the source where truth began.
And Plato, kindled by his failing breath,
    Revealed the Good, the Beautiful, the True—
    The inner light that lighteth every man.

6

JESUS

Not a mere priest to tend an altar flame,
    He led the spirit like a battle-cry,
    This man, who taught his fellows how to die;
Men call him God, but Jesus was his name:
He shunned the sage's and the warrior's fame;
    Free to resist his foreknown doom, or fly,
    He chose the inner voice and perished by
The utmost torture of a felon's shame.

"Forgive them, for they know not what they do!"
    Who could have trusted in the words till then,
    Or dared to tread the path that Jesus trod?
By Love's divine example now men know
    Not merely that God's spirit dwells in men
    But that, by God's grace, man himself is God.

Charles Wharton Stork

Lyra Mystica

THE ROSE AND GOD

Meditations of a Persian Mystic

American Contemporary

What are you, rose?—lips that lean back to meet
The June-long kiss of the sun? or fervid wine
Born of dark pangs, though trod out by the feet

Of spring's wild votaries; will the breeze incline
His waving curls and drink with tremulous hand,
Then lurch away to drowse at last supine

On yielding grasses? As your leaves expand,
Rose, you repay the dower that nature brought:
The sun begot you, and the warm breeze fanned

Your widening buds; till earth, whose womb was fraught
So patiently, might flaunt in recompense
A living ruby. Deeper must be sought

Your soul, that perfume of the inward sense
Which men call beauty, that red kiss of joy
Which bathes my being,—who knows how or whence?—

Till I am steeped in rapture. No mere toy
Of subterranean looms are you, sweet rose,
That frost or drouth or canker may destroy.

The color that exhales, the scent that glows,
Your many-petaled indivisible grace;—
Like mists the dawn-light wears but later throws

Aside—what were they but a withered face,
A starless night, a chord that felt no thrill
Of passion's fingers; could I neither trace

The light that from your bosom throbs to fill
Your emerald shine with awe, nor dream some tone
From which your deep thoughts limpidly distil

As music. Love is roused by love alone;
You, rose, unbarring paradise to me,
Are therefore God. How could He else be known

To mortals than in sensuous rhapsody?
Naught that is told us may we comprehend
Until we taste and breathe and hear and see

And handle. Rose, in you the ineffable Friend
Has three persuasive voices: perfume, touch
And color. Though your song may seem to end

Tonight, your petals whirled off in the clutch
Of winds, like wounded doves that hawks pursue;
Your beauty shall for me be ever such

As at this moment, when love speaks in you.
You blossom in my breast, as warm, as red
As my own heart. And my heart blossoms, too,

In God's heart. Through all time and space are spread
Roses unfading, ever-fragrant, more
And more; across the earth, and overhead,

Reflected on the ocean's tranquil floor;
Until the universe is one vast rose,
Nature and man, with God the flaming core
When love to every crimson petal flows.

Charles Wharton Stork

TO BE OLD

Against the quicksands of receding life to sink
    So broken, spent and wrenched to face thy death,
And then with sudden exaltation sweet to think,
    "The everlasting arms are underneath."

Helen Eldred Storke

THE VOICE

American Contemporary

Atoms as old as stars,
Mutation on mutation,
Millions and millions of cells
Dividing yet still the same,
From air and changing earth,
From ancient Eastern rivers,
From turquoise tropic seas,
Unto myself I came.

My spirit like my flesh
Sprang from a thousand sources,
From cave-man, hunter and shepherd,
From Karnak, Cyprus, Rome;
The living thoughts in me

Lyra Mystica

Spring from dead men and women,
Forgotten time out of mind
And many as bubbles of foam.

Here for a moment's space
Into the light out of darkness,
I come and they come with me
Finding words with my breath;
From the wisdom of many lifetimes
I hear them cry: "Forever
Seek for Beauty, she only
Fights with man against Death!"

Sara Teasdale

A STAR MAP

American Contemporary

All of heaven in my hands—
   With one finger I can turn
Till I sink Orion's bands,
   And the Lyre begins to burn.

I can make a night of spring,
   Shivering Spica, white Altair,
And above me I can swing
   Slowly Berenice's Hair.

Winter evening, autumn dawn
   Man has charted; I can see
How Midsummer Night moves on
   Tranquilly and terribly;

Lyra Mystica

Light lost in light, death lost in death,
    Time without end, Space without bound—
I, whose life is but a breath,
    Turn Infinity around.

Sara Teasdale

THY JOY IN SORROW

Give me thy joy in sorrow, gracious Lord,
    And sorrow's self shall like to joy appear!
Although the word should waver in its sphere
    I tremble not if Thou thy peace afford;
But, Thou withdrawn, I am but as a chord
That vibrates to the pulse of hope and fear:
Nor rest I more than harps which to the air
Must answer when we place their tuneful board
Against the blast, which thrill unmeaning woe
Even in their sweetness. So no earthly wing
E'er sweeps me but to sadden. Oh, place Thou
    My heart beyond the world's sad vibrating—
And where but in Thyself? Oh, circle me,
That I may feel no touches save of Thee.

Chauncey Hare Townshend

SILENCE

American Contemporary

I need not shout my faith. Thrice eloquent
    Are quiet trees and the green listening sod;
Hushed are the stars, whose power is never spent;
    The hills are mute: yet how they speak of God!

Charles Hanson Towne

Lyra Mystica

GOD OF THE OPEN AIR

American Contemporary

These are the things I prize
    And hold of dearest worth:
    Light of the sapphire skies,
    Peace of the silent hills,
Shelter of forests, comfort of the grass,
Music of birds, murmur of little rills,
Shadows of cloud that swiftly pass,
    And, after showers,
    The smell of flowers
    And of the good, brown earth—
And best of all, along the way, friendship and mirth.
    So let me keep
    These treasures of the humble heart
In true possession, owning them by love;
And when at last I can no longer move
    Among them freely, but must part
From the green fields and waters clear,
    Let me not creep
Into some darkened room and hide
From all that makes the world so bright and dear;
    But throw the windows wide
    To welcome in the light;
    And while I clasp a well-belovèd hand,
    Let me once more have sight
    Of the deep sky and the far-smiling land—
    Then gently fall on sleep,
And breathe my body back to Nature's care,
My spirit out to thee, God of the open air.

Henry van Dyke

Lyra Mystica

ACCEPTANCE

American Contemporary

I cannot think nor reason,
I only know he came
With hands and feet of healing
And wild heart all aflame.

With eyes that dimmed and softened
At all the things he saw,
And in his pillared singing
I read the marching law.

I only know he loves me,
Enfolds and understands—
And oh, his heart that holds me,
And oh, his certain hands!

Willard Wattles

BY EVERY EBB

American Contemporary

By every ebb of the river-tide
My heart to God hath daily cried;
By every shining shingle-bar
I found the pathway of a star;
By every dizzy mountain height
He touches me for cleaner sight,
As Moses' face hath shined to see
His intimate divinity;

Through desert sand I stumbling pass
To death's cool plot of friendly grass,
Knowing each painful step I trod
Hath brought me daily home to God.

Willard Wattles

LIFE

American Contemporary

Nay, lift me to thy lips, Life, and once more
Pour the wild music through me—

  I quivered in the reed-bed with my kind,
Rooted in Lethe-bank, when at the dawn
There came a groping shape of mystery
Moving among us, that with random stroke
Severed, and rapt me from my silent tribe,
Pierced, fashioned, lipped me, sounding for a voice,
Laughing on Lethe-bank—and in my throat
I felt the wing-beat of the fledgling notes,
The bubble of godlike laughter in my throat.

Such little songs she sang,
Pursing her lips to fit the tiny pipe,
They trickled from me like a slender spring
That strings frail wood-growths on its crystal thread,
Nor dreams of glassing cities, bearing ships.
She sang, and bore me through the April world
Matching the birds, doubling the insect-hum
In the meadows, under the low-moving airs,
And breathings of the scarce-articulate air

When it makes mouths of grasses—but when the sky
Burst into storm, and took great trees for pipes,
She thrust me in her breast, and warm beneath
Her cloudy vesture, on her terrible heart,
I shook, and heard the battle.
      But more oft,
Those early days, we moved in charmèd woods,
Where once, at dusk, she piped against a faun,
And one warm dawn a tree became a nymph
Listening; and trembled; and Life laughed and passed.
And once we came to a great stream that bore
The stars upon its bosom like a sea,
And ships like stars; so to the sea we came.
And there she raised me to her lips and sent
One wild pang through me; then refrained her hand,
And whispered: "Hear——" and into my frail flanks,
Into my bursting veins, the whole sea poured
Its spaces and its thunder; and I feared.

We came to cities, and Life piped on me
Low calls to dreaming girls,
In counting-house windows, through the chink of gold,
Flung cries that fired the captive brain of youth,
And made the heavy merchant at his desk
Curse us for a cracked hurdy-gurdy; Life
Mimicked the hurdy-gurdy, and we passed.

We climbed the slopes of solitude, and there
Life met a god, who challenged her and said:
"Thy pipe against my lyre"; But "Wait!" she laughed.
And in my live flank dug a finger-hole,
And wrung new music from it. Ah, the pain!

Lyra Mystica

We climbed and climbed, and left the god behind.
We saw the earth spread vaster than the sea,
With infinite surge of mountains surfed with snow,
And a silence that was louder than the deep;
But on the utmost pinnacle Life again
Hid me, and I heard the terror in her hair.
Safe in new vales, I ached for the old pang,
And clamored "Play me against a god again!"
 "Poor Marsyas-mortal—he shall bleed thee yet,"
 She breathed, and kissed me, stilling the dim need.
But evermore it woke, and stabbed my flank
With yearnings for new music and new pain.
"Another note against another god!"
I clamored; and she answered, "Bide my time.
Of every heart-wound I will make a stop,
And drink thy life in music, pang by pang.
But first thou must yield the notes I stored in thee
At dawn beside the river. Take my lips."
She kissed me like a lover, but wept,
Remembering that high song against the god,
And the old songs slept in me, and I was dumb.

We came to cavernous foul places, blind
With harpy-wings, and sulphurous with the glare
Of sinful furnaces—where hunger toiled,
And pleasure gathered in a starveling prey,
And death fed delicately on young bones.

"Now sing!" cried Life, and set her lips to me.
"Here are gods also. Wilt thou pipe for Dis?"
My cry was drowned beneath the furnace roar,

Choked by the sulphur-fumes; and beast-lipped gods
Laughed down on me, and mouthed the flutes of hell.

"Now sing!" said Life, reissuing to the stars;
And wrung a new note from my wounded side.

So came we to clear spaces, and the sea.
And now I felt its volume in my heart,
And my heart waxed with it, and Life played on me
The song of the Infinite. "Now the stars," she said.

Then from the utmost pinnacle again
She poured me on the wide sidereal stream,
And I grew with her great breathings, till we swept
The interstellar spaces like new worlds
Loosed from the fiery ruin of a star.

Edith Wharton

I DO NOT FEAR

American Contemporary

I do not fear to lay my body down
  In death, to share
The life of the dark earth and lose my own,
  If God is there.

I have so loved all sense of Him, sweet might
  Of color and of sound,—
His tangible loveliness and living light
  That robes me 'round.

Lyra Mystica

If to His heart in the hushed grave and dim
    We sink more near,
It shall be well—living we rest in Him.
    Only I fear

Lest from my God in lonely death I lapse,
    And the dumb clod
Lose Him; for God is life, and death perhaps
    Exile from God.

John Hall Wheelock

THE OTHER PLACE

American Contemporary

There is a far-off, closest place
  Where I stand tall as I was meant to be.
There I look into your shining face
  And see the light that you would have me see.

There is not Space as we know Space,
  For close your hand locks, your breath lies. . . .
(*Oh, how merciful with honor is your face,*
  How pure your eyes!)

My youth and age are one in me
  (*There is not Time as we know Time*)
Oh, look and feel and see!
  There are no miles to go, no steps to climb,
We see all-swift, all far,
For God is all this Other Place,
God in the briefest flower, the oldest star!

Lyra Mystica

(The fern I passed and did not wait to gather
   When I was young, I bend and gather now,
And oh, how beautiful the fruit and bud and blossom
   On the long-perished bough!)

I feel the fern's furred stem,
   Smell the dead peach-bough's sun-hot sharp perfume,
I can clasp you, clasp them,
   And, now there is no gloom,
Love the true soul that is the soul of you,
Knowing the darkest shattering hour's clear blue. . . .

Oh, sometimes we reach through
   With human eye and hand
To all, and know
   That once more we are in our own real land. . . .

This is a phantom-show,
This little three-wayed prison where we go.
Where blowing veils called Present and called Past
Dream-woven lock us fast—
Come! We shall break this painted film at last—
Here is our own real sky!

Margaret Widdemer

BARTER

American Contemporary

   If in that secret place
   Where thou hast hidden it, there yet is lying
   Thy dearest bitterness, thy fondest sin,

Though thou hast cherished it with hurt and crying,
Lift now thy face,
Unlock the bolted door and let God in
And lay it in His holy Hands to take. . . .
(How such an evil gift can please Him so
I do not know)
But, keeping it for wages, He shall make
Thy foul room sweet for thee with blowing wind
(He is so serviceable and so kind)
And set sweet water for thy soul's distress,
Instead of what thou hadst, of bitterness,
And He shall bend and spread
Green balsam boughs to make a scented bed
Soft for thy lying
Where thine own thorns pricked in. . . .

Who would not pay away his dearest sin
To let such service in?

Margaret Widdemer

THE PILGRIM

American Contemporary

I am my ancient self,
   Long paths I've trod,
The living light before,
   Behind, the rod:
And in the beam and blow
   The misty God.

I am my ancient self.
   My flesh is young,

But old, mysterious words
    Engage my tongue,
And weird, lost songs
    Old bards have sung.

I have not fared alone.
    In mount and dell
The one I fain would be
    Stands by me well,
And bids my man's heart list
    To the far bell.

Give me nor ease nor goal—
    Only the Way,
A bit of bread and sleep
    Where the white waters play,
The pines, the patient stars,
    And the new day.

Richard Wightman

THE SERVANTS

American Contemporary

Singers, sing! The hoary world
Needs reminder of its youth:
Prophet, tell! The darkness lies
On the labyrinths of truth:

Builder, build! Let rocks uprise
Into cities 'neath thy hand:
Farmer, till! The sun and rain

Hearken for the seed's demand:
Artist, paint! Thy canvases
Patiently convey thy soul:
Writer, write! With pen blood-dipped
Trace no segment, but the whole:
Teacher, teach! Thyself the creed—
Only that a child may know:
Dreamer, dream! Nor hide thy face
Though thy castles crumble low.
Where the toiler turns the sod
Man beholds the living God.

Richard Wightman

DEEP SEA SOUNDINGS

Mariner, what of the deep?
                    This of the deep:
Twilight is there, and solemn changeless calm;
Beauty is there, and tender, healing balm—
Balm with no root in earth, or air, or sea,
Poised by the finger of God, it floateth free,
And, as it threads the waves, the sound doth rise,—
Hither shall come no further sacrifice;
Never again the anguished clutch at life,
Never again great Love and Death in strife;
He who hath suffered all need fear no more;
Quiet his portion now forevermore.

Mariner, what of the deep?
                    This of the deep:
Solitude dwells not there, though silence reign,

Mighty is the brotherhood of loss and pain;
There is communion past the need of speech,
There is love no words of love can reach;
Heavy the waves that superincumbent press,
But as we labor here with constant stress,
Hand doth hold out to hand not help alone,
But the deep bliss of being fully known.
There are no kindred like the kin of sorrow,
There is no hope like theirs who know no morrow.

Mariner, what of the deep?
       This of the deep:
Though we have travelled past the line of day,
Glory of night doth light us on our way,
Radiance that comes not how nor whence,
Rainbows without rain, past duller sense,
Music of hidden reefs and waves long past,
Thunderous organ tones from far-off blast,
Harmony, victrix, throned in state sublime,
Couched on the wrecks be-gemmed with pearls of time;
Never a wreck but brings some beauty here;
Down where the waves are stilled the sun shines clear;
Deeper than life, the plan of life doth lie;
He who knows all, fears not. Great Death shall die.
         Sarah Williams

TENEBRAE

I cannot tell what psalms these voices sing,
 Each one more harsh and stern than that before,
 While at each chanted cadence answering

Lyra Mystica

A silent priest steps through the swinging door,
And there's one light the less, one candle gone.
My mind is wandered like the melody
Spun through these plaintive polyphonic strains,
And the gloom comes, sad as a threnody,
Yet as harmonious as April rains.
Tenebrae factae sunt: Thy Laws, O Lord,
To me, on pilgrimage, at eve, at dawn,
Have been my canticles, and what reward
Blessed my vigil? What fierce sacrament,
Passion or pain, is fixed to be my goal?
Here in the darkness, the last taper spent,
I wait the crucifixion of my soul.

Lawrence Wilson

A PAGAN RE-INVOKES THE TWENTY-THIRD PSALM

American Contemporary

I knock again and try the key,
I, who, enraged, fled from Thy temple's trees
Because the presence of my enemies
Around the table there offended me.
I, who laid up so long and bitterly
Complaints and old reproaches, on my knees
Offer regret for years misspent as these,
And wonder how such folly came to be.
Anoint again my head, and let me walk
The valley of the shadow, with the rod
Thou hast afforded for my comfort, God:

My soul restored, and singing through my veins.
Forgive the years of idle, foolish talk:
The cup that runneth over still remains.

Robert Wolf

WRITTEN IN A VOLUME OF THE IMITATION OF CHRIST

American Contemporary

Open the garden gate, walk in, my heart;
What pleasant herbs are these that sweetly smell?
Must I return from where I did depart?
The harsh, loud, crying world I bade farewell.

The garden shines with blossoms of delight,
The Lamb of God walks whitely through the grass;
Here with this little volume, quaintly bright,
I open gardens for my heart to pass.

Whose are those blessed figures clad in light?
What are the crimson flowers like raptures burning
Among the sacred lilies, cold and white,
Guiding my feet to paths of peace returning?

Open the garden gate, walk in, my heart!
What fires of peace! What sacred paths we took!
Enter the Heavenly Gardens, nor depart—
See, they are opened by a little book!

Marya Zaturenska

NOTES

1. "Death Is before Me Today." Doubtless this is the oldest poem in the Anthology. Mr. Walter de la Mare speaks of it as "the most ancient poem I know." It must have been composed at least five thousand years ago, yet it could have been written in our own day by someone whose soul was sure that "life is ever lord of death, and love can never lose its own."

1. "Hymn to Aton." This hymn, in the best sense a prayer, was found engraved on the coffin of Akhenaton. "Aton" is the ancient name for the sun, but that the term was used as a symbol of the eternal and spiritual God there can be no doubt. Among the fragments of the Aton faith which still survive are two Hymns to Aton, one of which, at least, bears a striking resemblance to one of the noblest of the Hebrew Psalms (CIV).

5. "This I Ask Thee." Translation by A. V. Williams Jackson.

5. "Hymn to Zeus." First Chorus from *Agamemnon*.

6. "Let Us Hasten, Let Us Fly." From *The Frogs*.

7. "Beauty." A paraphrase from *The Symposium* I. 581, 582. I have used Jowett's translation, and have only slightly altered the exact language of the text. "Fair bodies," I am led to believe, is a better translation than "fair boys and youths."

9. "All These Things Live." Ecclesiasticus XLII. 23–25; XLIII. 26–28.

9. "Inspiration." Translated by J. Rendel Harris. *The Odes of Solomon*, a collection of forty-two hymns,

Notes

is pseudonymous. The *Odes*, written in Greek, and the *Psalms of Solomon*, written in Hebrew, appear in the sixth century, A.D., in a list of books, including most of the Old Testament Apocrypha. The *Psalms of Solomon*, also pseudonymous, may be ascribed to the first century, B.C., and the *Odes* to the first century, A.D. The translator discovered the first complete manuscript of both the *Odes* and the *Psalms* in 1908 and published an English version of them in 1909.

11. "Love." I. Corinthians xiii. I have used Moffatt's New Translation, with only two or three minor changes, for the sake of euphony. "Know only in part" is a return to the more familiar version. "Passes away" more closely follows the text of the American Revision.

I make no apology for including only a single selection from the New Testament, a book incalculably rich in mysticism. The whole atmosphere of it is mystical. The reader will not forget that the name of St. Paul is first among the mystics of the Christian church. Back of St. Augustine are Plotinus and Plato; but between Plato and Plotinus is St. Paul, in whom—and in the writer of the Fourth Gospel—Christian mysticism first becomes articulate.

12–15. "Over All Presides the Universal Soul." From *Ennead* VI. 8. "We Are Not Cast Away." From *Ennead* V. 1. "The Soul Is in the Body as the Pilot in the Ship." From *Ennead* IV. 3. "We May Ascend to Him." From *Ennead* VI. 9. Paraphrased by the editor from translations by Kenneth Sylvan Guthrie.

15–17. "Great Art Thou, O Lord." From *Confessions* I. 1. "And How Shall I Call upon My God?" From *Confessions*. II. 2. Translations by J. G. Pilkington. Not a few of St. Augustine's Confessions are, vir-

Notes

tually, hymns of praise, and are written in such rhythmic prose that they fall quite naturally into verse form which, while irregular, may still be properly classified as poetry.

19. "Invocation." Translation by Israel Zangwill.
20. "Quatrains." Translation by Edward Granville Browne.
20–22. "Where Shall I Find Thee?" "The Lord Is My Portion." Translations by Nina Salaman.
22. "I Died." Translation by Edward Granville Browne.
23. "Canticle of the Sun." Translation by Maurice Francis Egan.
24–41. "Ineffable Love Divine." From *Lauda* XCI. "O Soul of Mine, How Noble Wert Thou Made!" From *Lauda* XXXV. "O Love Divine and Great." From *Lauda* LXXXII. Translations by Mrs. Theodore Beck.
44. "O Splendour of God!" From *The Divine Comedy (Paradiso)* XXX, ll. 97–120; XXXI, ll. 1–2; 13–15; 25–27.
45. "Passionate, with Longing in Mine Eyes." From *The Lâlla—Vakyani, or Wise Sayings of Lal Ded (or Lâlla) a Mystic Poetess of Ancient Kasmir*. Translation by Sir George Grierson and Dr. Lionel D. Barnett.
46. "The Gift of Intelligence." From *L'Ornament des Noces Spirituelles, de Ruysbroeck l'Admirable, Traduit du Flamand par Maurice Maeterlinck*. English translation by Jane T. Stoddart.
52–53. "O Servant, Where Dost Thou Seek Me?" "My Lord Hides Himself." "He Who Is Meek and Contented." Translations by Rabindranath Tagore.
53–55. "The Obscure Night of the Soul." "Living Flame of Love." Translations by Arthur Symons.

Notes

56. "Lines Written in Her Breviary." Translation by Henry W. Longfellow.

56. "If, Lord, Thy Love for Me Is Strong." Translation by Arthur Symons.

66. "Icarus." From *Robert Jones's Second Book of Songs and Airs*.

73. "A Little Bird I Am." Written in prison.

75. "'Tis Not the Skill of Human Art." Translation by T. C. Upham.

90. "Ode to God." Translation by Sir John Bowring.

95. "All Are but Parts." From *The Essay on Man*.

100. "There Is One Mind." From *Religious Musings*.

101. "He Is Made One with Nature." From "Adonais."

107. "Now That I Have Grown to Manhood." Translation by Norman Macleod. Though a recent *Critical Examination of the Poet and His Works* excludes Heine from the list of religious poets, we have only to read these and the following lines to give him a place among those whose lips have, at rare times, been touched with the mystic fire. This poem is, in a true sense, a confession of faith.

108. "Peace." From *Nordseebilder*. Translation by Jane T. Stoddart. These lines are difficult to translate, as the euphonies on which much of their beauty depends cannot at all be reproduced in English.

110. "L'Infinito." Translation by Lorna de Lucchi.

111. "The Prophet." Translation by Babette Deutsch and Avraham Yarmolinsky.

112. "Confession." Translation by Arthur Symons.

117. "Calm Soul of All Things." From "Lines Written in Kensington Gardens."

123. "Therefore to Whom Turn I but to Thee?" From "Abt Vogler."

Notes

127. "I Went to Sleep; and Now I Am Refreshed." From "The Dream of Gerontius."
133. "Prayer." From *In Memoriam*, CXXXI.
146. "For I Have Learned to Look on Nature." From "Lines Composed a Few Miles from Tintern Abbey."
148. "I Gaze Aloof." From "Second Day of Creation."
154–159. "God's Grandeur." "The Wreck of the Deutschland." "Pied Beauty." "A reader of Hopkins should expect obstacles; he must be prepared for difficulties that, at first, seem insuperable. He must be willing to accept a series of musical dissonances. . . . He must penetrate obscurities . . . but he will be rewarded. Behind the tortured constructions and heaped-up epithets there is magnificence," Louis Untermeyer, in *Modern British Poetry*.
171. "Death." Printed in *Ballou's Magazine*, June, 1858.
184. "Immortal." From *A White Sunday*.
187. "Eventide." The author should not be confused with Caroline Atwater Mason.
193. "The Starry Host." From *God and the Soul*.
199. "A Dance Chant." Translation by E. S. Parker.
232. "Where the Blessed Feet Have Trod." Michael Field was the pen-name adopted by two women, Katherine Harris Bradley and her niece, Edith Emma Cooper. *A Selection from the Poems of Michael Field* was published by The Poetry Bookshop in 1923.
243. "Let Us beside the River Rest Awhile." From *The House of Dreams*.
252. "At Beach St. Mary." From *Songs of Night and Day*.
302. "The Holy Face." From *La Ville*, in M.

Notes

Claudel's *Théâtre*. Translation by Henry Morton Robinson.

313. "Immortality." From *Songs of the World War*.

314. "The Fringe of Heaven." Written while flying.

327. "Thou Canst Choose the Eastern Circle." Quoted in *The Meaning and Value of Mysticism*, by E. Herman.

339. "By Those Heights We Dare to Dare." From *In Excelsis*.

342. "It Were Not Hard, We Think, to Serve Him." Quoted in *Voices of the Great Creator*, by Albert D. Belden.

344–347. "O Thou, in Whom We Live and Breathe." "Father, We Thank Thee." "O Thou Who Lovest with Divine Passion." From *A Book of Prayers Written for Use in an Indian College*. In the author's Foreword, Mr. Hoyland acknowledges his indebtedness to Rabindranath Tagore and "to one or two other modern authors for help in expressing the searchings after God of men belonging to several differing religious systems."

348. "In This, O Nature, Yield." Sir Ronald Ross is a physician and bacteriologist, Director in Chief of the Ross Institute and Hospital for Tropical Diseases in London. In 1892 he commenced a series of studies of malaria, and in 1895 carried to a successful conclusion, by elaborate experiments, the proof of his theory that micro-organisms of the disease are carried by mosquitoes. This was one of the most revolutionary discoveries in the history of medical science, affecting a vast population, especially in the tropics. These two poems indicate the spirit in which Sir Ronald approached the baffling problem, and his sense of spiritual victory when Nature yielded up her secret.

Notes

366. "The Guest." "Please regard my lines as a commentary on the Master's words in Matthew xxv. 40, 'Inasmuch as ye have done it unto the least of these, my brethren, ye have done it unto me.'" AUTHOR.

372. "The Frozen Grail." Dedicated to Robert Peary and his companions at the North Pole.

406. From *First Poems*, by "Henry K. Herbert." Privately printed, 1908.

432. "Psalm." From *The Lyric Year*.

455. The author's Foreword, a mid-volume preface to a group of mystical poems in *Collected Poems*, throws light on the poet's conception of the mystic sense—"the swinging open, little or much" of a door opening upon Reality:

"To many people there is only a blank wall at the world's end. And of these, many accept it contentedly, needing and desiring nothing more. There are others who will tell you that they have found a door in the wall, leading to another place. To most of us it only swings wide once or twice in a lifetime, because of the crash against it of some great joy or sorrow. To some lucky ones it is often open. And there have been a few men and women, like Siddhartha and St. Francis of Assisi and St. Teresa, who have said that there was not even any wall.

"The poems which follow here concern the swinging open, little or much, of that door. They might, I suppose, be called mystic. But the word has been used too loosely and mistakenly to be descriptive. I would rather call them poems of reality."

INDEX OF AUTHORS

	PAGE
Abu Sa'id Ibn Abi'l-Khayr.	
Quatrains	20
Adcock, A. St. John.	
Immortality	313
A. E. See George William Russell.	
Æschylus.	
Hymn to Zeus	5
Akhenaton (Amenhotep IV).	
Hymn to Aton	1
Albertson, Augusta.	
The Guest	366
Aldrich, Thomas Bailey.	
I vex me not	209
Ames, Charles G.	
Hidden life	166
Ames, Mary Clemmer.	
Go not away	167
Anonymous.	
A Ballade of the centre	211
The circuit of being	148
A dance chant	199
Death	171
Death is before me today	1
Hymn of Sivaite Puritans	18
Icarus	66
They list for me the things I may not know	210
Aristophanes.	
Let us hasten, let us fly	6
Arnold, Matthew.	
Calm Soul of all things	117
East London	116
Atkinson, Mary E.	
Lord, I have shut my door	168
Babcock, Maltbie D.	
No distant Lord	168
Baker, Karle Wilson.	
Pronouns	371

Index of Authors

	PAGE
Barker, Elsa.	
The frozen grail	372
Beaumont, Joseph.	
Seek no more abroad, say I	77
Benét, William Rose.	
The falconer of God	373
Ben-Sira (From the wisdom of).	
All these things live	9
Bewsher, Paul R.	
The fringe of heaven	314
Binyon, Laurence.	
A colloquy	315
Blackie, John Stuart.	
All things are full of God	153
Blackmore, R. D.	
Dominus illuminatio mea	117
Blake, William.	
Auguries of innocence	99
The divine image	98
(From) Milton	97
Bradford, Gamaliel.	
God	375
Bridges, Robert.	
Johannes Milton Senex	226
Brontë, Emily.	
Last lines	119
The visionary	118
Brown, Alice.	
A pagan's prayer	377
Brown, Thomas Edward.	
Land, ho!	161
My garden	163
Specula	162
Browne, Sir Thomas.	
The night is come	77
Browning, Elizabeth Barrett.	
(From) The soul's travelling	120
Browning, Robert.	
Prospice	122
Therefore to whom turn I but to Thee?	123
Bryant, William Cullen.	
To a waterfowl	169

Index of Authors

Buchanan, Robert.
(From) The city of dream (two extracts) 150, 151
Buckton, Alice Mary.
Before the dawn 375
Burroughs, John.
Waiting 213
Burt, Maxwell Struthers.
The hill-born 377
Burton, Richard Eugene.
God's garden 378
Bynner, Witter.
A little hill among New Hampshire hills 378
Calderón de la Barca, Pedro.
Thou art of all created things 72
Call, Mark W.
Renunciation 379
Canton, William.
Crying Abba, Father 229
Carlin, Francis.
Perfection 352
Carman, Bliss.
Veni Creator 265
Vestigia 264
Carpenter, Edward.
Over the city 316
So thin a veil 317
Carruth, William H.
Each in his own tongue 261
C. F.
Prayer 296
Childe, Wilfred Rowland.
Turris eburnea 317
Claudel, Paul.
The Holy Face 302
Cleaves, Charles Poole.
I have lifted my eyes 380
Cleghorn, Sarah N.
An air of coolness plays upon his face 283
The anodyne 284
Clough, Arthur Hugh.
With whom is no variableness, neither shadow of turning   125

Index of Authors

	PAGE
Coates, Florence Earle.	
Per aspera	233
Coleridge, Mary Elizabeth.	
After St. Augustine	262
Coleridge, Samuel Taylor.	
There is one mind	100
Collyer, Robert.	
Where is God?	163
Conolly, Myles E.	
Quo vadis?	381
Coolidge, Grace.	
The open door	381
Coolidge, Susan.	
Yea every day He comes	171
Cousins, James H.	
The quest	160
Crashaw, Richard.	
On Saint Teresa	78
A song	78
Crouse, M. Elizabeth.	
Light	190
Dante	
O splendour of God!	44
Da Todi, Jacopone.	
Ineffable Love Divine	24
O love divine and great	41
O soul of mine, how noble wert thou made!	37
David, King of Judah and Israel.	
The Lord is my shepherd	2
O Lord Thou hast searched me	3
Dawson, Richard Lew.	
Faith	382
Dawson, William James.	
Inspirations	242
Let us beside the river rest awhile	243
De Bary, Anna.	
Under a Wiltshire apple tree	319
Deland, Margaret.	
Deaf	383
De León, Luis.	
The heavenly light	57
A night of stars	59

Index of Authors

	PAGE
Derzhávin, Gavrila Románovich.	
Ode to God	90
De Vere, Aubrey Thomas.	
Implicit faith	201
Dickinson, Emily.	
Chartless	174
Dost thou remember me?	173
Eternity, I'm coming	172
My faith is larger than the hills	173
Dodge, Mary Mapes.	
The two mysteries	214
Dowden, Edward.	
A new hymn for solitude	222
Seeking God	222
Dowden, Mrs. Edward.	
Adrift	160
Drinkwater, John.	
A prayer	321
Earle, Mabel.	
The passer-by	384
Emerson, Ralph Waldo.	
The problem	176
(From) Threnody	174
Ericson, Eric.	
The cliff	203
Fechner, Theodore.	
In God my soul reposes	114
Field, Michael.	
Where the blessed feet have trod	232
Firkins, Chester.	
On a subway express	385
Fletcher, Phineas.	
(From) The Divine Lover	67
Flynn, Claire Wallace.	
The glory of the grass	386
Foulke, William Dudley.	
Life's evening	388
Fraser-Tytler, Christina Catherine.	
In summer fields	350
Fyleman, Rose.	
Enough	323

Index of Authors

	PAGE
Gabirol, Ibn.	
Invocation	19
Gale, Zona.	
Contours	391
The secret way	388
George, Stefan.	
Rapture	304
Gibran, Kahlil.	
Of children	289
Of reason and passion	290
Gibson, Elizabeth.	
I know not	323
Gilder, Richard Watson.	
Holy land	323
The invisible	225
Undying light	224
Gilman, Charlotte Perkins.	
Birth	393
Give way!	392
Goad, Harold E.	
Spring's sacrament	395
Golding, Louis.	
Ploughman at the plough	324
Goodwin, Grace Duffield.	
Love holds me	395
Gore-Booth, Eva.	
The quest	353
Guiney, Louise Imogen.	
Borderlands	262
Summum bonum	263
Guiterman, Arthur.	
In the hospital	396
Gunsaulus, Frank W.	
At Beach St. Mary	252
Guyon, Jeanne Marie.	
A little bird I am	73
'Tis not the skill of human art	75
Halevi, Jehudah.	
The Lord is my portion	22
Where shall I find Thee?	20
Haley, Molly Anderson.	
Miracles	397

Index of Authors

	PAGE
Haney, James P.	
A craftsman's creed	398
Havergal, Francis Ridley.	
(From) The thoughts of God	125
Heine, Heinrich.	
Now that I have grown to manhood	107
Peace	108
Henley, William Ernest.	
Thick is the darkness	126
Herbert, George.	
The elixir	69
Love bade me welcome	71
The pulley	71
Hodgson, William Noel.	
Before action	398
Hopkins, Gerard Manley.	
God's grandeur	154
Pied beauty	159
The wreck of the Deutschland	155
Hovey, Richard.	
The messenger	176
Hoyland, J. S.	
Father, we thank Thee	345
O Thou, in whom we live and breathe	344
O Thou who lovest with divine passion	347
Ingeman, B. S.	
Evening song	115
Jackson, Helen Hunt.	
Doubt	177
Jalal ud-Din Rumi.	
I died	22
Jones, Thomas. S., Jr.	
The ordeal	403
The parting	402
Prayer	401
Refuge	401
Saint Francis	400
Saint John of the Cross	399
Jordan, David Starr.	
Men told me, Lord!	233
Kabir	
He who is meek and contented	53

Index of Authors

	PAGE
My Lord hides Himself	52
O servant, where dost thou seek Me?	52

Keller, Helen.
In the garden of the Lord 403

Kemp, Harry.
The voices of Christmas 404

Kempis, Thomas à.
I will hearken what the Lord God will speak 48
Speak, Lord, for Thy servant heareth 50

Kilmer, Aline.
The gift 406

Kilmer, Joyce.
The soldier in France 292

Kimball, Harriet M.
The Guest 178

Knibbs, Henry Herbert.
He is the light 406

Lâlla.
Passionate, with longing in mine eyes 45

Lanier, Sidney.
(From) Florida Sunday 179
(From) The marshes of Glynn 180
A song of the future 182

Larcom, Lucy.
Immortal 184
Our Christ 183
The world we live in 185

Le Gallienne, Richard.
The second crucifixion 325

Leonard, William Ellery.
To the victor 407

Leopardi, Giacomo.
L'infinito 110

Lindsay, Ruth Temple.
Thou canst choose the eastern circle 327

Lindsay, Vachel.
Heart of God 284

Longley, Snow.
Sonnet 408

Lowell, James Russell.
God is not dumb 186
Longing 185

Index of Authors

	PAGE
L. W.	
Christ in Flanders	309
MacDonald, George.	
Lost and found	206
Obedience	205
A prayer for the past	203
Macleod, Fiona. See William Sharp.	
Markham, Edwin.	
Revelation	408
Masefield, John.	
(From) The Everlasting Mercy	328
Sonnets	329
Mason, Caroline Atherton.	
Eventide	187
Mason-Manheim, Madeline.	
Prayer	409
Meynell, Alice.	
Christmas Night	234
A general communion	235
I am the way	236
To a daisy	239
To the mother of Christ the Son of Man	236
The treasure	237
The unknown God	238
Millay, Edna St. Vincent.	
God's world	410
Monkhouse, Cosmo.	
The spectrum	215
Moody, William Vaughn.	
I stood within the heart of God	279
More, Paul Elmer.	
(From) A century of Indian epigrams	411
Morgan, Angela.	
Kinship	411
A song of thanksgiving	413
Morris, Kenneth.	
Dusk	414
Morris, Sir Lewis.	
A heathen hymn	207
Morton, David.	
Symbol	416
Who walks with beauty	415

Index of Authors

	PAGE
Muirhead, John Spencer.	
Quiet	416
Myers, Frederick William Henry.	
A cosmic outlook	218
A last appeal	219
Lo, as some bard	220
Naidu, Sarojini.	
In salutation to the eternal peace	300
The soul's prayer	301
Neihardt, John G.	
L'envoi	417
Prayer for pain	418
Newman, John Henry.	
I went to sleep; and now I am refreshed	127
Newton, Joseph Fort.	
The quest	419
Nichols, Robert.	
The secret garden	331
Noyes, Alfred.	
The origin of life	333
The paradox	335
Oppenheim, James.	
The cry of man	420
Palgrave, Francis Turner.	
The City of God	139
Palmer, Herbert E.	
The pilgrim	337
Patmore, Coventry Kersey Dighton.	
Sponsa Dei	137
Peabody, Josephine Preston.	
In the silence	282
The source	281
Percy, William Alexander.	
Overtones	425
Petrarch.	
Sonnet to Laura	45
Phillips, Stephen.	
The poet's prayer	276
Plato.	
Beauty	7
Plotinus.	
Over all presides the Universal Soul	12

Index of Authors

	PAGE
The soul is in the body as the pilot in the ship	14
We are not cast away	13
We may ascend to Him	15

Plunkett, Joseph M.
   I see His blood upon the rose 292

Poe, Edgar Allan.
   The goddess's song from "Al Aaraaf" 188

Pope, Alexander.
   All are but parts 95
   The universal prayer 95

Porter, Laura Spencer.
   Life and death 189

Pushkin, Alexander Sergeyevich.
   The prophet 111

Quarles, Francis.
   Ev'n like two little bank-dividing brooks 68

Realf, Richard.
   De mortuis nil nisi bonum 164
   The Word 164

Reese, Lizette Woodworth.
   Growth 427
   In praise of common things 425
   Trust 427

Rhoades, James.
   (From) Out of the silence 216

Rhys, Grace.
   Introit 274
   The pavilions of peace 273

Rice, Cale Young.
   A litany for latter-day mystics 430
   A rhapsodist's song 428

Robinson, Edwin Arlington.
   I had a dream last night 431

Rock, Madeleine Caron.
   He is the Lonely Greatness of the world 338

Rodd, Sir James Rennell.
   By those heights we dare to dare 339

Ross, Sir Ronald.
   In this, O nature, yield 348
   Reply 348

Rossetti, Christina.
   The goal in sight 141

Index of Authors

	PAGE
Up-hill	141

Russell, George William (A.E.)
By the margin of the great deep	353
The city	360
The divine vision	354
The twilight of earth	357
A vision of beauty	355

Ryan, Abram J.
The seen and the unseen	191

St. Augustine.
And how shall I call upon my God?	17
Great art Thou, O Lord	15

St. Francis of Assisi.
Canticle of the sun	23

St. John of the Cross.
Living flame of love	555
The obscure night of the soul	53

St. Paul.
Love	11

St. Teresa.
If, Lord, Thy love for me is strong	56
Lines written in her breviary	56

Salmon, Arthur L.
By Severn's banks	340

Sampter, Jessie E.
Psalm	432

Santayana, George.
Sonnet	366

Sassoon, Siegfried.
I lived my days apart	341

Schauffler, Robert Haven.
The White Comrade	435

Scheffler, Johann (Angelus Silesius).
In thine own heart	75

Scollard, Clinton.
First flight	434
The great voice	434
Sanctuary	435

Scudder, Eliza.
I cannot find Thee	202

Seebach, Margaret.
It were not hard, we think, to serve Him	342

Index of Authors

	PAGE

Shairp, John Campbell.
    I have a life with Christ to live 149
Sharp, William (Fiona Macleod).
    Desire 248
    The mystic's prayer 248
    The rune of age 248
    The valley of silence 250
    The white peace 251
    The white star of time 251
Shelley, Percy Bysshe.
    He is made one with nature 101
    Hymn to intellectual beauty 104
Silesius, Angelus. See Johann Scheffler.
Sill, Edward Rowland.
    Starlight 278
Solis-Cohen, Solomon.
    For I know that my Redeemer liveth 364
    O Lord, where shall I find Thee? 362
Solomon (From Ode VI).
    Inspiration 9
Solovev, Vladimir.
    Shadows 116
Southwell, Robert.
    The Burning Babe 63
    Of the blessed sacrament of the aulter 62
Spalding, John Lancaster.
    The starry host 193
Spenser, Edmund.
    (From) Hymn to heavenly beauty 65
Stead, W. Force.
    On Christmas eve 343
Stephens, James.
    The voice of God 343
Sterling, George.
    The final faith 280
Stork, Charles Wharton.
    The elder sacrament 438
    Falterings toward the unknown God 440
    The rose and God 444
Storke, Helen Eldred.
    To be old 446

Index of Authors

	PAGE
Suso, Henry.	
The knight of Jesus	47
Swinburne, Algernon Charles.	
Off shore	212
Symonds, John Addington.	
Adventante Deo	134
An invocation	135
The prism of life	137
Tabb, John Bannister.	
All in all	227
Christ and the pagan	228
An interpreter	228
Tagore, Rabindranath.	
Autumn	300
(From) Fruit-gathering	299
The oarsmen	297
Taylor, Rachel Annand.	
The immortal hour	350
Teasdale, Sara.	
A star map	447
The voice	446
Tennyson, Alfred, Lord.	
(From) The ancient sage	128
Crossing the bar	132
Flower in the crannied wall	133
The higher pantheism	130
The human cry	131
Prayer	133
Thomas, Edith M.	
Patmos	241
The reply of Socrates	240
Thompson, Francis.	
Desiderium indesideratum	257
The Hound of Heaven	253
The kingdom of God	257
Thompson, Maurice.	
(From) The final thought	194
Thomson, James.	
(From) The seasons	94
Towne, Charles Hanson.	
Silence	448

Index of Authors

	PAGE
Townshend, Chauncey Hare.	
Thy joy in sorrow	448
Traherne, Thomas.	
Amendment	80
The rapture	82
The vision	82
Trench, Richard Chenevix.	
If there had anywhere appeared	134
Tynan, Katharine.	
The flying wheel	271
The image	269
Of an orchard	270
Sanctuaries	267
Sheep and lambs	270
Underhill, Evelyn.	
Immanence	308
Supersensual	307
Uxbridge road	305
van Dyke, Henry.	
God of the open air	449
van Ruysbroeck, Jan.	
The gift of intelligence	46
Vaughan, Henry.	
The dwelling-place	88
The retreate	87
The world	85
They are all gone into the world of light	89
Verlaine, Paul.	
Confession	112
Waples, Annie Sophia.	
The every day of life	311
Ward, Frederick William Orde.	
Redemption	312
Warren, Henry W.	
Transfiguration	206
Watson, Sir William.	
Invention	313
Wattles, Willard.	
Acceptance	450
By every ebb	450
Wharton, Edith.	
Life	451

Index of Authors

	PAGE
Wheelock, John Hall.	
I do not fear	454
Whitman, Walt.	
(From) Passage to India	195
(From) Prayer of Columbus	195
Whittier, John Greenleaf.	
The Eternal Goodness	197
Whytehead, Thomas.	
I gaze aloof	148
Widdemer, Margaret.	
Barter	456
The other place	455
Wightman, Richard.	
The pilgrim	457
The servants	458
Wilkinson, Marguerite.	
A chant out of doors	285
Out of the dark	286
Sonnets of the new birth (2, 4, 12)	287
Williams, Roger.	
God makes a path	90
Williams, Sarah.	
Deep sea soundings	459
Wilson, Lawrence.	
Tenebrae	460
Wolfe, Robert.	
A pagan re-invokes the twenty-third psalm	461
Wordsworth, William.	
(From) The excursion	145
For I have learned to look on nature	146
(From) Ode: intimations of immortality	142
Yes, it was the mountain echo	147
Wylie, Elinor.	
This corruptible	293
Yeats, William Butler.	
The rose of the world	352
Zaturenska, Marya.	
Written in a volume of the Imitation of Christ	462
Zoroaster.	
This I ask Thee	5

INDEX TO FIRST LINES

	PAGE
Abba, in Thine eternal years	229
A fire-mist and a planet,	261
Against the quicksands of receding life to sink	446
A garden is a lovesome thing, God wot!	163
A little bird I am,	73
A little hill among New Hampshire hills	378
All are but parts of one stupendous whole,	95
All around him Patmos lies,	241
All in the April evening,	270
All living creatures' pain,	312
All of heaven in my hands—	447
All riches, goods and braveries never told	179
All sights and sounds of day and year,	203
All that began with God, in God must end:	137
All that is broken shall be mended;	335
All the birds shall sing to me,	428
All these things live and abide forever,	9
All things are full of God. Thus spoke	153
Alone I climb the hanging crags of prayer,	287
And a woman who held a babe against her bosom said,...	289
And did those feet in ancient time	97
And how shall I call upon my God—my God and my Lord?	17
And the priestess spoke again and said:	290
As I in hoary winter's night	63
As my soul has been dutiful	212
As the hand moves over the harp, and the strings speak,	9
At cool of day, with God I walk	187
Athirst in spirit, through the gloom	111
Atoms as old as stars,	446
At the dawn I seek Thee,	19
A wife at daybreak I shall be,	172
Backward!—beyond this momentary woe!—	218
Because on the branch that is tapping my pane	396
But whoso may, thrice happy man him hold	65

487

Index to First Lines

	PAGE
By all the glories of the day,	398
By every ebb of the river-tide	450
By those heights we dare to dare	339
Calm soul of all things! make it mine	117
Come in the glory of Thine excellence;	203
Cowering in fear, man felt himself alone	440
Day and night I wander widely through the wilderness of thought,	375
Dear friend, seest thou not	116
Death is before me today	1
De mortuis nil nisi bonum. When	164
Does the road wind up-hill all the way?	141
Do you hear the tumult of death afar,	297
Each love-thought in thy mind doth rise	251
Earth a transition underwent	343
Ev'n like two little bank-dividing brooks,	68
Fair realm of radiant light,	57
Fare not abroad, O Soul, to win	381
Father,	345
Father of all! In every age,	95
Fear death?—to feel the fog in my throat	122
Flight is but the preparative. The sigh	82
Flower in the crannied wall,	133
For he who has been taught in things of love so far,	7
For I have learned	146
For stock and stone;	425
For years I sought the Many in the One,	353
Frail petals fold about the weary bee	401
Give me thy joy in sorrow, gracious Lord,	448
Glory be to God for dappled things—	159
God, God!	120
God is not dumb, that he should speak no more;	186
God makes a path, provides a guide,	90
God of grave nights,	285
Go not away, Lord! Leave us not	167
Good is an orchard, the saint saith,	270
Great art Thou, O Lord, and greatly to be praised;	15
Greater than stars or suns,	195
Hail! Hail! Hail!	199
Hallowed be Thy name—Halleluiah!—	131
Happy those early dayes! when I	87
He, behind the straight plough, stands	324

Index to First Lines

	PAGE
He has taken away the things that I loved best:	406
He is made one with Nature: there is heard	101
He is the Light that fades not, never dies,	406
He is the lonely Greatness of the World—	338
He prayed, but to his prayer no answer came,	296
He who is meek and contented, he who has an equal	53
He who seeks that gift to light him	46
High in heaven stood the sun,	108
How many colors do we see set,	215
I always loved this solitary hill,	110
I am a stranger in the land	171
I am aware,	411
I am glad of the straight lines of the rain;	391
I am my ancient self,	457
I am Thy grass, O Lord!	427
I bent unto the ground	343
I cannot find Thee! Still on restless pinion	202
I cannot put the Presence by, of Him, the Crucified,	404
I cannot tell what psalms these voices sing,	460
I cannot think nor reason,	450
I climb that was a clod;	427
I come in the little things,	308
I died from mineral and plant became;	22
I do not fear to lay my body down	454
I do not pray for peace nor ease,	418
I dreamed I saw two angels hand in hand,	189
I dreamed last night I stood with God on high,	408
I envy not the Lark his song divine,	313
I feel a breath from other planets blowing	304
If in that secret place	456
I fled Him, down the nights and down the days;	253
If, Lord, Thy love for me is strong	56
I flung my soul to the air like a falcon flying,	373
I found Thee in my heart, O Lord,	222
If there had anywhere appeared in space	134
If thou would'st hear the Nameless, and wilt dive	128
I gaze aloof at the tissued roof,	148
I had a dream last night:	431
I had no God but these,	228
I have a life with Christ to live,	149
I have lifted my eyes to the strength of the hills	380
I have seen	145

489

Index to First Lines

	PAGE
I heard a bird at break of day	425
I hold with none who think not work a boon,	398
I knock again and try the key,	461
I know not where	323
I know Thee, O God!	382
I know 'tis but a loom of land,	161
I know, whatever God may be,	281
I lived my days apart,	341
I made a pilgrimage to find the God:	408
I may speak with the tongues of men and of angels,	11
I missed him when the sun began to bend;	206
In childhood's pride I said to Thee:	301
In Christ I feel the heart of God.	183
I need not shout my faith. Thrice eloquent	448
Ineffable Love Divine!	24
I never saw a moor,	174
In God my soul reposes;	114
In Jewry had I dwelt of old,	366
In the beginning slowly grope we back	333
In the full summer of that unearthly gleam	329
In the hour of death, after this life's whim,	117
In the late evening, when the house is still,	284
In the secret Valley of Silence	250
In this, O nature, yield, I pray, to me.	348
Into the heaven of Thy heart, O God,	184
In what far, green Judean field	386
I said, "I will find God," and forth I went	222
I said: "Let me walk in the fields."	205
I saw Eternity the other night	85
I saw the throng, so deeply separate,	235
I see His blood upon the rose	292
I shall breathe the sweet breath	1
I stood within the heart of God;	279
It fortifies my soul to know	125
I that had life ere I was born.	313
It is impossible to be alone here, even in this little cabin room,	414
It lies not on the sunlit hill	251
I took a day to search for God,	264
It were not hard, we think, to serve Him,	342
I vex me not with brooding on the years	209
I went seeking an unutterable Word	419

Index to First Lines

	PAGE
I went to sleep; and now I am refreshed,	127
I who have heard solemnities of sound—	434
I, who have lost the stars, the sod,	385
I will hearken what the Lord God will speak in me.	48
Lay me to sleep in sheltering flame,	248
Let be, O calling bird and rippling lake;	45
Let no one of Thy boundless Grace despair;	20
Let nothing disturb thee,	56
Let us beside the river rest awhile,	243
Let us hasten—let us fly—	6
Let us put by some hour of every day	435
Lift up your heads, gates of my heart, unfold	134
"Lift up your hearts!" The holy dews	395
Lo, as some bard on isles of the Ægean	220
Lo! in the vigils of the night, ere sped	216
Lord, I am born!	393
Lord, I have shut my door,—	168
Lord, not for light in darkness do we pray,	321
Lord of the grass and hill,	265
Lord, when the sense of thy sweet grace	78
Loud mockers in the roaring street	325
Love bade me welcome; yet my soul drew back,	71
Love holds me in the hollow of His hand,	395
Love wing'd my Hopes and taught me how to fly	66
Man's mind is larger than his brow of tears;	407
Mariner, what of the deep?	459
Men say the world is full of fear and hate,	300
Men told me, Lord, it was a vale of tears	233
My faith is all a doubtful thing,	416
My faith is larger than the hills,	173
My Lord hides himself, and my Lord wonderfully reveals himself:	52
My shoulders ache beneath my pack,	292
My soul is like a fencèd tower,	317
My terminus near,	195
Nature is but the outward vestibule	191
Nay, lift me to thy lips, Life, and once more	451
Night of the soul! Dark of divinest Fire!	399
No coward soul is mine,	119
No distant Lord have I	168
Not alone in Palestine those blessed Feet have trod,	232
Not often, when the carnal dance is mad—	280

Index to First Lines

	PAGE
Now have I left the world and all its tears,	314
Now that I have grown to manhood,	107
O Earth! Thou hast not any wind that blows	164
Of all great Nature's tones that sweep	201
Of all the myriad moods of mind	185
O flame of living love	55
O friends! with whom my feet have trod	197
O gain that lurk'st ungained in all gain!	259
O glory of the lighted mind	328
O great heart of God,	284
O heart, the equal poise of Love's both parts,	78
Oh, Lord, I cannot hear; didst speak, oh, Lord?	383
Oh Lord, my cup is small,	274
Oh, Most High, Almighty, Good Lord God, to Thee	23
Oh seek me not within a tomb;	417
Oh, sweet life's daily round;	311
"Oh, to be the Knight of Jesus!"	47
Oh, what is abroad in the marsh and the terminal sea?	180
"Oh! where is the sea?" the fishes cried,	163
O joy! that in our embers	142
O living well that shall endure	133
O Lord, the Giver of my days,	207
O Lord, thou hast searched me and known me.	3
O Lord, where shall I find Thee?	20
O Lord, where shall I find Thee?	362
O Love, Divine and Great,	41
O my God, thou hast wounded me with love,	112
O my soul, I would have you rest upon the bosom of the Infinite	409
One of the crowd went up,	238
One voice is from the homeland and the hills,	340
Open the garden gate, walk in, my heart;	462
O servant, where dost thou seek Me?	52
O somewhere, somewhere, God unknown,	219
O Soul of mine, how noble wert thou made!	37
O splendour of God! by means of which I saw	44
O Thou Eternal One! whose presence bright	90
O thou, in whom we live and breathe,	344
O Thou not made with hands,	139
O Thou that on the hills and wastes of Night art Shepherd,	248
O thou who lovest, with divine passion,	347
Out from the heart of nature rolled	176

Index to First Lines

	PAGE
Out of the four and twenty hours,	283
Out of the troubled dark I came	286
Out of the vastness that is God	430
Over all presides the Universal Soul.	12
Over the great city	316
O World, I cannot hold thee close enough!	410
O world invisible, we view thee,	259
O world, thou choosest not the better part!	366
Passionate, with longing in mine eyes,	45
Past this meadow on the shore	438
Sail fast, sail fast,	182
Saviour, I've no one else to tell	173
Seated within this body's car	411
Seek no more abroad, say I,	77
See, Lord, see, I am dead:	67
Serene, I fold my hands and wait,	213
Servants of time, lo! these be slaves of slaves;	22
Shall the mole, in his night underground, call the beasts from the day-glare to flee?	364
Shall we not open the human heart	392
Should Fate command me to the farthest verge	94
Silent is the house: all are laid asleep:	118
Since Eden it keeps the secret!	166
Since I believe in God the Father Almighty,	226
Singers, sing! The hoary world	458
Slight as thou art, thou art enough to hide	239
Some folks as can afford,	319
Sometimes, as in the summer fields	350
Sometimes, I know not why, nor how, nor whence,	242
So thin a veil divides	317
"Speak, Lord, for Thy servant heareth,	50
"Speechless sorrow sat with me;	178
Spirit! that dwellest where,	188
Stark on the window's early gray	388
Still as the great waters lying in the West,	350
Strong angel of the peace of God,	176
Such pictures of the heavens were never seen	225
Sunset and evening star,	132
Sunshine let it be or frost,	262
Sweet Infancy!	82
Teach me, my God and King,	69
Thank God, a man can grow!	233

Index to First Lines

	PAGE
Thank God, I can rejoice	413
That all things should be mine,	80
That He might better of Love's mystery tell	402
That I have felt the rushing wind of Thee:	276
The angells' eyes, whome veyles cannot deceive,	62
The awful shadow of some unseen Power	104
The Body, long oppressed,	293
The countless stars, which to our human eye	193
The desire of love, joy:	248
The goal in sight! Look up and sing,	141
The harp is ever singing to itself	206
The long brown arm thrusts out to sea	252
The Lord is my shepherd;	2
The Lord said,	371
The mossy paths that bore the patient herd	400
The night is come, like to the day,	77
Therefore to whom turn I but to thee, the ineffable Name?	123
There is a far-off, closest place	455
There is a flame within me that has stood	416
There is a Garden birds seek without knowing,	401
There is one Mind, one omnipresent Mind,	100
There is somewhere a Secret Garden, which none hath seen	331
These are the things I prize	449
The snowflake that glistens at morn on Kailasa,	148
The soul is in the body as the pilot in the ship,—	14
The sun in beauty left the hill	115
The sun, the moon, the stars, the seas, the hills and the plains—	130
The Western Road goes streaming out to seek the cleanly wild,	305
The wonder of the world is o'er:	357
The Woof that I weave not	150
The word of God came unto me,	403
The world is charged with the grandeur of God	154
The world we live in wholly is redeemed,	185
They are all gone into the world of light!	89
They bade me cast the thing away,	177
The years are flowers and bloom within	378
They have burned to Thee many tapers in many temples:	432
They list for me the things I may not know:	210
They said: "She dwelleth in some place apart,	160
They say there is a hollow, safe and still,	125

Index to First Lines

	PAGE
They think me daft, who nightly meet	278
Thick is the darkness—	126
This day relenting God	348
This from that soul incorrupt whom Athens had doomed to the death,	240
This I ask Thee—tell it to me truly, Lord!	5
This is the earth He walked on; not alone	223
This mood hath known all beauty, for it sees	354
This was the dream I saw before I woke;	384
Thou art of all created things,	72
Thou art the Way	236
Thou canst choose the Eastern Circle for thy part,	327
Thou, for whom words have exhausted their sweetness—	375
Though Christ a thousand times	75
Thou givest me greenest sanctuaries,	267
Thou mastering me	155
Thou one all perfect Light,	190
Three score and ten! The tumult of the world	388
Three times have I beheld	237
Through all the evening,	262
Thy miracles in Galilee	397
'Tis not the skill of human art	75
Today the peace of autumn pervades the world.	300
To God, the everlasting, who abides,	135
To Mercy, Pity, Peace, and Love	98
To see a World in a grain of sand,	99
"Toward the last outpost of the world I ride:	403
'Twas August, and the fierce sun overhead	116
Under our curtain of fire,	435
Unto my faith as to a spar, I bind	160
Upon an obscure night	53
Waiting on Him who knows us and our need,	263
Wakeful all night I lay and thought of God,	379
We are not cast away, not separate;	13
We do not find Him on the difficult Earth,	234
We had forgotten You, or very nearly—	309
"We know not what it is, dear, this sleep so deep and still;	214
We know Thee, each in part—	227
We may ascend to Him, and grasp Him	15
We too (one cried), we too,	236
What are you, rose?—lips that lean back to meet	444
What domination of what darkness dies this hour,	360

Index to First Lines

	PAGE
What happy, secret fountain,	88
"What is there but the sky, O Sun, that can hold thine image?"	299
What is this maiden fair,	137
What, O Eternity,	228
What roar as of breaking of Oceans, what cry as of seas on the iron-clanging coasts?	420
When all the shores of knowledge fade	211
When a wild grace I see,	269
When first the busy, clumsy tongue is stilled,	307
When God at first made man,	71
When He appoints to meet thee, go thou forth—	162
When I am recompensed and lean secure,	337
When I behold the sky	59
When in the golden western summer skies	224
When I was young the days were long,	271
When once I knew the Lord,	18
When the breath of twilight blows to flame the misty skies,	353
Where didst Thou tarry, Lord, Lord,	282
Where we sat at dawn together, while the star-rich heavens shifted,	355
Which way are my feet set?	194
Whither, midst falling dew,	169
Whither, when freed from fetters of the clay,	434
Who dreamed that beauty passes like a dream?	352
Who seeks perfection in the art	352
Who walks with beauty has no need of fear;	415
Why hurt so hard by little pricks,	315
Why sing the legends of the Holy Grail,	372
Wilt thou not ope thy heart to know	174
Within the circle of His peace	273
Yea every day he comes!	171
Yes, it was the mountain Echo,	147
Yonder the veil'd Musician sits, His feet	151
You cannot efface from your heart a certain image,	302
You, my son, have shown me God	381
You that uphold the world,	377
"You toil in your attic the whole day long	323
You who are born of the hills,	377
Zeus,—by what name soe'er	5